BATTLES
—IN—
BRITAIN

BATTLES
— IN —
BRITAIN

Glen Lyndon Dodds

Tell me not, Sweet, I am unkind,
*   That from the nunnery*
Of thy chaste breast and quiet mind
*   To war and arms I fly.*

True, a new mistress now I chase,
*   The first foe in the field;*
And with a stronger faith embrace
*   A sword, a horse, a shield.*

Yet this inconstancy is such
*   As thou too shalt adore;*
I could not love thee, Dear, so much,
*   Loved I not Honour more.*

—Richard Lovelace (1618-1658)

ARMS AND
ARMOUR

For my brothers,
Shaun and Gavin

Arms and Armour Press
An Imprint of the Cassell Group
Wellington House, 125 Strand, London WC2R 0BB

Distributed in the USA by Sterling Publishing Co. Inc.,
387 Park Avenue South, New York, NY 10016-8810.

Distributed in Australia by Capricorn Link (Australia) Pty.
Ltd, 2/13 Carrington Road, Castle Hill, NSW 2154.

British Library Cataloguing-in-Publication Data:
a catalogue record for this book is available from
the British Library

ISBN 1-85409-297-9

Designed and edited by DAG Publications Ltd.
Designed by David Gibbons; edited by G. W. A. Napier;
printed and bound in Great Britain.

CONTENTS

INTRODUCTION

Battles have played a decisive part in determining the course of history. Hence military history is a subject worthy of serious attention. Students of Britain's past have a rich military heritage to explore, for over the centuries many engagements have been waged on this island and although the details of some of these are unknown, the course of others can be ascertained with varying degrees of accuracy from relevant source material.

In this book I have dealt at some length with nine battles fought in the period 1066–1746 and, moreover, have summarised another nineteen engagements from within the same period. In the main accounts I have said something about the character and background of the commanders, and have discussed the composition and weaponry of the forces they led, thereby hopefully giving a more rounded out view than is sometimes the case in books of this nature.

This is also true of the political dimension. Frequently scant regard is paid to what led to the battles, but they were not fought in a vacuum and I have thus endeavoured to place them in their historical context. Furthermore, where space has permitted I have analysed the part the battles played in determining the course of events.

Finally, I wish to thank my family and friends for their support and encouragement. In particular, I wish to thank my brother, Gavin Dodds, for preparing the maps. I also wish to thank the staff of Sunderland City Library and Monkwearmouth Library for obtaining books and articles requested by me.

Glen Lyndon Dodds
Sunderland, 27 August 1995

1

HASTINGS
14 OCTOBER 1066

'If anyone desires to know what kind of man he was or in what honour he was held...then we will write of him just as we perceived him....King William, of whom we speak, was a man of great wisdom and power, and surpassed in honour and strength all those who had gone before him. He was mild with good men who loved God, though stern beyond measure to those who opposed his will.'
—Anglo-Saxon Chronicle

According to the twelfth century historian, Wace, William of Normandy was preparing to hunt near Rouen when he received news that his cousin Edward the Confessor, England's king, had died and had been replaced by his brother-in-law, Harold Godwineson, Earl of Wessex. It is reported that the news, which arrived on or around 10 January 1066, threw the duke into such a fearful temper that only William fitz Osbern, one of his closest friends, dared talk to him.

Just where William received the news of Harold's accession is in fact uncertain. What is beyond doubt is that he reacted angrily. He felt that he had been cheated – the crown should have been his. William had a number of reasons for believing that the kingdom of England should have passed to him upon the death of the Confessor. It is evident that in 1051 or 1052 Edward had promised the succession to him, a natural enough promise for the childless monarch to have made to his cousin, for Edward had grown up in Normandy while living as an exile and thus had strong Norman sympathies. Furthermore, in 1064 or 1065 Harold himself had promised, while in the duchy, to help William secure the English crown upon the demise of the Confessor.

It is highly probable that Harold was expressly sent to Normandy by Edward to make this promise for he was the most powerful nobleman in England and without his backing the duke's chances of ascending the throne were slim. According to a biography of William written c.1074 by his chaplain, William of Poitiers, while an honoured guest in the duchy Harold swore an oath that he would do all in his power 'to assure [Duke William] the possession of the English kingdom after the death of Edward', and some other sources, such as the Bayeux Tapestry, (which likely dates from c.1080), maintain that he swore the oath whilst touching holy relics. Subsequent events, however, proved that this was not a promise the Englishman intended to honour. It was, he later claimed, sworn under duress. Consequently, Harold had no qualms about ascending the

English throne himself upon Edward's death on 5 January 1066: if William wanted the crown he would have to fight for it.

William was equal to the challenge. Following the news of Harold's accession he began planning to take by war what he considered his by right. An adroit politician, he fully realised the importance of creating a favourable atmosphere for his endeavours. Thus a delegation was sent to Rome to gain papal approval for an invasion of England and there can be little doubt that the duke fully expected to receive support. He had tried to bring about a peaceful settlement, (an embassy had been sent to England to demand that Harold step down in his favour) but had only met with intransigence from Harold. Furthermore, William was in favour with the papacy for he had been very generous to the Church, while for various reasons England's ecclesiastics were out of favour in Rome. Not surprisingly, things went William's way. He received authorisation for an invasion and a papal bull excommunicating Harold and his supporters. His planned campaign had the seal of approval: it was to be a Holy Crusade.

William now set about winning the support of his barons for he needed their backing if he were to carry out his projected military venture. He had little difficulty with his greatest vassals. They were generally closest to him and in many cases owed their wealth and position to his patronage. However, the lesser barons were not so easily won over. After failing to gain their collective support at a great meeting at Lillebonne, William resorted to seeing them individually, promising them wealth and glory in return for their services if the invasion were a success. By such means the hitherto unwilling barons pledged their assistance.

It is understandable why many were uneasy about the planned campaign. Warfare is after all a risky business, and a seaborne invasion in particular would be daunting. Furthermore, Harold was a fine warrior. He had fought alongside William against the Count of Brittany during his visit to Normandy and had distinguished himself while doing so. He would no doubt prove a worthy adversary, and could be expected to lead a formidable army.

Though William now had the backing of the Pope and his barons, was Normandy strong enough and sufficiently wealthy for the massive undertaking it faced? Moreover, it is worth asking, who were the Normans?

The duchy of Normandy originated in 911 when a Viking ancestor of William's, a chieftain by the name of Rollo, made an agreement with the French king, Charles III, whereby he and his followers would accept Charles' sovereignty and renounce paganism in return for his recognition of their possession of lands which they had occupied in the valley of the River Seine. Then, in later years, the Norsemen gained control of neighbouring territory which included places such as Bayeux, Caen and Falaise.

For much of its history the duchy was weakened by internal strife and threatened by hostile neighbours, but by 1066 Normandy was more powerful and more wealthy than it had ever been. This was due to the leadership of William.

He took steps to curb private warfare, dealt successfully with external threats to his position, and ensured that local administration was conducted by trusted subordinates from whom he received a substantial regular income. Moreover, owing to his dynamic personality and achievements, he retained the services of men of knightly rank who might otherwise have forsaken the duchy to serve elsewhere, as had happened in the past.

Nonetheless, Normandy's resources were insufficient for an invasion of England. Hence the duke resorted to enlisting support and such was his reputation that he attracted volunteers from Maine and Brittany (both of which were subject to him), and from lands such as France, Flanders and Aquitaine.

It is sometimes said that the Normans were Vikings, but in fact they were of mixed blood. The Scandinavian settlers had not driven out the numerically superior indigenous populations of the lands which came under their sway and intermarriage had occurred. The descendants of Rollo and his followers were therefore essentially French in their customs, speech and dress. They were also influenced by the French in the field of warfare, for unlike their Viking forebears who fought on foot, William and his principal warriors were knights, and men trained to fight whilst mounted had been a feature of warfare in France since Carolingian times.

It has often been maintained that Norman lords and senior churchmen had to provide the duke with quotas of knights imposed by him to serve for a set period. Research has shown that this was not the case. Feudalism in Normandy was not as advanced as it was to become (one of the methods by which knights were provided to serve the duke seems to have been individual agreements between lord and vassal), and an eminent Anglo-Norman scholar, Marjorie Chibnall, has suggested that the change to systematised service commenced on the eve of the Conquest during the preparations for the invasion of England.

Once William was sure that he had the backing of his barons, he set to work with them to provide a fleet sufficient for transporting a sizeable army to England. Some ships were commandeered, but many others had to be built and for months craftsmen along the coast of the duchy laboured to provide the requisite vessels.

By mid August William's army and fleet were assembled at Dives-sur-Mer where there was an excellent anchorage. Just how many craft there were is uncertain. Wace, for instance, states that there were 696 ships. It is, however, possible that there were as many as 900 vessels of various kinds. Not surprisingly, the size of the army is also a moot point. A realistic figure is nearly 9,000 men, though not all of these would have been combatants.

William remained at Dives well into September. According to Poitiers, he was waiting for a favourable wind which would enable him to sail to England. This may have been the case. However, Chibnall has recently suggested that the duke's stay at Dives was deliberate and intended to perplex Harold.

An insight into the high degree of control William exercised over his army at this time is provided by Poitiers: 'He made generous provision both for his own knights and those from other parts, and did not permit any of them to take their sustenance by force. The neighbouring peasantry could pasture their cattle and sheep in peace... or...move about the district...without trembling at the sight of soldiers.'

On 12 September William and his armada sailed from Dives and headed north-east up the coast, either intending to turn due north for a short crossing of the English Channel from the vicinity of St Valéry, or to put in at that port for additional provisions before setting out for England. A storm blew up, however, and several ships were lost before the fleet arrived at St Valéry as planned or owing to a change of plan brought about by the inclement weather.

Once again, or perhaps for the first time, contrary winds blew for days on end. (It may well be significant that according to William of Poitiers and William of Jumièges it was only after the duke arrived at St Valéry that prayers for a favourable wind were made). To make matters worse, rain set in.

Then, suddenly, on 27 September, the wind began blowing from the south. Elated, William ordered his men to embark. This was done under welcome sunshine. Embarkation took many hours and it was nightfall when the fleet put to sea with William leading the way in his ship, *Mora*.

During the course of the crossing the duke's vessel outdistanced the rest of the fleet and when dawn broke the *Mora* was alone in the middle of the Channel. William thus hove to and awaited the fleet. If English warships had borne down on the duke his enterprise would have ended in disaster but fortunately for him Harold's fleet, (which had been stationed off the Isle of Wight for months in expectation of invasion), had sailed to London earlier in the month owing to the deteriorating weather conditions and the fact that provisions had run low.

At about 9.00am on Thursday 28th William landed at Pevensey. Here members of his army likewise disembarked, while others did so in the vicinity. Although William and his men came ashore in Harold's home county, Sussex, the landing was unopposed. England's king and his army were not in the neighbourhood, or indeed anywhere else in the south-east. Instead, Harold was hundreds of miles away, for although he had spent several months on the south coast awaiting William, he had recently dashed north to confront a formidable army under Norway's king, Hardrada, which had landed in Yorkshire in mid September intent on conquest. Hardrada was a notable warrior, but on 25 September Harold had surprised and annihilated him and his army in an epic encounter at Stamford Bridge.

Upon landing, William carried out a reconnaissance of the neighbourhood and concluded that Pevensey was not a suitable base. For one thing, it was bounded to the north and east by marshy levels. He thus soon moved east to

Hastings, which was a more advantageous location, for among other things it had an excellent harbour. Here a fortress of earth and timber was hastily constructed.

News of William's arrival was soon received by Harold. According to the most probable accounts, the king heard of the duke's landing while attending a banquet in York on the evening of 1 October celebrating the destruction of Hardrada and his army. However, some believe that by this date Harold was en route south and so received the news while riding towards London. This is unlikely. After all, following their recent exploits Harold and his men must have been in dire need of rest. Furthermore, the king had to ensure that the inhabitants of the north were loyal to him for it appears that many of them had been prepared to throw in their lot with Hardrada. Consequently, it seems reasonable to believe that Harold was indeed in York when he received the unwelcome news of William's landing.

What is certain is that the information made him dash towards London. He was probably 200 miles from the city: William was closer, much closer, and could easily have arrived first if he had wished to do so. Instead, he remained at Hastings, watching and waiting.

Harold entered London on or around 6 October. Here his weary army was reinforced by fresh fighting men, members of the select levies of London and the local shires which had not participated in the northern campaign. Furthermore, Edwin and Morcar, the young Earls of Mercia and Northumbria who had unsuccessfully confronted Hardrada in a battle at Fulford on 20 September, were raising their men once again.

In London Harold was faced with questions of strategy. Should he remain in the city and await the expected reinforcements? Or should he move against William as soon as possible and hopefully take him by surprise? He chose the latter. According to some sources, Harold's younger brother, Gyrth, offered to lead the army and suggested that Harold should remain in London and await the reinforcements. His reason for making the offer is said to have been his belief that England could afford to lose an army but not its king. Harold, however was determined to confront William himself, and exact vengeance for devastation the duke had wrought in Sussex since his landing.

Harold probably left London on the morning of 12 October, and just prior to doing so he ordered a number of warships to sail to Hastings to prevent William escaping by sea. Some historians are of the opinion that the king was at the head of about 5,000 men, and this seems reasonable. What is clear is that it was only a fraction of the force he could have commanded had he stayed in London longer, but he evidently wished to trap William on the Hastings peninsula, (at this date Hastings was situated at the southern end of a peninsula formed by the estuaries of the Brede and Bulverhythe), and bring him to battle on his own terms.

From London Harold rode to Rochester where he crossed the Medway. He then moved south along the Hastings road and entered a great forest known as the Andredsweald a mile or so beyond Maidstone. His destination was Caldbec Hill, a prominent and well known junction for roads, which dominated the exit from the Hastings peninsula. There he would rendezvous with select units from the south-eastern shires which had been ordered to congregate at that location.

Harold is generally believed to have arrived at Caldbec Hill on the evening of the 13th. He was just seven miles from William's base and it is possible that it was his intention to launch a lightning attack, reminiscent of that which had surprised Hardrada, as soon as his men were rested. On the other hand, some historians believe that he intended to remain on the high ground in the vicinity of Caldbec Hill and allow the Normans to attack his strong defensive position, thereby limiting the effectiveness of William's cavalry, after which a counterattack could be launched with the hope of routing the invaders.

However, according to the C version of the *Anglo-Saxon Chronicle*, it was William who now called the tune. He was aware of the proximity of the English army and was determined to meet it on his terms. At dawn on Saturday 14 October, he began marching towards Harold's position: a battle which would decide the destiny of England was soon to begin.

But before discussing what transpired, something needs to be said about the background and character of the opposing commanders and of the composition, weaponry and tactics of the armies they led.

WILLIAM AND HIS ARMY

William was born in 1027 or 1028, the illegitimate son of Duke Robert the Magnificent and Herleve, a tanner's daughter. In 1035 he succeeded to the duchy and his accession was followed by a period of intense anarchy in which several factions fought for supremacy. William's chances of survival were slim: more than once his guardians were murdered, more than once he had to flee for his life. In part, his survival was due to his overlord, Henry of France, who came to his assistance in 1047 when William faced a major revolt, and crushed the rebels at Val-es-Dunes.

In the years which followed, William consolidated his position by, for example, displacing those who had opposed him and giving their lands to faithful companions. Furthermore, in the early 1050s he married the daughter of the count of neighbouring Flanders, thereby allying himself with a potential adversary.

In 1053 William again faced a major challenge when one of his uncles proclaimed himself the rightful duke and received support from Henry who had turned against William. Henry invaded the duchy but withdrew following a reverse at St Aubin-le-Caulf. The following year he invaded again in a two-pronged attack, with one of the armies led by his brother, but again withdrew after the latter's defeat at Mortemer by one of William's vassals. Another expedition in 1057 also ended in failure when William fell on part of the French army at Varaville and cut it to pieces.

William also fought outside his duchy. In 1063, for example, after repeated ravaging over many years, he finally conquered Maine, and in the following year he overcame the Bretons. Thus by 1066 William was an experienced commander whose exploits had earned him the fear and respect of others, so much so that he was known as William the Great. It is worth noting, however, that he did not have any experience of commanding a set engagement. He avoided battle where possible, preferring either to ravage enemy territory before withdrawing or, when on the defensive, to shadow and harass his opponents.

From the above it is axiomatic that William was tough, resourceful, courageous and indomitable. He was, moreover, remarkably dynamic and methodical; a man who could inspire others and exercise discipline effectively. He was also deeply religious, but could nonetheless behave with great ferocity when crossed.

In view of the campaigns referred to above, William's invasion force inevitably contained many seasoned warriors, the most important of whom were knights. The Bayeux Tapestry vividly portrays the knights whom William brought to England in 1066. It shows that they fought with a variety of weapons. Among these were spears which could either be thrown at opponents or, more often it seems, be used in hand-to-hand fighting. Some knights, moreover, apparently fought with couched lances. Knights also carried a sword, though some preferred to have an axe or mace instead. The swords had broad, two-edged blades, while the hilts were often elaborate, for instance, being inlaid with gold, copper, silver, or niello.

The knights wore coats of mail for protection. These weighed about 14kg, reached to the knees, and were slit from hem to crotch at the front so that they could be worn while mounted. Furthermore, the Tapestry shows that William and his leading associates also wore mail leggings and that all knights wore iron helmets which were conical in form and had nose guards. Kite-shaped shields afforded additional protection, and were about 1.25m long and 55cm wide.

The Tapestry indicates that the knights' mounts were almost all stallions trained to join in the fighting with hooves, teeth and forehead. As can be imagined, it required horsemanship of a very high order to retain control of a mount and fight at the same time.

The knights were undoubtedly the elite warriors of William's army. They were born and bred to arms and were used to fighting alongside fellow knights in the contingents of their respective lords. 'Such units,' as the late R. A. Brown has commented, 'trained together over long, arduous years, and bound by the companionship of expertise, had ample discipline and the capacity not only to work and fight together but also to combine with other similar units'.

The infantry consisted of heavy infantry and archers. The principal weapon of the heavy infantry was the sword. For protection the men wore caps and hauberks (some of the latter, like hauberks worn by knights, were coats of mail, though most wore coats of stout leather girded around the waist), and all no doubt carried shields. Some of the 29 archers depicted on the Bayeux Tapestry are well dressed or even armoured in contrast to the others shown and probably represent professionals. The lesser archers present were likely sailors from the Norman fleet who accompanied the army into battle. The Tapestry shows the archers using ordinary bows but it may well have been the case that some used crossbows for these were used in Norman armies during this period.

HAROLD AND HIS ARMY

Harold Godwineson was a confident man with much to be confident about. Born c.1022, he was the second son of Earl Godwine of Wessex whom he succeeded in 1053. By the time of his accession to that important earldom Harold was already an experienced and prominent figure, well aware of the dangers and vicissitudes of political life. In 1051, for instance, Godwine and his two eldest sons (Harold was Earl of East Anglia at the time) assembled their forces after Godwine had fallen out with King Edward. The situation was tense: bloodshed seemed inevitable. However, many of their supporters melted away rather than fight against the king and so Godwine and his sons resorted to flight. Harold made for Ireland while his father and brother fled to Flanders. The following year they returned to England at the head of mercenary forces and gained significant support, for in the interval Edward had alienated many people by showing favouritism to Normans in his court. A reconciliation of sorts thus occurred and Godwine and his sons were restored to their positions.

As Earl of Wessex, Harold led English armies on lightning campaigns in Wales in 1062 and 1063. The campaigns resulted in the regaining of lost territory, the death of the Welsh leader, Gruffydd ap Llywelyn, and greatly enhanced Harold's reputation. In 1062 the Earl of Mercia, the head of the country's other most powerful noble family, had died leaving his earldom to a young son, Edwin. Hence an eminent Anglo-Saxonist, the late Sir Frank Stenton, has observed of Harold's standing at this time: 'No subject of the English crown had ever been at once so powerful in relation to other noblemen and so great a figure in the country at large'.

Although he came from a very ambitious, and at times very ruthless family, Harold is generally perceived as an essentially decent man. A contemporary, William of Jumièges, tells us that 'he was extremely brave and bold' and was 'very handsome...agreeable...and affable with everybody'.

Harold Godwineson was a very able man then, brave, decisive, resourceful and a born leader. But what of his army? Was it a formidable force?

Harold's army, or fyrd, was a fine one consisting of his housecarls, those of his loyal brothers, Gyrth and Leofwine, Danish mercenaries, and shire levies.

Until recently the royal housecarls were generally viewed as the corps d'élite of Harold's army, a standing force of some 3,000 or so men founded by King Cnut (1016–35) and set aside from the rest of society by its professionalism and by its own rigid rules. In 1985, however, Nicholas Hooper challenged this view in a stimulating article in which he argues against the importance and uniqueness of the royal housecarls: they were not as numerous as has often been supposed and were little or no different from the household retainers who had served Anglo-Saxon kings militarily and in other ways before the days of Cnut.

Hooper's contention that the royal housecarls did not form a powerful standing army is persuasive. Nonetheless, they may have constituted a law-bound guild for these were not unknown in late Anglo-Saxon England, and it is moreover probable, as a number of historians have maintained, that some were garrisoned at Wallingford. Furthermore, it is reasonable to believe that the housecarls, like the military households of past kings, formed or at least partly comprised, the spearhead of Harold's army.

The housecarls' principal weapons were swords, axes and spears. The swords had broad, two-edged blades, which were usually some 75 to 80cm long and were primarily slashing weapons of which Peter Bone has commented: 'Surviving archaeological evidence confirms that powerful sword cuts, backed by the flow of adrenalin in combat, could shear through skulls and cut through iron mail'. Some of the axes were small, single-handed weapons, but many were two-handed battleaxes with cutting edges up to a foot in length and handles over three feet long. For protection housecarls wore iron helmets and coats of mail (which reached to the knees), and carried kite-shaped shields.

The arms and equipment of the housecarls of Harold's brothers were no doubt identical to those of the royal housecarls, while the mercenaries must likewise have been well equipped, though most if not all of them probably had traditional round shields.

The bulk of Harold's army has often been said to have consisted of ill-armed peasants. This was not the case. A system operated in the kingdom which ensured that the king was provided with a well-armed force when occasion demanded. *Domesday Book* contains an entry which states how this system operated in Berkshire: 'If the king sent an army anywhere, only one soldier went from five hides [a hide was a unit by which land was rated for military service and taxation], and four shillings were given him from each hide as subsistence and wages for two months'. Elsewhere in England under the hide system the principle of one warrior from a given number of hides – perhaps again, every five – evidently operated and it is apparent that in other parts of the country such as the Danelaw, where carucates were a means of assessment, the principle of one man from a given number of such units also existed.

Some of the men who served in the fyrd were peasants, but most of these appear to have been drawn from the 'aristocratic' element of the peasantry. Within the host they served alongside men of more exalted rank in shire units which were normally led by their respective sheriffs.

That the shire levies were generally well-armed is indicated by the rate of pay given to warriors from Berkshire, £1 each for two months' service, for as Richard Abels has commented this 'was far from a negligible sum of money' at this time and 'was even comparable to the wages paid to Anglo-Norman stipendiary knights throughout the twelfth century'.

Many of the shire levies must have possessed swords. The principal weapons of others, however, would have been spears. There were two types: one for thrusting at an opponent; the other, a light throwing spear. Some levies were probably archers and if so, like all members of the fyrd, they would also have carried a knife which could be used to finish off a felled opponent or in lieu of a sword. Many of the levies no doubt possessed coats of mail, helmets and kite-shaped shields. The rest would have fought in their everyday clothes (except perhaps for wearing stout leather jerkins), and would have had round shields.

DESCRIPTION

As has been noted earlier, at dawn on Saturday 14 October 1066 William left his base at Hastings and marched towards Harold's army on Caldbec Hill intent on engaging it on his own terms. According to the C version of the *Anglo-Saxon Chronicle*, William's decision to take the initiative resulted in his coming upon Harold before the king's 'army was set in order'.

It is perfectly reasonable to accept that Harold was surprised by William's advance. Hence, upon hearing of the duke's approach, Harold hurriedly began preparing for battle. He chose to make his stand on a ridge which lies east-west a short distance to the south of Caldbec Hill to which it is connected by a narrow neck of land. It was a strong defensive position, for owing to the lie of the ground and the fact that there were streams on either side of the isthmus, Harold could not be outflanked. Moreover it is likely that some of the ground to the south of the ridge, like that to the east and west, was marshy. Furthermore, the central section of the south slope of the ridge has a gradient of one in fifteen, sufficient to reduce the effectiveness of an assault against a force defensively arrayed, as Harold's was, on the top of the hill.

Nonetheless, the position was not ideal. The size of the ridge necessitated that Harold deploy his men in very close formation and according to Florence of Worcester, (whose account was written before 1118), owing to the cramped conditions which prevailed, some of the king's warriors deserted. The possibility that there was discontent in the ranks of the English army is strengthened by a statement in the *Anglo-Saxon Chronicle* which records that in the battle Harold fought very bravely with those of his men 'who would stand by him', a comment which indicates that there were others who forsook the king. William of Malmesbury, (who wrote his account of the battle c.1120), explicitly states that some of Harold's men deserted and attributes this to the fact that the king had failed to share Hardrada's captured treasure with his soldiers following Stamford Bridge.

Nevertheless, despite the strong probability that some of Harold's warriors had deserted, there can be no doubt that the army with which he engaged William was formidable. It probably numbered about 7,000 men and, as noted, the overwhelming majority were well armed warriors, housecarls, mercenaries and select levies. The Bayeux Tapestry does portray a few members of the host as lacking good equipment and perhaps they are meant to represent local rustics who may have participated in the battle in order to exact revenge for the harrying done by William's army.

Harold's position can be identified. It is known that he chose to stand near the highest point of the ridge, and William the Conqueror subsequently ordered that the high altar of a monastery he founded here – Battle Abbey – should mark the spot. Beside the king stood at least a contingent of his housecarls and above flew two standards, Harold's own banner, *The Fighting Man*, and the

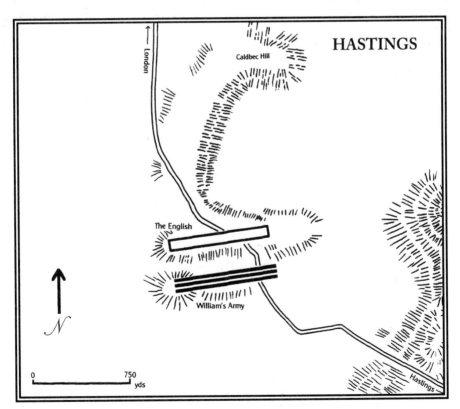

Dragon of Wessex. The remainder of the housecarls were probably positioned to the fore with the mercenaries to form the front ranks of the army.

By now William was busy marshalling his own forces for battle to the south of the English position and with the front ranks about 200 yards from it. We know that his army, which probably numbered about 8,000 men, of whom perhaps around 2,400 were knights, was drawn up in three lines with the archers in front, the heavy infantry behind, and knights to the rear. It may have been the case that the army was also drawn up in three divisions, with that on the left commanded by Count Alan of Brittany, the centre under William, and the division on the right by Roger of Montgomery. This is said to have been the case by an unreliable source, the *Carmen de Hastingae Proelio*, whose authorship and date of composition are uncertain.

The battle is said to have commenced at 9.00am but most historians are of the opinion, and probably correctly so, that it did so about half an hour later than this. Hostilities commenced when William's archers moved forward until they were within effective range and began firing at the massed ranks of Harold's army. Their efforts produced little result. Most of the arrows failed to penetrate the shield wall and so after a while the archers fell back, leaving behind them the bodies of unfortunate comrades who had been hit by an assortment of missiles including arrows fired by Harold's few bowmen.

It was now the turn of the heavily armed infantry to go into action. As they approached the English they were also met by a shower of missiles. Some screamed and fell, but the rest pressed on determined to exact vengeance. Thus hand-to-hand combat ensued and the greatest slaughter began, with Harold's finest warriors dealing out death and destruction to many of those who dared to assail them.

Upon seeing that the heavy infantry needed assistance, William rode forward with his knights. It is probable that the knights on the left, many of whom were Bretons, arrived on the scene first for the gradient here is only 1 in 33. What is certain is that it was they, and the infantry to whose assistance they rode, who broke first for William of Poitiers (whose account of the battle is the finest narrative source), relates that they fell back in disorder 'panic-stricken by the violence of the assault' which they had encountered.

The rout of the left exposed the flank of the centre, and so it too began giving ground. Soon the entire line was falling back. Then, to make matters worse, among all the fear and confusion, the cry went up that William himself had been cut down. This was a crucial moment. The duke proved equal to the occasion. He removed his helmet and, according to Poitiers, shouted: 'Look at me. I am living and with God's help I shall be victor!'

In so doing, William rallied at least some of the knights. With them he then rode against English soldiers who had charged down the hill after their enemies and cut them to pieces. It is often said that the Englishmen were undisciplined peasants who had acted on their own volition. However the Bayeux Tapestry portrays the deaths of Harold's brothers, Gyrth and Leofwine, at about this stage of the proceedings and it has therefore been plausibly suggested that the event was a deliberate counterattack led by them. Of this we can be certain: Harold and the bulk of his army remained firmly in position at this time and William still had to deal with them effectively if he wished to win the day.

It is very likely that a lull now occurred in the fighting for the battle – which proved long and bloody – would not have continued without letup, for it would have been beyond the capability of the armies to have done so. During the proposed lull both commanders would have restored order in their ranks. Harold for instance, had to strengthen his weakened right flank and this would have necessitated thinning the ranks elsewhere.

That he managed to restore the situation is evident from what happened next. William launched another attack by his knights and once again stiff resistance was encountered. Poitiers records, 'the English fought confidently with all their strength, striving in particular to prevent the attackers from penetrating within their ranks, which indeed were so closely ranked together that even the dead had not space in which to fall'.

During this phase of the battle William's knights made repeated attempts to break the English shield wall but made little headway. Consequently, according to Poitiers, a new tactic was employed: 'Realizing that they could not without severe loss overcome an army massed so strongly in close formation, the Normans and their allies feigned flight ...the Barbarians thinking victory within their grasp...gave rapid pursuit...but the Normans suddenly wheeling their horses surrounded them and cut down their pursuers so that not one was left alive'.

William of Poitiers' account of the battle is not the only one in which the invaders are said to have pretended to flee in order to draw English soldiers after them, and it may thus have been the case that general feigned flights did occur. Some historians though, have suggested that instead of occurring en masse, feigned flights were conducted by individual lords and their knights or in concert with the contingents of a number of other lords. That feigned flights did happen need not be doubted for they are a well-attested part of continental warfare of this era.

In view of the cavalry's failure to destroy the shield wall, William decided to change tactics. Time was running out and he could not afford to let the battle end in stalemate. In a final bid for victory, he ordered a general advance at about 4.00pm.

In this assault the archers are often said to have fired on a higher trajectory than before. Perhaps this was the case. That they did so is first mentioned by Henry of Huntingdon (whose account dates from c.1130), who may have derived the idea from the Bayeux Tapestry which shows some of the archers shooting high at this point.

The battle now slowly but surely began turning in William's favour. At last the shield wall was crumbling; at last his men were gaining a foothold on the top of the ridge for there were not enough Englishmen left to prevent them doing so.

The Tapestry portrays several English warriors who have been struck in the face and neck by arrows, but what of King Harold? Was he hit by an arrow as is commonly thought? The earliest narrative accounts do not state how the king died but English tradition of the following generation attributed his death to an arrow which pierced one of his eyes, and some historians are of the opinion that this view is substantiated by the Tapestry for under the words 'Hic Harold rex interfectus est', ('Here King Harold was killed'), an English soldier is portrayed as having been struck in, or just above, the eye by an arrow. However, under the same inscription can be seen another English warrior, this time one being cut down by a knight, and some contend that this figure is meant to be the king.

It has been demonstrated that at times important individuals appear twice in the same scene. Thus another school of thought maintains that Harold was first wounded by an arrow and then killed. The recent discovery of evidence in the much restored Tapestry for the former presence of an arrow just above the right eye of the second figure can be taken to support this view. Against this it has been argued that the weaponry of the two figures is different. The former has a spear, sword and shield; the latter a sword and axe. Of this, however, David Bernstein has commented: 'Placing the Tapestry in the artistic conventions of the time allows us to accept more readily the apparent unnaturalness of Harold shown twice within the length of a horse wearing different stockings and having changed weapons'.

Bernstein is of the opinion that both figures are meant to be Harold but maintains that the idea that the king was blinded was invented by the Tapestry's designer: 'In medieval lore there were...famous tales recounting how kings were miraculously blinded by an arrow because they had offended the divine order....Thus, without explicitly depicting God's presence at Hastings, the artist could give pictorial expression to the widely held belief that the king's defeat was a fitting punishment for his perjury on holy relics'.

Though we shall never know just how Harold was slain what really matters is that he perished and that his death was followed by the flight of many of the tired and dispirited warriors who had fought so valiantly in the ranks of his army. Others, however, did not join them in their attempt to gain the sanctuary of the Andredsweald. Disdaining flight, they fought on beside their fallen lord and died fighting heroically.

Upon destroying those who fought to the end, William sent Eustace of Boulogne and a force of knights after the warriors who had taken to their heels. According to an account written in the early twelfth century by Ordericus Vitalis, while pursuing the English many of Eustace's men rode headlong into a ditch of whose presence they were unaware and suffered heavy losses as a result. In contrast, Poitier's more reliable account relates that Eustace came across a force of English soldiers who had rallied by 'a broken entrenchment and a labyrinth of ditches' and thus turned back. Upon meeting the oncoming duke, he advised him also to withdraw. But while speaking, Eustace was wounded between the shoulder blades by a missile, after which William rode against the English and overcame them.

The Battle of Hastings was an extremely prolonged affair and the number of casualties sustained was considerable. It is probable that William's losses amounted to at least 2,500 men killed or incapacitated. Indeed, in the 1090s Eadmer, (a monk of Canterbury who discussed the matter with veterans of Hastings), wrote that Norman casualties were such that they attributed their success entirely 'to a miracle of God'.

The number of English warriors who perished, or escaped the battle wounded, may very well have exceeded the casualties sustained by William's army. More importantly, in addition to Harold and his brothers, many other Englishmen of note lost their lives in the engagement and subsequent events were to show that there was no one left in England of sufficient character and stature to lead effective large-scale resistance to William.

The victors spent the day after the battle, Sunday 15 October, burying their dead and tending their wounded. The bodies of the fallen English, with the exception of that of Harold, and perhaps those of his brothers, were left to rot and Vitalis records seeing their bones many years later. Legend has it that Harold's body was so badly mutilated that only his devoted mistress of many years, Edith Swanneck, could identify it by means of some marks known only to her. What is certain is that in due course the king's body (or at least one believed to be his) was buried at Waltham Abbey in Essex, an establishment which he had founded.

After burying his dead William returned to Hastings, (whose name was in time given to the battle), and rested his weary army for five days. Then, as the *Anglo-Saxon Chronicle* records, 'he marched inland with what was left of his host, together with reinforcements lately come from oversea, and harried that part of the country through which he advanced until he came to Berkhamsted'. There, following his circuitous and intimidating march, William received the submission of, among others, Edwin and Morcar, and senior citizens of London.

Shortly after this, on Christmas Day 1066, William was crowned in Westminster Abbey. Hastings had won him the throne but not the allegiance of all his new subjects. Some no doubt believed that he owed his victory to divine favour and recalled the appearance of Halley's Comet earlier in the year, 'a portent such as men had never seen before' as evidence that God had indeed spoken in William's favour. Others, though, were not prepared to submit, and it was several years, and several ruthlessly crushed rebellions later, before William could truly regard himself as England's master. Indeed, in the far north his hold was always tenuous.

Hastings is none the less one of the most important battles in history. It was the crucial stage in the last successful invasion of England by a foreign power and paved the way for the introduction of a rigid feudal system and a massive redistribution of wealth from English to Norman hands. Moreover, William's success at Hastings and the conquest of England it made possible, resulted in England's being brought more firmly into the mainstream of European affairs and culture than had been the case.

However, although Hastings led to Norman dominance and some significant changes, it was not followed by large scale immigration. The Normans never settled in England in considerable numbers as had earlier invaders such as the Anglo-Saxons and Vikings. Hence a number of things remained the same, or little altered, in the years which followed the battle. In view of this an eminent Victorian historian, E. A. Freeman, wrote: 'The fiery trial which England went through was a fire which did not destroy, but only purified. She came forth once more the England of old'.

Though it subsequently became fashionable to deride Freeman (whose view was undoubtedly too extreme), it is nevertheless now generally accepted that the Norman Conquest had a less calamitous effect on Anglo-Saxon civilisation than was once thought. Place names, for instance, retained their overwhelmingly Germanic character and the speech of ordinary folk remained essentially Anglo-Saxon. Furthermore, many native institutions survived the Conquest, and in connection with this fact a distinguished medievalist H. R. Loyn has recently observed: 'Only in their feudal attributes do the Normans appear as conspicuous innovators. Elsewhere it is as constructive builders on solid Anglo-Saxon achievements that their principal virtues find expression'.

Finally, it is time to discuss the performance of the armies at Hastings and to assess the leadership of their commanders. In his account of the battle, Poitiers refers to Harold's soldiers as 'barbarians' and some modern historians have likewise portrayed the English army as an undisciplined and backward force. Harold's army certainly lacked cavalry and was weak in archers but it is nevertheless wrong to dismiss it in a cursory manner. Hastings was a long and closely contested engagement in which Harold's followers in general proved themselves courageous and formidable. There was nothing inevitable about William's victory.

Harold has been criticised for being over confident during the campaign. His confidence is understandable when one remembers that he had just destroyed Hardrada at Stamford Bridge. That victory was, after all, the most resounding success achieved by an English king since another great Viking force and its allies had been annihilated at Brunanburh in 937 by King Athelstan. Nonetheless, Harold's decision to move against William with only part of his army was a rash one and suggests that he perhaps underestimated his opponent or, more probably, the strength of the duke's forces.

Some historians have also criticised Harold for not counterattacking at Hastings when William's army was in a state of confusion following the rout of the soldiers on the left. This may be a valid point. If the situation among the invaders was as chaotic as it has been portrayed, a counterattack by Harold would very likely have proved decisive. On the other hand, it has to be borne in mind that the extent of the confusion may have been exaggerated by Poitiers, among others, in order to enhance William's achievement at Hastings, for he relates that the duke restored the critical situation. Moreover, we should also bear in mind that time was on Harold's side. His army could more readily be reinforced and provisioned than William's. He could afford to simply deny his opponent victory on the 14th if need be, aware of his superior logistical position and the fact that the morale of his army would not disintegrate in such circumstances.

And what of William's performance? He showed tremendous powers of leadership and administrative ability during the crucial months which preceded the invasion and, after landing in England, wisely stayed near his fleet. Furthermore, upon hearing of Harold's approach, he boldly took the initiative by advancing against him, and he retained the initiative throughout the following proceedings. His success at Hastings was in large part due to the courage, decision and tactical ability he displayed. In short, William was a dynamic and able commander, and Hastings was his greatest triumph.

The courage and ability of the men under his command must not be forgotten. They had undertaken a daunting task and had acquitted themselves very well, thereby making William's triumph possible.

However, luck also played a considerable part in bringing about William's success. Hardrada's northern invasion opened the way for the Normans and, in retrospect, signed the death warrant for Anglo-Saxon England. It drew Harold away from the south and inflicted heavy losses on his army. Had it not been for Hardrada and the Battle of Stamford Bridge, it is almost certain that William of Normandy would not have conquered.

2

THE STANDARD
22 AUGUST 1138

In 1135 Henry I of England died. He had compelled the barons to accept his only surviving legitimate child, Matilda, as his heir, but following his death the majority of them gave their allegiance instead to her popular cousin, Stephen of Blois, who had spent much of his time in England and had extensive estates here. For much of his reign England was torn apart by a bitter civil war, known as the Anarchy, in which Stephen and Matilda fought each other in order to retain or gain power. It was a time, so says the *Anglo-Saxon Chronicle*, when: 'It was said openly that Christ and his saints were asleep'.

To add to the country's woes, David I of Scotland had designs on English territory. Indeed, in 1138, before hostilities in England began in earnest, David crossed the border at the head of a formidable army 'more barbarous than any race of pagans' according to a contemporary, Richard of Hexham, who witnessed its depredations outside his Northumbrian monastery. Stephen was preoccupied by affairs in the south and so resistance to the invasion was organised by Archbishop Thurstan of York and some northern barons. At 6.00am on the misty morning of 22 August, the invaders came face to face with an army under the archbishop on Cowton Moor three miles north of Northallerton.

The English front line consisted of archers interspersed with dismounted knights; the second of spearmen; and the third of more knights and men-at-arms. In the middle of the army was a large ship's mast mounted on a wagon. Attached to the mast was a pyx containing the consecrated host, and several banners, and it was this mast, or standard, which gave its name to the battle. The English army probably numbered about 10,000 men.

Some scholars believe that David's force numbered around 12,000 men, others that it was approximately 15,000 strong. The centre was under the personal command of the monarch. His son, Henry, led the right wing while Alan de Percy commanded the left.

Wild men from Galloway were in the forefront of the Scottish host, and as these lightly armed individuals charged towards the English position they suffered terrible casualties at the hands of the English bowmen. They subsequently broke against what Henry of Huntingdon called the 'iron wall' of their adversaries and began to flee. Seeing this, Prince Henry charged against the English left wing. It was a brave move but it did not turn the tide of battle. The English were in determined mood, eager to exact revenge for the atrocities committed by the invaders since their arrival in England. By 9.00am it was all over and the remnant of the Scottish army, including the king and his son, was in full flight, 'scattered as sheep without a shepherd' according to Richard of Hexham, leaving behind a battlefield 'strewed with corpses'. It is said that 10,000 men perished. Even allowing for exaggeration, the slaughter was great and the vast majority of the slain were Scottish.

Although David subsequently concluded a peace treaty with Stephen, (9 April 1139), this did not prevent him shortly thereafter trying unsuccessfully to impose his chancellor William Cumin upon the vacant and strategic see of Durham.

3

LINCOLN
20 MAY 1217

In October 1216 King John died at Newark Castle. In June of the previous year he had granted disaffected barons a charter of liberties, Magna Carta, but distrust between the parties had been such that by the autumn of 1215 civil war had commenced with both monarch and rebels looking abroad for assistance. John hired mercenaries: the barons asked Louis, heir of Philip Augustus of France, to come and replace John as king. He landed at Thanet in May 1216 and his arrival greatly boosted the prospects of success for the rebels, who controlled much of eastern England.

It was in such circumstances, with the majority of the baronage in revolt and a foreign prince intent on gaining England's throne, that John breathed his last. His successor was his nine-year-old son, Henry III, who was crowned at Gloucester on 28 October by the Bishop of Winchester in the presence of loyal prelates and barons. On the following day it was agreed that one of them, the veteran Earl of Pembroke, William Marshal, would serve as regent and take the lead in waging war on the youngster's behalf.

In the ensuing fighting neither side really gained the upper hand. Then, in the spring of 1217, at the behest of some of his supporters, Louis agreed to divide his army. He remained in the south and proceeded to besiege Dover Castle – which had enjoyed a temporary respite from rebel siege operations – while the rest of his army under the Earl of Winchester and the Count of Perche moved to relieve Mountsorrel Castle in Leicestershire. The siege had been raised by the time they arrived. Hence they moved east and augmented forces investing Lincoln Castle from within the city.

News of events reached the regent at Northampton on 13 May and he decided to march against the enemy assembled in Lincoln. His forces gathered at Newark a few days later, and early on the morning of the 20th the regent arrived outside the north wall of Lincoln.

The north part of the city occupied high ground and was enclosed by walls dating from Roman times: on lower ground to the south was the medieval part of Lincoln. The castle was built along part of the Roman west wall and occupied much of the south-west quarter of the Roman city.

While part of the regent's army assaulted the north gate of the city other troops entered the castle through the fortress' west gate and proceeded to sally into Lincoln via the castle's east gate. As this was happening, Lincoln's blocked west gate – a short distance to the north of the castle – was forced open and the regent entered the city. He was subsequently reinforced when the north gate was at last forced.

In fierce fighting, the adherents of Louis were driven down into the lower part of Lincoln, and though they tried to regain the high ground were repulsed. Eventually, they fled southwards out of the city leaving behind many dead, including the Count of Perche and many persons of rank, captive.

The engagement was a disaster for Henry III's opponents and was followed by peace negotiations. As D. A. Carpenter has observed: 'The heart had been ripped from Louis's party in England. The battle of Lincoln, one of the most decisive in English history, meant that England would be ruled by the Angevin, not the Capetian, dynasty'.

4
LEWES
14 MAY 1264

In 1258 a group of leading nobles who were disaffected by Henry III's irresponsible and ineffective rule, forced Henry to accept the Provisions of Oxford which resulted in significant changes. For instance, a council was established to control and reform the government. However, subsequent events showed that Henry – who had the support of the Pope – was not prepared to abide by the Provisions and this led to civil war.

Fighting broke out in the spring of 1264. By this date the leader of the disenchanted members of the baronage was the king's brother-in-law, Simon de Montfort, Earl of Leicester. Simon left London on 6 May and moved south against Henry who was campaigning in the south-east. On 11 May he reached Fletching. On the same day the king arrived at the little town of Lewes some ten miles to the south, further down the valley of the Sussex Ouse.

During the course of the following two days, Montfort opened negotiations with Henry to avoid bloodshed, but when it became evident that the king was still not prepared to maintain the Provisions he decided to take the offensive. A great medievalist, the late Sir Maurice Powicke, has said of this period, 'a sense of beauty lingers over those days in May when the great earl waited among the woods of the Weald. High spirits and anxious forebodings, eager exaltation and solemn resolve had brought bishops, friars, barons, and Londoners together in a transient mood of high purpose....In the words of the St. Albans chronicler, Earl Simon's followers were united in faith and will and courage to die for their country'.

During the night of the 13th Simon marched towards Lewes. At around dawn the following day he began deploying on high ground overlooking the town. He divided his army into four divisions. Nicholas de Segrave commanded the left wing, the Earl of Gloucester the centre, and Henry de Montfort the right wing: Simon led the reserve. The army probably numbered approximately 5,000 men, of whom about 500 were cavalry.

Henry's force was around 10,000 strong and included some 1,500 or so cavalry. Prince Edward, Henry's heir, seems to have attacked with the cavalry before the rest of the host was ready. He defeated the opposing left wing, and in the words of the *Chronicle of the Mayors and Sheriffs of London,* drove 'the greater part of the Londoners...as well as certain knights and barons' off the field. But while Edward was in pursuit, the remainder of the royal army, which consisted of battles (divisions) under Henry and his brother the Earl of Cornwall, was routed either after advancing up to engage the enemy or, as some historians think, after coming to blows with the Montfortians who came down to attack them. Thus, by the time Edward returned, Lewes was occupied by the enemy and his father was in the Cluniac priory on the southern edge of the town to where he had fled following his defeat.

Many prisoners were taken at Lewes, among them the king, (he soon gave himself up), Edward, and many other persons of consequence. The number of slain is uncertain, but included few persons of rank. However, the Battle Abbey chronicler relates that Royalists who 'were dispersed through flight, were everywhere slaughtered by villeins living in the countryside'.

5

EVESHAM
4 AUGUST 1265

After Lewes, King Henry and Prince Edward were prisoners of Simon de Montfort and the country was governed by the earl and a number of associates, most notably the Bishop of Chichester and the young Earl of Gloucester. It was a provisional administration with the task of running the country until a settlement agreeable to all parties was reached.

But peace was far from the minds of some men. Hence in early May 1265 Simon moved to Hereford (with Henry and Edward), for a number of royalist exiles had landed in Pembrokeshire at the head of a small force, intent on joining other opponents of Montfort headed by Roger Mortimer of Wigmore. Then, on 28 May, Edward managed to escape from captivity at Hereford. He made his way to Ludlow where he was joined by Mortimer and Gloucester. By this date the latter had turned against Montfort. He had grown to hate Simon's sons and to resent the dominance of the aged earl.

Faced with an increasing number of adversaries, Simon eventually decided to head east to join one of his sons – Simon the younger – at Kenilworth. On 2 August he crossed the Severn. On the evening of the 3rd he arrived at Evesham and settled down for the night at the head of a tired and hungry army of about 6,000 men.

Evesham was a death trap: it is virtually surrounded by the River Avon which loops around it in the shape of a U. This became all too obvious on the morning of the 4th. Edward trapped Montfort at Evesham after carrying out a night march from Worcester – it is said that Simon's movements had been betrayed to the prince. Edward's army probably numbered nearly 10,000 men and the bulk of it was drawn up on Green Hill to the north of Evesham, with the Avon to the east and west. The remainder was stationed to the south, on the east bank of the river, to prevent Simon escaping via a bridge across the Avon.

Accounts of battles often differ, and so it is with Evesham. The generally accepted version is that Montfort moved towards Edward's position at about 9.00am and that he formed his army into a column with cavalry in the van, English infantry in the centre, and Welsh spearmen to the rear, intent on smashing his way through the centre of the enemy line. The column clashed with the enemy at about the junction of Edward and Gloucester's battles. At first, progress was made, but when the wings of the royal army moved against Montfort's flanks the battle turned in Edward's favour. Simon's army began to collapse as the Welsh broke and fled – many may have deserted before the battle was joined – and no doubt Englishmen likewise tried to escape. The rest fought doggedly but by about 11.00am King Henry had been rescued and Simon's army destroyed.

Some favour another version of events: Montfort fought a defensive battle by forming his men into a circle which succumbed to charges by Edward and Gloucester. The important fact is that Simon's army was destroyed and that the earl and many of his supporters were among the slain, said to have numbered eighteen barons, 160 knights and 4,000 soldiers, most of whom had belonged to the vanquished force. The great days of the baronial party were well and truly over.

6

FALKIRK
22 JULY 1298

Edward I was a prepossessing figure, tall and athletic, formidable and able, a man determined to uphold his rights. He regarded himself as the overlord of Scotland, and in early 1296 began planning a Scottish campaign after being angered by the refusal of Scotland's king to obey summonses to his court, and by the fact that the Scots had decided to ally themselves to his enemy, Philip IV of France: a treaty of alliance between the Scots and French was ratified in February 1296, shortly after Edward had summoned his forces. A campaign that year led to the abdication of John Balliol, and Englishmen were placed in positions of authority. (For a fuller account see Chapter 7.) However, many Scots were not prepared to accept English domination. They revolted in 1297, led by William Wallace and Andrew Murray, and routed an English army at Stirling Bridge.

1297 was a year of political discord in England owing to disaffection with some of Edward's policies. The defeat concentrated people's minds: it had to be avenged. A formidable army was summoned to assemble at Roxburgh on 25 June 1298. The cavalry probably numbered 3,000, while pay rolls show that Edward had 14,800 infantry and about 10,900 Welsh foot.

On 15 July Edward arrived at Kirkliston, a few miles west of Edinburgh. Here he was rejoined by the Bishop of Durham, Antony Bek, 'the most valiant clerk in Christendom', who had taken Dirleton and two other castles after being sent to clear the coastlands south of the Forth.

Supplies were scarce for the Scots had laid waste much of the countryside. Hunger led to depression and acrimony: bad feeling occurred between the English and the Welsh. In such circumstances, Edward decided to return to Edinburgh and await supplies. Upon hearing however that the Scottish army was near Falkirk, he moved against it and spent the night of 21/22 July just east of Linlithgow.

Before sunrise, Edward was on the move again. He soon caught sight of the Scots, whom Wallace had prepared for battle. It seems that they were arrayed on a natural defensive position immediately south of Callendar Wood where the ground slopes down to the confluence of two burns. He had grouped his men in four schiltroms – densely packed formations bristling with spears, and in between these were companies of archers. Wallace also had some cavalry.

Two English divisions of cavalry, one under the Earls of Lincoln, Norfolk, and Hereford, the other under Bek, advanced to the attack, moving in respectively from the west and east after avoiding boggy ground before Wallace's position. They converged and proceeded to drive off the isolated Scottish horse and overwhelm Wallace's archers. In due course, the static schiltroms were destroyed, and this was most probably primarily due to the fire of the English archers. The Welsh, who stood aloof for most of the battle, joined in when it was evident that the Scots were beaten.

Only one knight perished on the English side but many others must have been wounded. Casualties among the foot probably approached 2,000. The number of Scots slain and wounded was horrific. Wallace escaped, but his military reputation was destroyed, or at least seriously damaged.

7

BANNOCKBURN
24 JUNE 1314

*'From his youth he devoted himself in private to the art of rowing
and driving carts, of digging ditches and thatching houses, as was
commonly said...and other pointless and trivial occupations unsuitable
for the son of a king.'*
—Lanercost Chronicle

Of whom was the chronicler speaking? None other than Edward, Prince of
Wales, the unconventional son and heir of one of England's most conventional kings, Edward I. In July 1307 the prince succeeded to the throne when
his redoubtable father died on the eve of a Scottish expedition, an event
which raised this question: would the new king follow in his predecessor's
footsteps and continue vigorously trying to hammer the Scots into submission?

But before dealing with this question, another should be asked: what had led
to Edward I's policy of attempting the subjugation of Scotland? This question
has been touched upon in Chapter Six but for a fuller answer we need to go back
to 1286 when that small but prospering nation was ruled by Alexander III. In
March of that year he died after falling from his horse, leaving his young granddaughter Margaret as the rightful heir to the Scottish throne. Then, in 1290, an
agreement was ratified whereby Margaret would marry Edward I's heir, but in
the autumn she followed her grandfather to the grave and with her death the
royal line of Scotland failed.

Thirteen claimants to the throne came forward and overtures were made to
Edward of England, requesting his involvement in the proceedings so that the
succession could be determined without recourse to civil war. On 17 November
1292 Edward, who was accepted as the overlord of Scotland by the claimants,
chose one of them, John Balliol, to be the new king and subsequently received his
homage.

For a while relations between Edward and Balliol were cordial, but the Scots
in general were not prepared to accept Edward's suzerainty and were not
impressed by their new king who was no born leader. In mid 1295 the Scottish
parliament wrested power from Balliol and vested it in a council which proceeded to ratify (February 1296) an alliance with the French – with whom
Edward had been at war since 1294 – promising mutual support if needed. This
development, combined with Balliol's failure to appear at Edward's court to

answer charges brought against him by a Scot, resulted in an English invasion of Scotland in March 1296.

The campaign led to the defeat of a Scottish force at Dunbar and Balliol's subsequent surrender and abdication in the summer after which Edward held a parliament at Berwick where he received the homage of many important Scots. He then returned to England leaving the governance of Scotland to trusted English subordinates.

However, in 1297 widespread rebellion broke out and an English army was routed at Stirling Bridge on 11 September by a force under William Wallace, a man of knightly family, and the aristocratic Andrew Murray. In response, Edward led a campaign in Scotland the following year and inflicted a major defeat on Wallace at Falkirk on 22 July. Nonetheless resistance continued, and though many Scots of consequence subsequently surrendered, Wallace remained a thorn in Edward's flesh as a guerrilla leader until his capture and execution in 1305, by which date Scotland had been to all intents and purposes subjugated.

But then, suddenly, the situation was transformed. By whom? By Robert Bruce, the grandson of one of the claimants to the Scottish throne in the early 1290s. Where, when and how? At Dumfries and Scone in February and March 1306; firstly when Bruce murdered Balliol's nephew, John Comyn, following an argument in which the latter evidently refused to support a plan by Robert to seize the throne; and secondly, when Bruce was enthroned as King of Scotland at Scone.

News of events in Scotland infuriated England's ageing and increasingly vengeful king. Once again he made plans to crush his Scottish enemies. His kinsman, Aymer de Valence, (who was married to a sister of Comyn), and Henry Percy were appointed to command forces in operations against Bruce. In early June, Aymer arrived at Perth. His advance had been unopposed. Indeed, he had been augmented en route by relatives of Comyn. He secured the town, with an army some 6,000 strong. On 19 June Bruce arrived outside Perth with an army mainly raised in the north-east of Scotland. Lacking siege engines, and sufficient manpower, Bruce could not attempt to take Perth and so fell back for the night near Methven, after challenging de Valence either to come out and fight or to surrender. Aymer had replied that he would engage Bruce in battle the following morning. But, at dusk, he fell upon the Scottish camp and shattered the surprised Scots.

Bruce managed to flee the battle, but within months was forced to shelter in Ireland or the Inner Hebrides. In early 1307 he returned to Scotland and, in the spring, defeated Valence at both Glentrool and Loudoun Hill before putting a force under the Earl of Gloucester to flight. According to Walter of Guisborough, Edward I was 'much enraged' by Bruce's successes and understandably so. Although the encounters had been little more than skirmishes their outcome had undermined English morale and had brought fresh recruits to Bruce's side: the tide had turned. But had it turned permanently?

Edward was determined that it had not. But he was nearing his end – he had just spent several months in poor health at Lanercost Priory near the border. Nevertheless, the tenacious but weary old warrior set out from Carlisle on 3 July to campaign in Scotland. But, on the 7th, he expired nearby at Burgh-upon-the-Sands.

This brings us back to the question raised earlier: would Edward I's successor continue vigorously trying to subjugate Scotland? At first necessity demanded otherwise: matters such as a state funeral, coronation, and consequent holding of a parliament, required his attention: the planned Scottish expedition was abandoned. Nonetheless, Edward II showed that he was not indifferent to affairs north of the border for he appointed Aymer de Valence and the Earl of Richmond as his lieutenants in Scotland to continue the struggle against the nationalists under Bruce.

But as an eminent medievalist, the late May McKisack has observed: 'Edward II had not been many months on the throne before it became apparent that English policy towards Scotland would no longer be guided by any consistent or statesmanlike purpose...Scottish affairs and the defence of the northern border would always be subordinate to his private loves and hates.'

The same could be said of other aspects of royal policy. In short, Edward soon showed that he was unfitted for kingship and his irresponsible behaviour, such as his addiction to a favourite, Piers Gaveston, ('the king would speak to no one save in his presence,' states the *Vita Edwardi Secundi*), produced a reaction. In 1311 the king was forced to accept the Ordinances, regulations ordained by a committee of magnates intended to safeguard the interests of the realm. Among other things, Gaveston was banished. He soon returned however, but was subsequently captured by a group of earls and executed on 19 June 1312. 'From that day,' Edward's biographer records, 'a perpetual enmity grew up between the king and the earls.'

Obviously Edward's incapacity and the problems it caused, presented Bruce with a golden opportunity to further his aims and he seized it with both hands; besieging castles in Scotland held by the English; waging war against the relatives and friends of Comyn ranged against him; and raiding the north of England thereby gaining great sums of money for his war-treasury from the local populace who purchased truces.

In fairness, on occasion Edward did make an effort in Scotland during this period. In 1310, for example, he advanced through the Scottish Lowlands at the head of an army towards Linlithgow. If he had expected to be confronted by Bruce, he was disappointed. Robert proved elusive, keeping to 'caves and wooded places' as states Edward's biographer, and limited his response to attacking foraging parties.

By 1313 most of Scotland was controlled by Bruce and early in that year his campaign to oust the English resulted in the capture of the castles of Perth,

Roxburgh and Edinburgh. By spring, Stirling Castle was the only fortress of any consequence and strategic importance still in English hands.

Its commander was Sir Philip Mowbray, and in the summer shortage of supplies led him to come to an agreement with Bruce's brother, Edward, who was besieging the castle. Edward agreed to raise the siege on condition that Mowbray would surrender Stirling if a relieving English army did not appear within three leagues (nine miles) of the castle by Midsummer Day, 1314.

Mowbray subsequently hastened south to make Edward II aware of how vitally important it was that Stirling be saved. Hence, by late 1313 Edward was planning to lead an army north, and he proceeded to raise a formidable force without obtaining parliament's consent. This was an infraction of the Ordinances, but since Gaveston's death the king's position had been strengthened somewhat because a number of formerly disaffected nobles had aligned themselves with him. One such was Aymer de Valence, who had become Earl of Pembroke in 1308.

Edward Bruce's chivalrous decision to accept Mowbray's proposition therefore placed his brother in a difficult position. Hitherto, as has been seen, Robert had deliberately avoided fighting a pitched battle with the English. Falkirk had destroyed, or at least seriously damaged, Wallace's reputation and Bruce was not eager to risk all he had achieved by confronting an English army in view of what had transpired on that occasion. However, if he failed to confront the expected English army then perhaps his position among the Scots would be undermined. The stage had been set for a showdown: Bruce decided to accept the challenge.

By mid June the English army had mustered on the border. On the 17th Edward crossed the Tweed at Berwick and began marching towards Edinburgh. Some have maintained that he did so along the coast, via Dunbar. However, though slight, the evidence – such as an order issued by the king at Soutre in Lauderdale within days of leaving Berwick – points in another direction: up the Tweed valley and then north through Lauderdale. Edward entered Edinburgh on the 21st. On Saturday 22nd he pressed on again and arrived at Falkirk that evening. He was twenty miles west of Edinburgh, and ten miles from Stirling to the north-west.

Meanwhile, Bruce had assembled his forces in Torwood, a forest between Falkirk and the Bannock burn, a tributary stream of the Forth about two and a quarter miles from Stirling. He had then taken up a position on a fairly well wooded plateau north of the burn to counter a move by Edward up the road from Falkirk to Stirling. To strengthen his position Bruce had a series of pits dug on either side of the road. They may have contained pointed stakes and were camouflaged by grass laid on sticks. Moreover, although Bruce could not be outflanked to the west owing to the densely wooded nature of the terrain, there was a possibility that the English would attempt to reach Stirling by making their way across low ground to the east – the Carse – and thus part of Bruce's army was deployed to overlook the area. This is especially true of a battle under

Bruce's nephew, Thomas Randolph, Lord Moray, who was stationed to the rear of the army beside a church, St Ninian's.

On the afternoon of the 23rd the English army approached the open ground in the valley of the burn separating Torwood from the area where Bruce was stationed. Edward was now joined by Sir Philip Mowbray, who had returned to Stirling following his visit to England. Mowbray reminded him that under the terms of the agreement with the Scots, Stirling Castle was now relieved because the English army was within three leagues of it: Edward did not have to press forward. However the king and his captains were intent on confronting and destroying Bruce. Nothing less would do.

Lord Robert Clifford and Sir Henry de Beaumont were subsequently despatched with a force of about 300 men-at-arms to make their way across the Carse and head for Stirling Castle. There they would temporarily augment the garrison and be well placed to harass the Scots if they commenced withdrawing.

When they were not far from St Ninian's Kirk, Clifford and Beaumont saw that Moray was moving against them, having been ordered to do so by Bruce. The English thus prepared to charge. One source for the Battle of Bannockburn is the *Scalacronica*, composed in 1355 by an English knight, Sir Thomas Gray of Heton, whose father (also called Thomas), was with Clifford and Beaumont. From this we hear that Beaumont commented as the Scots approached: 'Let us wait a little and let them come on', and that Gray then observed: 'Whatever you give them I doubt not that they will have all soon enough'. Then, stung by Beaumont's rejoinder that he could quit the field if he wished, Gray charged alone and was captured after his horse had been brought down by the Scottish pikes. Another knight, Sir William Deyncourt, followed Gray and was killed.

Soon the rest of the cavalry force charged Moray's schiltrom. Fierce fighting ensued. Repeatedly the English men-at-arms tried to penetrate the ranks of their opponents. Despite their efforts, they failed. Indeed, they were thrown onto the defensive and sooner or later were put to flight. Some made for the castle. The rest headed back to rejoin the king. During the encounter, James Douglas, the commander of one of Bruce's other schiltroms, had begun moving to assist Moray and it is possible that the sight of his approach may have played a part in undermining the morale of the men under Clifford and Beaumont.

While these events were unfolding, the English van under the Earls of Hereford and Gloucester crossed the Bannock burn and began ascending the ground leading to Bruce's position. As it did so, a knight at the head of the column, Hereford's nephew, Sir Henry de Bohun, spotted the Scottish king mounted on a grey palfrey and distinguished by a crown worn over his helmet. Bruce was in an exposed position. He is often said to have been reviewing his lines, but it is possible that he deliberately rode out to challenge the Englishman. Upon seeing the king, de Bohun spurred his charger forward, his lance aimed at Bruce.

The king responded calmly. At the last moment he swerved aside, and thus John Barbour (whose work, *The Brus*, was written in 1385), records: 'Sher Henry myssit the nobill Kyng'. Bruce, however, found his target. He turned in his saddle and cleft de Bohun 'to the brisket'. The exultant Scots who witnessed the incident then rushed forward against the dead knight's shaken colleagues and inflicted some loss on them as they withdrew to the main body of the army south of the burn. According to the *Vita Edwardi Secundi*, Gloucester was unhorsed during this rather humiliating episode for the English.

Evidently, Edward and his captains decided that it was too dangerous to move directly against Bruce's strong defensive position. Thus, on the evening of the 23rd, the English army began making its way across the Bannock burn somewhere to the east of the Falkirk-Stirling road and proceeded to spend the night, (or what remained of it, for the crossing would have been time consuming), somewhere on the Carse. As the *Scalacronica* comments, 'they came out on a plain fronting the Water of Forth, beyond Bannock Burn, a bad, deep, streamy morass, where the said host of the English settled down'. Most of the extensive baggage train was no doubt left on the south side of the burn. Indeed, some of it may already have been left at Edinburgh.

EDWARD II AND HIS ARMY

Edward was born at Caernarvon on 25 April 1284, the fourth son of Edward I by his much loved wife Eleanor of Castile. Like his father, he had a strong physical presence for he was tall and muscular, but unlike him he was not a martial figure. For instance, he did not love tournaments. He did, however, excel at horsemanship, but most of his pursuits were more plebeian such as digging, thatching and boating. Nonetheless, Edward was not uncultured. He loved listening to minstrels, had literary interests, and was interested in architecture.

Edward became heir to the throne in 1284, within months of his birth, and was granted the royal lands in Wales and the earldom of Chester by his father on 7 February 1301. From May of that year until his accession he was termed Prince of Wales. Though disinclined to military matters, he participated in four Scottish campaigns while heir to the throne. In July, 1306, for example, he led an army into Scotland from Carlisle, received the surrender of Lochmaben Castle, and marched to Perth ravaging the countryside as he did so.

The *Lanercost Chronicle* describes Edward as 'chicken-hearted,' but in fact he was no coward. However as this comment makes clear, he did not command respect. His rustic pursuits and almost certain homosexual relationship with Gaveston (the son of a Gascon knight who had served in Edward I's household), alienated people. His addiction to Gaveston, for instance, resulted in his not treating his 'natural counsellors' the barons with the attention and respect that they deserved. Edward's laziness, lack of judgement and extravagance only added to the low opinion many of his subjects had for him. Michael Prestwich has plausibly suggested that Edward's personal inadequacy was perhaps partly 'the result of his relationship with his formidable father, who must have been a hard man to live up to'.

The size of Edward's army at Bannockburn is uncertain. Barbour states that it numbered 190,000 men but he clearly inflated its strength to reflect glory on his hero, Bruce. Some modern writers are of the opinion that Edward had 2–3,000 cavalry and around 20,000 infantry. On the other hand, in a stimulating account of Bannockburn Major Becke has argued that the cavalry probably did not exceed 550 men and that the infantry was between 6,000 and 6,500 strong.

It is true that Edward's earls, with the exceptions of Hereford, Pembroke and Gloucester, refused to participate in the campaign and only sent their feudal quotas. It is also true that the writs – issued at Newminster near Morpeth on 27 May – which summoned 21,540 foot were issued at a late date and that not all men requested for a campaign made an appearance anyway: in 1300, of 16,000 infantry called upon for a Scottish expedition only 9,000 mustered at the rendezvous. Nonetheless, Becke's figures are too low. 12,500 infantry alone had been summoned from the northern counties where many communities had suffered from Scottish raids and where a desire for revenge no doubt resulted in a positive response. In short, it seems reasonable to conclude that Edward had nearly 2,000 cavalry and about 16,000 infantry. Indeed these figures may be slightly too low.

The core of the army was formed by the royal household cavalry. This consisted of the bannerets (knights who could bring a retinue to the field under their own banners), knights, squires and sergeants-at-arms of the king's household, and the retinues of the bannerets and knights in question. The royal household could provide a substantial cavalry force. It provided 800 cavalry for the Falkirk campaign of 1298 (at which time the total cavalry force may have numbered 3,000), whilst two years later some 850 men-at-arms participated in another Scottish campaign.

The rest of the cavalry included men-at-arms brought on campaign by lords performing feudal service – men who had to serve at their own expense for 40 days, after which they could return home or stay in royal pay. Furthermore, there were men-at-arms brought by lords on a voluntary basis in addition to their obligatory quotas.

The heavy cavalry formed the elite component of the army. They rode great war-horses which often had splendid names and both horse and rider were protected by armour. They must have been an impressive sight. This would have been particularly true of the lords, bannerets and knights, with their emblazoned surcoats and shields, and their banners (in the case of the first two categories), and pennons fluttering from their lances.

Most men-at-arms possessed a lance and sword, and all would have had a dagger. For protection they wore coats of mail, though plate armour was used to protect knees, elbows, shoulders and shins. Shields afforded additional protection, as did helmets, many of which completely enclosed the head.

At a later stage in the Scottish wars it became common for English men-at-arms to fight on foot. They did so for instance at Halidon Hill in 1333, 'contrary to the old habits of their fathers' as Geoffrey le Baker noted. But in 1314 they still fought on horseback, the traditional mode of fighting for chivalry, and a charge by heavy cavalry was an awesome spectacle which often struck fear into opposing infantry.

The infantry in Edward's army came from Wales, the northern counties of England, Lincolnshire, Warwickshire, and Leicestershire. The men were recruited by commissioners of array acting in accordance with the summonses issued on 27 May. It was the commissioners' duty to select the best men available, and the communities from which the men came were supposed to provide them with suitable equipment for war.

A notable weapon common among the infantry was the longbow, a weapon which is first recorded as having been used by the men of South Wales in the twelfth century and was subsequently adopted by the English. The longbow, which was often made of yew, could be a potent weapon in strong and experienced hands. Indeed, the penetrative power of an arrow fired from such a bow is said to equal that of a rifle bullet. The accurate range of the longbow was about 250 yards and a skilled archer could loose off up to twelve arrows a minute, and when a large number of archers fired in unison the noise of the arrows as they flew through the air frequently frightened adversaries and their mounts.

In addition to his bow and quiver of arrows, an archer carried a sword or axe for close combat. Spears and swords, of course, would have been the principal weapons of infantrymen who were not archers. The infantry wore thick quilted jackets which afforded them some protection, as well as headgear such as the chapelle-de-fer, an iron hat with a brim and low comb.

ROBERT BRUCE AND HIS ARMY

Robert Bruce was born in Scotland on 11 July 1274, into a family which held estates in both England and Scotland. The Bruces were of Norman origin – they had come to Britain with the Conqueror – and in common with some other Norman families had acquired land in Scotland during the reign of David I (1124–53), a man who had spent much time in England and of whom the late A. L. Poole observed: 'David's court was a Norman court and in his reign Scotland became a feudal country'.

Thus Bruce had an Anglo-Scottish background and this helps to explain why he was not a constant Scottish nationalist in his early years. For example, like his father, he supported Edward I against Balliol in 1296 and swore fealty to him at Berwick on 24 August. In the following year, however, he sided with Wallace and laid waste lands of adherents of the English king. There is no evidence that he fought at Stirling Bridge or Falkirk, but what is known is that shortly after the latter he was appointed one of the Guardians of Scotland by the nationalists and though he subsequently resigned, remained opposed to Edward until 1302 when he came to terms with the king and fought on his behalf against the nationalists in 1303–4. Edward I was not the most generous of English kings and it may well have been the case that Bruce did not feel that he received adequate reward for his services. This seems likely in view of the fact that in early 1306 he risked all by leading the rising which led to his enthronement.

There is no doubt that Robert Bruce was a brave man. We also know that he was physically prepossessing for he was 6ft tall and powerfully built. Though at times impetuous, he was shrewd and intelligent, a born leader who could endure hardship and prove resourceful, a man to be reckoned with.

At Bannockburn Bruce had about 500 cavalry and around 6,000 infantry. Moreover, there was a miscellaneous body, perhaps 3,000 strong, of camp followers and ill-equipped and inexperienced patriots, the 'small folk'.

Bruce's army had many veterans in its ranks. This is certainly true of its commanders for his lieutenants included able and experienced figures such as James Douglas, whose exploits had earned him an heroic reputation. As W. M. MacKenzie has commented: 'Years of common activity had given these men knowledge of each other's qualities and respect for them, and their reputations were buttresses to the host....Hard circumstances had developed and given edge to what was most necessary in the Scottish leaders; in comparison, the English, equally brave and high spirited, were but amateurs or of undeveloped talents, with a few veterans'.

Furthermore, the army was a determined force. According to Barbour, Bruce had told any faint-hearted individuals to depart. Only men who would 'wyn all or de with honour' were to stay. What is certain is that the majority of the men present were tough individuals with a real sense of purpose.

Although the Scottish knights and men-at-arms wore armour, Bruce's cavalry was inferior to that of the English for many of the mounts were smaller than those of Edward II's men and few of the horses had armour. The infantry were armed with pikes 16 to 18ft long, had shields, and wore protective gear, some of it armoured. Moreover, some had an axe as their principal weapon: others still, were archers.

At Falkirk, the Scottish infantry had been formed into schiltroms. These were densely packed formations of pike-and axemen walled by their shields, and with the pikes protruding in all directions. The schiltrom could be a strong defensive formation, effective against cavalry, and not surprisingly Bruce decided to form his infantry into schiltroms at Bannockburn.

DESCRIPTION

It will be remembered that the English army spent the night of 23–24 June on the Carse. But just where it encamped on this large plain, which was very marshy in places, is uncertain. Some are of the opinion that it was between the Bannock burn and its tributary, the Pelstream and this view is accepted here. Such a position, with streams on three sides and a narrow front, is in accord with statements that the battle was fought in a very restricted area. Barbour, for example, emphasises the 'great stratnes of the plase' upon which the engagement occurred.

Though Edward's army was formidable when day dawned at about 4.00am on Monday 24th, few of his men can have felt eager for battle. For one thing, the strenuous march of the previous day had sapped their strength. Moreover, the reverses of the 23rd had undermined morale. Sir Thomas Gray records that the 'English had been put out of countenance and were exceedingly dispirited by what had occurred'. The *Lanercost Chronicle* makes the same point, referring to 'great fear...among the English'. In fact, during the course of the night Sir Alexander Seton, a Scot serving in the army, had deserted to Bruce and informed him that he only needed to attack to gain victory.

Early on the morning of the 24th Bruce did just that. He advanced towards the English with his army in echelon. The foremost battle was that of Edward

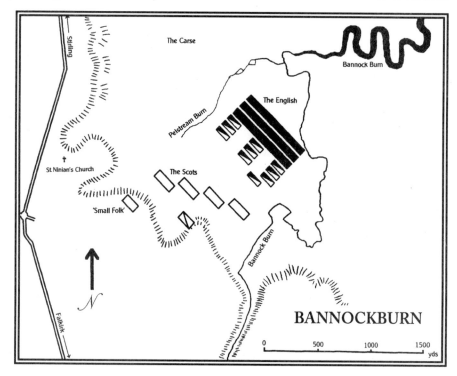

Bruce on the right, then came that of Moray, then Sir James Douglas' battle, and behind, that of the king. The cavalry, to the rear, was commanded by Sir Robert Keith. As the army proper advanced, the 'small folk' moved to the eastern rim of the high ground from which their countrymen had descended and halted to watch as events unfolded below.

The Scots' advance was an unpleasant surprise for Edward's congested army which was only in the process of arraying, and necessitated speedy action on its part. According to Barbour there were ten 'battles' of cavalry. As Sir Charles Oman has written, these were 'probably in three lines of three each, with the tenth forming an advance guard'. Behind the cavalry was the bulk of Edward's force, the infantry.

According to the *Lanercost Chronicle*, as the Scots moved across the Carse they suddenly halted and 'fell on their knees, repeating Pater Noster and commending themselves to God, after which they advanced boldly against the enemy'. Reportedly, as Edward II watched this he commented: 'Those men kneel to ask for mercy'. To which Sir Ingram de Umfraville responded: 'You are right, they ask for mercy, but not from you. They ask it from God for their sins.'

Earlier in the morning, Edward had angered the 23-year-old Earl of Gloucester – who was in joint command of the English van with his rival, Hereford – by accusing him of prevarication and treachery for not being eager enough to come to blows with the enemy. Smarting from this, and perhaps eager to upstage Hereford, Gloucester now charged against Edward Bruce's oncoming schiltrom without even waiting to don his surcoat and was soon slain.

The *Lanercost Chronicle* relates that in the subsequent clash between the van and Edward Bruce's men, 'the great steeds of the knights dashed into the Scottish pikes as into a thick wood; there arose a great and horrible crash from rending lances and dying horses'. The Scottish pikes took a heavy toll. Many were directed at the steeds of their assailants which were thus horribly wounded, bringing both the mounts and their hapless riders crashing to the ground. More and more limbs and lives were destroyed, and though the English fought bravely they could not break the schiltrom of their determined opponents.

The other English cavalry battles had by now also become engaged or had attempted to do so. Some had ridden forward to support the van; the rest had moved against the schiltroms of Moray and Douglas which (from the English point of view), were to the right of Edward Bruce. According to the *Lanercost Chronicle* the English were so densely packed that the rear ranks 'could not help' their colleagues. Again, fierce combat occurred. Valiantly the English desperately tried to break the formations of the stubborn Scots, but once more their attempts proved fruitless.

While the above conflict was raging some, if not all, of Edward's archers took up a position to the north of the Scots and commenced firing. Barbour tells us that: 'The English shot so fast that, if only their shooting had lasted, it would have been hard for the Scots'. Seeing this, Robert Bruce sent in his cavalry under Sir Robert Keith and scattered the unfortunate bowmen, some of whom fled the field whilst others fell back behind the fighting line.

Elsewhere, the battle was also going in the Scots' favour. Confusion, frustration and fear, were becoming increasingly prevalent in the ranks of Edward's hardpressed army. Geoffrey le Baker states that some of the English archers fired arrows at a high trajectory over the cavalry in front of them and in so doing 'hit some few Scots in the breast, but struck many more English in the back'. If so, this would understandably have had a disconcerting effect on the congested cavalry whose morale had already been damaged by its failure to break the schiltroms of Edward Bruce, Moray and Douglas.

Then, to make things worse, Robert Bruce moved forward, almost certainly against the English right, thereby increasing the pressure. Soon, according to Barbour, the cry 'On them! On them! On them! They fail!' could be heard along the battlefront as the Scots realised that Edward's once proud army was faltering.

As the battle was drawing to a close the 'small folk', who had been eagerly watching events, commenced moving forward, having tied sheets to poles to serve as banners. They were mistaken by the demoralised English as fresh Scottish soldiers. Resistance thus began crumbling.

At this juncture, with many of his men taking to their heels, and himself in danger of capture, King Edward was persuaded by Pembroke and a celebrated knight, Sir Giles de Argentine, to quit the field. According to the *Scalacronica*, as the king made his way to safety he had to fend off some of the enemy with his mace. Edward headed for Stirling Castle accompanied by Pembroke, Sir Giles, and a cavalry escort. However, proud Sir Giles disdained flight for himself. Once he was sure that the king had escaped, he turned around and charged against the enemy. 'Thus died', as Major Becke has commented, 'one of the bravest and finest knights of the Christendom of his day'.

The departure of the king seems to have hastened the complete collapse of his army. Men began fleeing in all directions, including towards the castle, desperate to escape the carnage. Many never made it. They were either cut down by pursuing Scots, or drowned in the Forth or while attempting to cross Bannock burn. Indeed, it is said that so many perished in the latter that it became possible for others to cross dryshod.

And what of King Edward and his escort? Sir Philip Mowbray refused to let them enter Stirling Castle for the stronghold now had to be surrendered to the Scots. Consequently they rode circuitously past the victors and, pursued by Douglas, then headed east towards Dunbar from where they sailed to Berwick.

Bannockburn is sometimes said to have been the worst defeat ever suffered by an English army. This is going too far. Nonetheless, a great reverse it most certainly was. At least 37 lords, bannerets and knights perished, either in the skirmishes of the 23rd, the battle proper, or the pursuit, and likely hundreds of ordinary men-at-arms likewise fell. Losses among the infantry were also severe, though just how severe is unknown.

Furthermore, many prisoners of note were taken in the battle or while in flight. Among them was the Earl of Hereford who was subsequently exchanged for Bruce's wife, sister and daughter who had been held by the English since 1306. Another captive was the keeper of the privy seal, Roger Northburgh, a highly important governmental official.

In addition the victors also seized much plunder in the English camp, including rich fabrics and gilt and silver vessels. Edward's biographer estimated the value of the losses at £200,000. Whatever the true figure, it was a significant prize for the Scots and undoubtedly sweetened the taste of victory.

Bruce's own losses seem to have been relatively slight. In fact according to Barbour only two Scottish knights perished in the battle, and there is little reason to doubt this figure.

Sir Charles Oman has observed of Edward II, 'to be attacked and beaten when, by your own fault, you have no power to utilize superior numbers and armament is the mark of a bad general'. The king's performance was indeed lamentable. For instance, he committed the cardinal error of underestimating his opponent and was thus surprised when Bruce advanced against him on the 24th, with the result that he was forced to fight on ground which was not ideal. Moreover, he failed to deploy his archers properly.

In contrast, Bruce deserves admiration. He exercised discipline over his men, chose a strong position on which to confront Edward initially and then, instead of remaining on the defensive, boldly seized the initiative by advancing against his opponent's larger army on the Carse. It was a decisive and skilful performance.

Finally, something must be said about Bannockburn's historical significance militarily and politically. At Falkirk in 1298 the English cavalry had evidently found Wallace's schiltroms formidable, and according to one account of the battle, Edward I's army only made headway after he had used his archers against them. What is certain is that Bannockburn, like Courtrai in 1302, (when Flemish infantry routed the chivalry of France), and Morgarten in 1315, (when Swiss pikemen defeated the heavy cavalry of the Habsburgs), showed clearly that the nature of warfare had changed. For generations mounted knights had been dominant, but those days were over. The French were slow to grasp the fact. The English soon did so. In future battles such as Halidon Hill (1333) and Crécy (1346), they were to emerge victorious by combining dismounted knights and men-at-arms with archers deployed in such a way that they could use their longbows effectively.

The *Lanercost Chronicle* relates that following Bannockburn 'Robert de Bruce was commonly called King of Scotland by all men, because he had acquired

Scotland by force of arms'. It is undoubtedly true that Bannockburn consolidated his position and greatly enhanced his reputation.

In contrast, Edward's reputation sank even lower, and following his return to England he was at the mercy of his political enemies. His biographer informs us that Edward 'made for York and there took counsel with the Earl of Lancaster and the other magnates,' and that 'the earls said that the Ordinances had not been observed and therefore events had turned out badly for the king'. Edward thus promised to observe the Ordinances, and in subsequent months watched helplessly as positions of importance were filled by friends and supporters of his principal English opponent, Lancaster.

Fortunately for the king, Lancaster's dominance soon waned. He proved an inept figure and more moderate men such as Pembroke came to the fore. Then, in 1322, Lancaster was defeated at Boroughbridge in Yorkshire whilst in revolt and was soon executed. Hence Edward's position became stronger than it had been for years and the Ordinances were consequently annulled in parliament. But the king soon squandered his chance of redeeming himself in the eyes of his people – largely through the favouritism he showed to the avaricious Despenser family. In 1327, following a revolt led by his embittered wife Isabella, (whom he had married in 1308) and her aristocratic lover, Roger Mortimer of Wigmore, he was forced to abdicate in favour of his son and then murdered in Berkeley Castle.

Since Bannockburn, (save during periods of truce), the Scots had repeatedly raided the north of England, thereby devastating the region. Mortimer and Isabella therefore decided to make peace with the Scots once and for all (England's new king, Edward III, was just a youngster), and in the Treaty of Northampton (1328), Bruce was recognised as the King of the Scots and Scotland was acknowledged to be an independent realm in no way subject to England. Furthermore, it was agreed that Bruce's four-year-old son, David, would marry Edward III's young sister, Joan.

By this date Robert Bruce was ailing, and in the following year he died. Through his courageous and skilful leadership he had secured the independence of his country and won for himself everlasting renown: 'in the art of fighting and in the vigour of body,' wrote the chronicler John Fordhun, 'Robert had not his match in his time in any clime.'

8

HALIDON HILL
10 JULY 1333

In 1329 Scotland's king, Robert Bruce, died and was succeeded by his five-year-old son, David II. As David was too young to rule, the Earl of Moray became regent and governed the country on his behalf. In the summer of 1332 Moray died and was succeeded by the Earl of Mar. He had to face an invasion from England led by Edward Balliol (the son of John Balliol, Scotland's king from 1292–96), and a number of exiles whose land in Scotland had been forfeited through treason. Mar was killed in battle at Dupplin Moor on 11 August and in September Balliol was crowned King of Scotland at Scone after which, in November, he acknowledged Edward III of England as his liege lord. But Balliol was far from secure, and was soon driven back across the border by Scots loyal to David.

Balliol was determined to recover his throne, and in the spring of 1333 he moved north at the head of an English army with Edward's blessing. He besieged the strategic border town of Berwick upon Tweed, and was soon joined by Edward himself, for the English king was an adventurous young man eager for military glory and intent on avenging the ignominious defeat experienced by his father at Bannockburn in 1314.

By this date Sir Archibald Douglas was regent of Scotland, and he moved south to relieve Berwick. He failed to dislodge the English army entrenched around the town and so moved into Northumberland where he began plundering the countryside, no doubt hoping that Edward III would raise the siege and pursue him. He was wrong. Edward stood firm, determined not to ease the pressure on Berwick.

It had been agreed between the investing forces and the garrison that if the town were not relieved by a certain date the latter would surrender. To ensure that this would occur a number of hostages had been sent to the English camp. In order to increase pressure on the garrison the king now unjustifiably threatened to hang one of the hostages, Thomas Seton, the son of Berwick's governor, in the hope of forcing the governor to surrender early to save his son. The threat failed – Thomas was hanged in view of the garrison.

Upon hearing of this outrage, Douglas returned to Scotland and proceeded to march on Berwick. At Halidon Hill, two miles north-west of the town, he was confronted by Edward, who had marched from Berwick to oppose him with the bulk of his army.

Edward's men were deployed on a hill with marshy ground before it. They were arrayed in three battles with small wings. The right was commanded by the

Earl of Norfolk, the centre by Edward, and the left by Balliol. The army consisted of archers and dismounted knights and men-at-arms.

As the Scottish cavalry advanced towards the English position their progress was slowed down by the marshy ground, and as they ascended the hill they suffered severely from the fire of the English archers. Few of the cavalry, or of the infantry who likewise advanced, reached the English lines, and the battle ended when Edward's knights and men-at-arms mounted and charged, putting the Scots to flight.

Few Englishmen died at Halidon Hill. Scottish losses numbered into the thousands and included Douglas and many of Scotland's other noblest men.

9

NEVILLE'S CROSS
17 OCTOBER 1346

Following Edward III of England's victory at Crécy in 1346 Philip VI of France turned to Scotland, a traditional ally, for assistance. According to the English historian, Henry Knighton, Philip 'suggested to the Scots [that] there did not remain in England any unless husbandmen and shepherds, and imbecile and decrepit chaplains' because all the fighting men were in France with Edward. After receiving word that Philip required support, Scotland's young king, David II, invaded England being 'right jolly, and desirous to see fighting', according to Andrew Wyntoun.

David wasted Lanercost Priory in Cumbria, and Hexham in Northumberland, before entering Durham. He halted at Beaurepaire, just north-west of Durham City.

Edward had placed the Archbishop of York and two important northern barons, Ralph Neville and Henry Percy, in charge of defending England during his absence. Hence, on Monday 16 October, an English army summoned to oppose David arrived at Bishop Auckland about thirteen miles south of Beaurepaire.

A large body of Scottish cavalry made its way to Ferryhill about five miles north-east of Bishop Auckland, perhaps intent on raiding. However English cavalry appeared and the Scots fell back. They were pursued and a fierce clash occurred at Sunderland Bridge at a crossing of the River Wear. The badly mauled Scots then returned to the Scottish camp.

David proceeded to assemble his army and took up a position on Durham Moor a short distance south-west of Beaurepaire. If, as seems likely, the exploits referred to above occurred on the 16th rather than early on the 17th, a night passed before the English army appeared on the scene. It made its way onto high ground just beyond Neville's Cross a short distance to the west of Durham between the River Wear, which flows through the historic city, and its tributary the Browney.

The English were arrayed in three main divisions, with archers stationed to the fore and flanking each division. Sir Thomas Rokeby led the left wing. Ralph Neville, described by the *Lanercost Chronicle* as 'strong, truthful, cautious and brave,' led the centre and was in overall command. Percy commanded the right wing. A reserve of cavalry was to the rear.

The Scots then began moving towards the English position. The right was under the Earl of Moray and Sir William Douglas, David led the centre, while the left wing was commanded by Robert the Steward and the Earl of March. The army reportedly numbered between 15,000–18,000 men: the English force was of comparable strength.

The battle began at about 9.00am. As Moray and Douglas advanced they were impeded by the confined nature of the terrain and the presence of ditches and fences. Terrible execution was done by English archers, and the Scottish division broke when Rokeby closed in for the kill. Moray was slain and Douglas captured. Rokeby then turned against the right flank of David's division which was engaged in a stubborn contest with Neville. Meanwhile, on the left, the invaders threw the opposing English into some confusion only to be driven back following a charge by the English reserve which fell upon their left flank. Soon the exposed centre likewise began collapsing. A general rout ensued and many fleeing Scots perished in the Browney.

Among the significant number of important prisoners taken was King David, who had displayed 'great personal valour'. He was taken south and imprisoned in the Tower of London where he remained until 1357.

10

OTTERBURN
5 AUGUST 1388

In 1377 Edward III of England died. During his reign much of southern Scotland had been occupied by English forces. Attempts were made by the Scots to regain this territory as Edward neared his end, and campaigning increased following his death and the accession of a minor, Richard II. Hence much of the occupied zone was wrested from English hands. Then, in 1388, England was riven by discord between the king and a number of senior nobles – the appellants – who dominated the 'Merciless Parliament' which sentenced the principal members of his administration to death, exile or imprisonment.

In the summer of 1388 a large Scottish army assembled in the forest of Jedburgh intent on taking advantage of England's problems, likely with the aim of securing a peace treaty favourable to Scotland. The army divided in two. The main body invaded Cumbria and Westmorland while the young Earl of Douglas invaded the north-east.

The most influential account of the Otterburn campaign was written a year or so later by Jean Froissart, a French chronicler who talked to participants from both sides but was also given to invention. He states that once across the border Douglas moved quickly through Northumberland into Durham where he began to 'slay people and to burn villages'. (Douglas' entry into Durham is uncertain: the point is not corroborated by other chroniclers). Then, states Froissart, laden with plunder Douglas moved north towards Newcastle where an English force had assembled under the Earl of Northumberland's son, Henry Percy, 'Harry Hotspur,' an individual of martial renown. After a skirmish outside the strongly fortified town in which Douglas reportedly seized Percy's pennon, the Scots moved north.

Eager for revenge, Hotspur soon gave chase. On an August evening, most likely that of the 5th, he came upon Douglas who was evidently encamped about half a mile north-west of Otterburn astride the road to Scotland, with wooded hills to the north and a bend of the River Rede to the south. According to Froissart, Douglas had no more than 3,000 men while Percy had about 9,000: the latter figure is no doubt inflated.

After sending Sir Thomas Umfraville on a wide detour to attack the Scottish camp from the flank or rear, Percy moved forward while Douglas hurriedly sent men to hold a ridge some 500 yards in front of his camp. Battle was joined in failing light, and the fighting was fierce. Then, 'at the swynnys downe-gangyng', states *Wyntoun's Chronicle*, Douglas fell upon the English right flank after leading a detachment along a depression just to the north of the ridge. The assault threw the English off balance; they began to be pushed down towards the river. Though Douglas fell mortally wounded, the Scots fought on unaware of his fate. Meanwhile, Umfraville had fallen upon the Scottish camp and routed its guards. However, he then failed to support Percy and the battle ended in a magnificent victory for the Scots. Many Englishmen of rank, including Hotspur, were taken captive.

Otterburn was not merely an event of regional significance, as is often said. It was an important battle. For one thing, it had long-term effects on Border society and on the politics of both kingdoms. Froissart was greatly impressed by the spirit of the participants: 'Of all the bataylles...that I have made mencion of...this...was one of the sorest and best foughten, without cowardes or faynte hertes.'

11

SHREWSBURY
21 JULY 1403

Some historians believe that Richard II became mad in his final years. He certainly made a number of major blunders. One such was his decision to go on an expedition to Ireland in 1399, for he left behind a country seething with discontent. So much so that when his kinsman Henry of Lancaster (whom he had exiled), returned during his absence, large numbers of people alienated by Richard's increasingly tyrannical behaviour flocked to his side. Thus when Richard returned from Ireland he was captured, forced to abdicate in Henry's favour, and finally murdered in early 1400 following an unsuccessful rising on his behalf by a few adherents.

This rising was not the only one Henry IV faced. His reign proved far from tranquil. In September 1400, for example, a revolt broke out in Wales and, under the leadership of Owen Glendower, became a prolonged and bloody national uprising. Henry also had to deal with the Percies. This powerful northern family had played a major part in bringing about his accession, but soon turned against him, claiming among other things, that he was not providing enough money to pay the men they used to defend the border. By 1403 relations had declined so much that the Percies allied themselves with Glendower and his son-in-law Edmund Mortimer, with the intention of overthrowing Henry and placing Mortimer's nephew, the young Earl of March, on the throne.

Hence in July the Earl of Northumberland's son, Henry Percy, 'Harry Hotspur', and Northumberland's brother, Thomas Percy, Earl of Worcester, marched south to rendezvous with Glendower and Mortimer, accompanied by a Scottish ally, the Earl of Douglas. Henry moved against the Percies and on Saturday 21 July confronted them about two miles north-west of Shrewsbury. Henry's army probably numbered around 14,000 men and was deployed in three divisions, with the young Prince of Wales (the future Henry V) in command of the left wing. The Percies' force probably numbered about 10,000 men and was arrayed on high ground to the north.

Henry sent the Abbot of Shrewsbury to talk to the rebels: if they dispersed he was willing to consider any statement of grievances they might send. The attempt at avoiding bloodshed failed, and so the royal army advanced. A fierce archery duel ensued: the first such duel on English soil between archers using the longbow. This resulted in the king's men recoiling somewhat. During the bitter hand-to-hand fighting which followed, Hotspur and Douglas charged toward the royal standard intent on slaying Henry, but failed to do so. Meanwhile, the Prince of Wales moved against the rebels' right flank and rear, and while doing so was wounded by an arrow. Nonetheless, the assault put the rebels under pressure and their resistance collapsed after Hotspur was killed.

It is believed that around 1,600 died on both sides during the fighting and pursuit, and that many of the wounded were dispatched by villagers during the night. Moreover, some important prisoners, Thomas Percy for one, subsequently suffered a traitor's fate.

12

TOWTON
29 MARCH 1461

'They do so interrupt me that by day or night I can hardly snatch
a moment to be refreshed by the reading of any holy teaching.'
—Henry VI

Whether or not Henry actually stated the above, (the quotation is from a life of the king by John Blacman, his confessor), there is no doubt that he was a pious and peace-loving man prone to neglect the affairs of state. In short, in many respects he was a very different man to his redoubtable father, Henry V, the victor of Agincourt, and his incapacity for kingship was a major cause of the Wars of the Roses which commenced in the 1450s.

The Wars of the Roses have long been viewed as one of the greatest periods of strife in English history; a time when the armigerous families of the land sallied forth to settle old scores and to gain, or retain, power while fighting on behalf of rival branches of the royal family, Lancaster and York, and a time when lesser folk suffered grievously due to circumstances beyond their control. This view was forcefully expressed by William Denton in the late nineteenth century. He believed that the 'baronage of England was almost extirpated' and that 'want, exposure, and disease' killed a considerable number of ordinary people, more indeed, than had 'the most murderous weapons of war'.

More recent scholarship has shown that England in the latter half of the fifteenth century was not as greatly affected by the Wars of the Roses as Denton had thought. In fact some of his contemporaries expressed such opinions. T. L. Kington Oliphant, for instance, did not believe that the 'old nobility' was almost exterminated, whilst J. R. Green contended that: 'For the most part the trading and agricultural classes stood wholly apart', leaving the upper orders and their retainers to deal out death and destruction upon one another. The late Charles Ross was of similar opinion: 'England in the later fifteenth century was...the home of a rich, varied and vigorous civilization. To study it is to remain largely unaware that it was an age of political violence, which did nothing to hinder its steady development'.

That the period witnessed violence, and on a significant scale, is certain. Indeed, when the Battle of Towton was fought in early 1461 several engagements had already occurred: the stage had been set for a period of great risk and uncertainty for the politically elite section of English society.

57

What circumstances brought about such a situation? For what reasons did men gather to fight and perhaps die at Towton, and for that matter, the battles which preceded it?

Mention has already been made of Henry VI's incapacity for kingship and that this was a major cause of the commencement of the Wars of the Roses. It is now time to say a little more about the king and to mention the problems of this era. Henry belonged to the Lancastrian branch of the royal family – which had gained the throne in 1399 when his grandfather, the Duke of Lancaster, deposed tyrannical Richard II – and through Lancaster he was descended from John of Gaunt, the fourth son of Edward III. Henry ascended the throne in 1422 when only nine months old, and so for many years the governance of the country was conducted on his behalf by a council. From the late 1430s however, Henry began to play an active part in political affairs. It was a role to which he was ill-suited. To say the least, he was not overendowed with sagacity. Moreover he was malleable, a weak and recklessly generous man who soon fell under the sway of an unscrupulous court faction.

The House of Commons was not impressed, and was thus reluctant to grant taxation. Inevitably, this greatly added to the financial difficulties being experienced by the Crown, and lack of resources was a major factor which contributed to the loss of Normandy to the French in 1450.

The loss of Normandy greatly added to the discredit of a regime already viewed with widespread disfavour for corruption and misgovernment at home, and was soon followed by a rising in the south-east in late May intended to remove 'the false traytours about his hyghnesse,' that is, Henry's ministers.

Shortly after the rising was crushed, an important man arrived on the scene. His name? Richard, Duke of York. His purpose? To play a major role in the political life of the nation, a role to which he rightly believed himself entitled for he was heir presumptive to the throne (Henry was childless) being descended through his father from Edmund, the fifth son of Edward III, and through his mother, from Lionel, Edward's third son.

Since 1447 York had been Henry's lieutenant in Ireland, 'the great slum of the fifteenth century political system' as J. R. Lander has commented. He had been sent to that troubled land by his enemies, the king's ministers, who wished to keep him out of the way, (previously he had been virtually excluded from the royal council). Now he was back, a bitter man, determined to assert himself. Initially he made little impression. Indeed it was not until April 1454 that he achieved a central role in political affairs when he was appointed Protector of England after Henry had become insane in August of the previous year. Several months of uncertainty had followed the onset of the king's madness, but as the situation was comparable to that of a minority, with the king quite incapable of performing the duties incumbent on him, York, as the senior adult member of the royal family was eventually appointed Protector.

This was not to the liking of Henry's wife, Margaret of Anjou, for she had recently given birth to a son and evidently feared that York had designs on the throne. Tension was increased by the fact that the great Percy family, (whose head was the Earl of Northumberland), had become embroiled in a private war with a cadet branch of the Neville family, a branch represented by the Earl of Salisbury and his son, the Earl of Warwick. Moreover, Warwick was also at loggerheads with the Duke of Somerset, York's bitter foe. The Protector's mother was a Neville, and consequently when York intervened to restore order he was viewed by some as partisan and rightly so. For her part, Margaret allied herself to the Percies and Somerset, as well as others hostile to York and the Nevilles in question.

York's protectorate ended in February 1455 following Henry's recovery and after this the duke and his associates withdrew from court. Shortly after doing so they were summoned to appear before a great council which was to meet at Leicester. Fearful that their opponents intended destroying them, they resorted to arms. On 22 May they clashed with a Lancastrian force at St Albans and routed it: Somerset and Northumberland were among the Lancastrian notables slain.

The victors had succeeded in destroying several of their personal enemies but they were still loyal to Henry, who had been little more than a cipher in the hands of men such as Somerset, and immediately after the engagement they protested their loyalty to him. Then, not long after St Albans, Henry once again became mentally incapacitated and the protectorate was briefly restored. During this period Warwick became Captain of Calais and this greatly strengthened the York-ists for though, as events were to show, some of Calais' strong garrison were pro-Lancastrian, many were to support Warwick and his associates thereby not only providing them with important fighting material, but a refuge in times of peril.

During 1456 the court party, which was dominated by the queen, regained the ascendancy, ended York's protectorate and subsequently removed his supporters from office. There was one exception – Warwick. He refused to relinquish the captaincy of Calais. As for York, he withdrew to his estates, no doubt sullen and apprehensive.

Though few persons wished for a fresh outbreak of warfare, hostility and suspicion were still very strong. Indeed, a 'Loveday' in March 1458 when the rival factions made their way to St Paul's side-by-side in a display of reconciliation, was a sham. Both were preparing for a renewal of military conflict.

Margaret was primarily responsible for the resumption of bloodshed. Her animosity towards York and his associates seems to have become increasingly strong, so strong that in 1459 she gave orders for Lancastrian forces to assemble. Her preparations were over: it was time to destroy the Yorkists.

Not surprisingly, the Yorkists likewise resorted to arms. York was at Ludlow and sent word to Salisbury, who was at Middleham in Yorkshire, to join him. Warwick was to do likewise from Calais. En route the former was intercepted by Lord Audley at Blore Heath, Shropshire, on 23 September. Audley had been ordered by the queen to prevent Salisbury from joining York, but in the ensuing engagement his force came off worst and thus the earl managed to press on to his destination. Soon after this, Warwick also arrived at Ludlow.

However, during the night of 12/13 October most of the Yorkist rank and file, including members of Calais' garrison, deserted after being confronted by a large force led by the king. Consequently, York made for Ireland whilst Salisbury, Warwick and others, including York's eldest son, Edward, the Earl of March, fled to Calais. Then in November parliament assembled at Coventry and attainted the Yorkist leaders – they were declared rebels and their lives, estates and other possessions, were forfeited to the Crown.

York and his colleagues could only return by force, and return by force they did. In June 1460 Salisbury and Warwick landed in Kent after waging a skilful propaganda campaign in which they had, among other things, denounced the king's ministers as corrupt and oppressive thereby winning greater support in England than they had hitherto enjoyed. The invaders entered London on 2 July. While part of their force proceeded to blockade the Lancastrian garrison in the Tower, Warwick moved on and encountered and defeated the king's army at Northampton on 10 July. Many leading figures in the Lancastrian force were slain and Henry himself was captured.

He was conducted back to London where the victors assumed office, ruling in his name. They sent out writs summoning a parliament to meet at Westminster in October with the intention of obtaining the reversal of the attainders passed at Coventry.

Before parliament assembled, York returned from Ireland on about 8 September and slowly made his way towards London. He reached the capital on 10 October – three days after parliament had assembled – and caused great consternation. He strolled into Westminster Hall and laid his hand on the empty throne as if claiming it as his by right. He expected acclamation. He received none. Even Salisbury and Warwick were evidently surprised and angered by his action. During their recent propaganda campaign they had once again professed loyalty to Henry, stating that they only wished to remove his 'evil counsellors'. Hence, like their fellow peers, they refused to accept York's demand that Henry be deposed and he, York, be accepted as the true king by right of descent. (If a claim to the throne through a female were allowed, as York wished – there was no ruling in English law on this point – his title to the crown was indeed superior to that of Henry).

Nonetheless, as has been noted, no one of consequence wished to depose Henry in favour of York. All were of course aware of the king's ineffectiveness. Previously it has been said that Henry's incapacity for kingship was a major cause of the commencement of the Wars of the Roses, but we can go further. His shortcomings were the chief cause. He had, after all, allowed himself to be dominated by a court faction which not only lost the lands in France won by his father, but was also oppressive and unscrupulous. Furthermore, he had allowed

York to become alienated and had failed to control his own wife. In short, as the late K. B. MacFarlane commented, Henry's 'head was too small for his father's crown'. Nevertheless, he was still the anointed king to whom the lords had sworn allegiance and therefore, much to York's annoyance, they determined that king he would remain.

A compromise ensued. On 25 October it was declared that Henry would retain the throne but that York would be his heir instead of the king's young son, Edward. York was disappointed and angered by this limited success. But what of Margaret? Was she prepared to accept the disinheritance of her son? Far from it. She was adamant – York would never wear the crown in his place. Others felt likewise. It soon became apparent that the compromise would not bring peace, but renewed war.

Indeed, the queen soon had a formidable following gathered in Yorkshire. On 8 December York and Salisbury marched north to confront her, while Warwick remained in London. On 30 December the Yorkists were defeated at Wakefield: York and one of his young sons, Rutland, were slain, while Salisbury was killed soon after. Among the victors were the Duke of Somerset and the Earl of Northumberland, men whose fathers had perished at St Albans: their deaths had been avenged.

The stage was now set for a showdown with Warwick. He had also been at St Albans: his time of reckoning had come. Thus Margaret began moving south. On 17 February she defeated Warwick in the Second Battle of St Albans and in so doing recaptured her feeble husband. She could then have moved on London – whose inhabitants had been greatly alarmed by reports which had reached them of her army's rapacious behaviour when moving south – but did not do so. After a week or so of indecision she began moving north to York. En route her army reportedly behaved licentiously again. A contemporary source, the *Old English Chronicle*, relates that the Lancastrians 'did harms innumerable, taking men's carts, wagons, horses, and beasts...robbed the people and led their pillage into the north country, so that men of the shires that they passed by had almost left no beasts to till their land'.

And what of the Yorkists? Though Warwick had been defeated at St Albans he was very much alive. Moreover, the late Duke of York's eldest son, Edward Plantagenet, had routed a Lancastrian force at Mortimer's Cross near Wigmore on 2 or 3 February before joining forces with Warwick in the Cotswolds on about the 22nd.

On the 26th Warwick and his young kinsman entered London unopposed. With Henry back in the hands of their opponents the Yorkists realised that they had little choice other than to set up their own king in his stead for without Henry they had no claim to the obedience of his subjects. Hence, on 4 March, Edward was acclaimed by his followers and the citizens of London as king and then enthroned at Westminster.

Though the Yorkists had secured London and installed Edward as monarch, their position was far from secure. Most of the nobility remained loyal to Henry, and thus the Lancastrian army at York was growing in strength as more and more loyal lords and knights rallied to the cause. In such circumstances the Yorkists could not afford to waste time. Aware of this, they soon began assembling an army to engage the Lancastrians' big battalions.

On 6 March Edward issued proclamations to areas generally favourable to the Yorkist cause calling, among other things, for recognition of him as king and stipulating that nobody was to offer help or comfort to his adversaries. Then, while Edward remained in London for some days to raise funds, a task which proved fruitful, a number of his lieutenants, including Warwick, dispersed to begin assembling a powerful army.

On 11 March Warwick's uncle, Lord Fauconberg, left London and began moving north at the head of a force comprised of infantry. Two days later Edward himself rode out of London accompanied by the Duke of Norfolk and at the head of a force which included a Burgundian contingent sent by Duke Philip of Burgundy.

Edward arrived at Pontefract in Yorkshire on the 27th, having been joined en route by a number of contingents, including one under Warwick raised in the midlands. Upon doing so, he sent a detachment under Lord FitzWalter to reconnoitre a crossing of the River Aire at Ferrybridge a short distance to the north and, if possible, seize and hold it. FitzWalter found the crossing unguarded and the bridge destroyed. He thus effected repairs, perhaps by straddling the ruined structure with planks of wood.

However, unbeknown to FitzWalter and his party, the grim reaper was about to draw near. It did so in the person of a senior Lancastrian nobleman, Lord Clifford, a warlike young man who made his way to Ferrybridge from the Lancastrian army – which by now was likely in the vicinity of Towton, about ten miles to the north, having marched from York via a crossing of the Wharfe at Tadcaster. Edward Hall, (whose account was written c.1540), states that Clifford did so at the head of a detachment of 'light horsemen', intent on attacking 'such as kept the passage at Ferrybridge'. Hence, 'early before his enemies were awake,' Clifford 'got the bridge, and slew the keepers of the same, and all such as would withstand him', including FitzWalter.

According to Hall, Edward responded promptly upon receiving news of events. Fauconberg and the van were sent to cross the river three miles upstream at Castleford with the purpose of cutting off Clifford's line of retreat from Ferrybridge, and when the latter realised this he 'departed in great haste towards King Henry's army', whereupon Edward crossed the Aire.

It is normally held that this was all that transpired in the vicinity of Ferrybridge on 28 March 1461. But is this correct? Or is it merely only part of the canvas, not the whole picture?

Andrew Boardman has recently argued in *The Battle of Towton* that Edward moved against Clifford after hearing of the attack on FitzWalter, and that this resulted in a more serious encounter at Ferrybridge. It is a contention which the admittedly rather sparse and generally garbled sources appear to warrant.

For instance, Warwick's brother, George Neville, the Bishop of Exeter, who received word of events from 'messengers and letters, as well as by popular report,' wrote on 7 April that: 'Our adversaries had broken the bridge which was our way across, and were strongly posted on the other side, so that our men could only cross by a narrow way which they had made themselves after the bridge was broken. But our men forced a way by the sword, and many were slain on both sides. Finally the enemy took to flight, and very many of them were slain as they fled'. Neville dated this event to 29 March, but as will be seen, it is reasonable to conclude that the 28th was the true date. Moreover, in view of what he says, it is also reasonable to assume that he was referring to an event other than the FitzWalter/Clifford incident.

Bearing this in mind, it is interesting to note the following by a Burgundian chronicler, Jean de Waurin, who met Warwick some years after Towton and wrote about the campaign in his *Recueil des Chroniques D' Engleterre*. He states that on Friday before Palm Sunday (i.e., 27 March), Edward received word that Ferrybridge had been secured by the enemy. A 'small company' was thus sent 'to find out the strength of the enemy, but...went so far...that a guard saw them and raised the alarm'. Consequently, the 'small party was in so much danger of being routed that [Edward] had to send reinforcements for his reconnaissance troops'.

Is de Waurin's reference to a small forward party of Yorkists being threatened with destruction a garbled reference to the FitzWalter incident? It seems likely. What is interesting, in this context, is that he proceeds to mention that a battle was then fought to secure a river crossing. He relates that the reinforcements sent to the assistance of the reconnaissance party drove 'the enemy back to the bridge where they formed a defensive line', and that upon hearing of this Edward advanced with the bulk of his army and gave the order 'to attack the bridge which had been fortified by the enemy, and it so happened the battle lasted from midday to six o'clock in the evening and there died more than 3,000 men on both sides'.

In view of the above, and allowing for a degree of inaccuracy and exaggeration on the part of our sources, it does seem, as noted earlier, reasonable to conclude that two encounters occurred at Ferrybridge on 28 March. If so, it also appears likely that the second followed close on the heels of the first, for although the Clifford/FitzWalter incident is sometimes said by historians to have been a walkover, it is probable that FitzWalter's force was larger than some believe and that members of it put up a fight. For instance, Hearne's Fragment, a fifteenth century source, states that FitzWalter was killed in 'a great skirmish'. Consequently, it is probable that Edward arrived on the scene shortly after Clifford had overcome FitzWalter's party, and that shortly thereafter he sent Fauconberg and the vanguard to Castleford to outflank the Lancastrian.

Sooner or later Clifford began withdrawing to rejoin his colleagues. En route, however, he was surprised and attacked (presumably by the mounted contingent of the Yorkist van), in Dintingdale, a shallow valley some 2.5 miles or so from Towton and below the southern edge of a plateau upon which Towton is situated. According to Hall, Clifford's party was ambushed and 'almost all' of the Lancastrians were killed. What is certain is that Clifford perished in the encounter, as did another prominent adherent of the House of Lancaster, John Neville, the brother of the Earl of Westmorland.

It is generally assumed that by now the day was drawing to a close and that Fauconberg and the van thus settled down for the night nearby, most probably on high ground just to the south-east of the village of Saxton. And what of Edward? Where did he spend the night? According to de Waurin, Edward encamped four miles from the enemy, and it has thus been suggested that he did so at Sherburn in Elmet. However, it has to be borne in mind that medieval writers frequently provide inaccurate mileages, and that it is probable that Edward was closer to the subsequent battlesite than this. Indeed, it is generally assumed that he spent the night near Saxton, having linked up en route with Fauconberg (scouts would have kept them in touch), and this seems most probable. For one thing, it is unlikely that Edward would have been prepared to allow himself to become separated from the van in the heart of enemy country: he had done so earlier in the day only out of necessity.

THE COMMANDERS AND THEIR ARMIES

Though only nineteen, Edward was an imposing figure, 6ft 3in tall and strikingly good looking, a fact mentioned by many of his contemporaries. The *Croyland Chronicle*, for example, comments that he was 'of most elegant appearance, and remarkable beyond all others for the attractions of his person': 'of visage louelye, of body myghtie, strong and cleane made' states a writer of the next generation, Sir Thomas More. Intelligent and able, he was a man of great charm and a born leader. As the late E. F. Jacob has observed, 'in personal relationships he had little sense of class; there was nothing stuffy about Edward'. He was fond of the good life – to put it mildly celibacy was little to his taste – and was generous and good-natured.

Although young, Edward had of course tasted battle. He was a confident and able soldier of whom More rightly states, in war he was 'sharpe and fyerce, in the fielde bolde and hardye'. No doubt as he settled down for the night of 28–29 March he wondered what was going through the mind of the man in command of the army against which he was to do battle.

Evidently, his opponent was the Duke of Somerset. Like Edward, he was young (he was born in about April 1436), and was also no stranger to armed conflict. He was for instance a veteran of the First Battle of St Albans, where he was severely wounded, and according to the *Paston Letters* had had to be 'caryede hom in a cart'. He was appointed to the captaincy of Calais (October 1459) and unsuccessfully endeavoured to oust his predecessor, Warwick, from the town. In England, Somerset's military undertakings proved more successful. He commanded the Lancastrian army at Wakefield and evidently did so again at the Second Battle of St Albans. It is reasonable to conclude that he was a courageous and confident young man.

According to some sources, Edward's army numbered around 200,000 men, a figure which has to be discounted as grossly inflated. On the other hand, Hall states that the Yorkist force was 48,660 strong and the Lancastrian, 60,000. However, when it its borne in mind that England's population was only about 2.5 million it becomes clear that these figures must also be erroneous.

Not surprisingly, modern estimates for the strength of the armies have been significantly reduced. E. F. Jacob, for instance, was of the opinion that the Lancastrian force numbered over 22,000 men and was much larger than that of the Yorkists. Other historians, though, while rejecting the early figures, have made or agreed with higher estimates than this, (in some cases maintaining that the combined strength of the armies was about 80,000 men). Charles Ross was one such. He wrote, 'given the unparalleled number of notables present at the battle – they included some three-quarters of the surviving adult peerage – it is not at all unlikely that as many as 50,000 men were engaged' at Towton.

The figure of approximately 50,000 combatants all told, seems the most reasonable estimate. The Lancastrian army, which included the most men of rank, probably numbered around 28,000 men and was thus stronger than that of the Yorkists, especially prior to the arrival of the Duke of Norfolk's contingent some time after battle had been joined. Some historians maintain that Norfolk had been taken ill at Pontefract, and had thus been left behind with his men by Edward on the undertaking that he would follow the next day, perhaps having been augmented by any late arrivals; while others hold that for one reason or another he was a day's march behind the rest of the Yorkist army and thus only arrived at Pontefract on 28 March.

Both armies, like those which fought at the other battles of the Wars of the Roses, included the private forces of the principal men present. A lord's affinity, i.e., his following, whose members wore his livery or at least his badge, was composed of men who served him in return for protection and payment. Indentured life retainers formed its core. These were men who had contracted to serve in both peace and war (save their allegiance to the king), and among such were knightly tenants of the lord who owing to the traditional allegiance of their house, or fear of retribution, allied themselves to him. Important personages, however, were not only accompanied by their affinities: the bulk of their forces was made up from ordinary able-bodied members of their tenantry.

In addition to the private 'armies' of the baronage, were forces from crown lands and contingents from the towns of England. The latter were brought into being through commissions of array. The commissioners inspected the able-bodied adult males in the towns in which they were authorised to act and chose the men they believed best suited to military service. The communities had to provide the requisite equipment for those chosen.

Members of Calais' garrison were also present at Towton. Some had come to England in 1459 under Warwick and shortly after had deserted to the Lancastrians. Most though, had accompanied Salisbury and Warwick in June 1460 and were ranked among the Yorkist forces. These men were professional English soldiers but foreign troops were also present for as noted earlier the Yorkist army included a contingent of Burgundians sent by Duke Philip the Good, while some foreigners were also present in Lancastrian ranks, including men from France and perhaps Scotland.

Among men-at-arms, that is persons who possessed a full harness (suit of armour), were aristocrats and wealthy members of the gentry with harnesses of the highest quality (most of which came from northern Italy and Germany). By this date full suits of plate armour were in vogue and had been for several decades. Armour had reached such a high level of sophistication that the longbow, which had proved so effective in battles such as Crécy (1346) and Agincourt (1415), was no longer regarded as much of a threat unless used at close quarters. By this date shields were no longer generally used by men-at-arms and suits of armour usually had thicker plates on the left and most vulnerable side.

The plate armour worn during the Wars of the Roses was generally lighter and more articulated than that of previous decades, thereby providing greater freedom of movement. It is certainly erroneous to believe that once encased in a harness the man-at-arms of this era was rendered ponderous. He could, for example, mount his charger without assistance and experiments have demonstrated that a very fit man can even perform certain gymnastics when wearing armour of this period.

A vital part of the harness was the helmet. The most popular style was evidently the sallet, a continental introduction which came in a variety of shapes and sizes and often had a movable visor and an elongated neck-guard. It was worn in conjunction with a mentonnière, a plate fastened to the breastplate and moulded so that it protected the throat and lower part of the face.

The mounts of men-at-arms were sometimes provided with plate armour which protected the face, neck and body. The piece which protected the face was the chamfron, and this often had a spike projecting from the forehead.

Men-at-arms fought with a variety of weapons: swords, battleaxes, poleaxes, maces, lances, war hammers and flails. When fighting on foot, as they usually did, they evidently favoured poleaxes. These came in a variety of shapes and sizes, (the shafts were usually between three and five feet long), but the most common poleaxe had a head combining a hatchet, serrated hammer and pike, and inflicted wounds comparable to those of the sword, mace and lance. Daggers were used to finish off the felled opponent.

And what of the rank and file? Archers were of course numerous on both sides at Towton and their favourite weapon was the longbow, a weapon which had done so much to win English armies glorious victories in the past but one which, as noted, was no longer as effective against men-at-arms as had been the case. Longbows were made of yew and could be effective at a range of up to 250 yards. A competent archer could discharge about twelve arrows a minute. On the other hand some archers, notably foreign mercenaries, preferred crossbows. These were more cumbersome and had a slower rate of fire – four quarrels (short, heavy bolts or arrows) a minute evidently being the maximum – but had greater powers of penetration and could be effective at a range of about 300 yards.

Additionally, archers were usually armed with swords and daggers so that they could defend themselves in close combat. Furthermore, shields were common. Protection was also provided by a variety of helmets, and while some archers had plate armour to protect parts of the body such as the arms and chest, brigandines (flexible armour essentially consisting of rows of small overlapping plates riveted between two or more layers of canvas or leather) and padded leather jackets were more usual.

Levies who were not archers fought with a variety of weapons: swords, spears, pikes and halberds, for instance, and many would have fought in their everyday clothing save for rudimentary protective gear.

As has been mentioned, Burgundians were present in the ranks of the Yorkist army and some of these were armed with handguns. These were not particularly efficient or reliable weapons. The petards used by some of the Burgundians (and Englishmen too for that matter), were likewise of dubious worth. They were perforated earthenware pots containing Greek fire, which once ignited, were thrown towards the enemy to explode.

And what of artillery? Cannon were used during the Wars of the Roses but do not feature in accounts of Towton. Moreover, as yet no archaeological evidence to support their presence has been uncovered on the battlefield.

Normally, armies were deployed in three wards or battles, and these were usually in line abreast or in line astern. Tactics tended to be straightforward. Most engagements commenced with an exchange of fire by the archers. During the Hundred Years War English armies had fared well in such contests because, unlike the French, they favoured the longbow with its superior rate of fire to the crossbow, but during the Wars of the Roses the longbow seldom played as decisive a part in determining the outcome of engagements for the simple reason that it was used by both sides and its value was thus largely cancelled out.

After an archery duel, armies closed and hand-to-hand fighting commenced. At times, commanders of armies kept a detachment in reserve which could be led forward into the fray if required, but in general once close combat began there was little that commanders could do other than fight bravely to inspire their men. On the whole, commanders and their lieutenants who led the 'battles,' did just that and were often killed whilst doing so.

DESCRIPTION

Shortly after dawn on 29 March, Edward advanced towards the Lancastrians, and thus began ascending the plateau north of Saxton upon which his opponents were preparing to give battle. (The Lancastrians were without Henry and Margaret, for they had stayed at York). The weather must have tempered whatever martial ardour existed in both armies for it was bitterly cold and snow was either falling or threatening to fall.

Before discussing the battle, something must be said about the terrain. The plateau rises to 150ft above sea level out of the great plain of York and is the highest ground between Pontefract and York. To the west the ground falls away steeply towards a stream – the Cock Beck – which meanders north to join the River Wharfe near Tadcaster, and along which some of the ground consists (and presumably consisted) of water-meadows. Moreover, on the east side of the Cock are areas of woodland, namely Renshaw Wood and Castle Hill Wood,

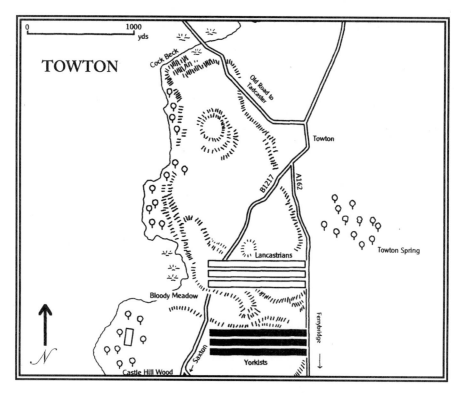

both of which were no doubt rather more extensive in 1461: the latter is the southernmost and partially extends onto the plateau. To the east, the plateau falls away more gently than it does to the west, and includes areas of low-lying land which were probably marshy at the time of the battle.

As for the windswept plateau itself, it is now largely given over to cultivation but in 1461 it was essentially heathland, though there may have been patches of arable, hedgerows, and of course some trees.

The top of the plateau is bisected by an east–west depression and the Lancastrians and Yorkists are generally believed, and almost certainly correctly so, to have been deployed to the north and south of this respectively. On the east side the depression is only slight, but on the west it is deeper, and of course, drops towards the Cock Beck.

How the armies were deployed is uncertain. The late A. H. Burne believed that both were arrayed 'in great depth, one ward behind another' and this view is accepted here. Furthermore, it is normally held that the Lancastrians probably placed an ambush party in Castle Hill Wood to the left of the Yorkist line. This is merely an assumption, though a plausible one.

What is undoubted is that the opposing armies were, as noted earlier, unusually large. Both sides knew that the stakes were high and had made a tremendous effort, the greatest of the Wars, to raise formidable forces. For the Yorkists the task had been made easier by the depredations recently wrought by the Lancastrians while marching through the midlands, something which swelled Yorkists ranks with men eager for revenge.

Just when the battle commenced is uncertain. Likely, it did not do so earlier than about 9.00am and it may have done so an hour or so later than this.

It did so in the midst of a snowstorm, and Polydore Vergil (who briefly discussed the battle in his *History of England*, written c.1510) states that 'the archers began the battle, but when their arrows were spent the matter was dealt by hand strokes'. That the archers opened proceedings was, of course, normal procedure, and it is generally accepted that it was Fauconberg who initiated the archery duel. A graphic description of what transpired is provided by Hall: 'The Lord Fauconberg, which led the forward of King Edward's battle...caused every archer under his standard to shoot one flight and then made them stand still. The northern men [Lancastrians], feeling the shoot, but by reason of the snow, [which was blown into their faces by a south wind], not perfectly viewing the distance between them and their enemies, like hardy men shot their sheaf arrows as fast as they might, but all their shot was lost and their labour in vain for they came not near the southern men by 40 tailors yards. When their shot was almost spent the Lord Fauconberg marched forward with his archers, who not only shot their own sheaves, but also gathered the arrows of their enemies and let a great part of them fly against their own masters, and another part they let stand on the ground which sore annoyed the legs of the owners when battle was joined'.

Allowing for some exaggeration, and indeed perhaps invention on Hall's part, it does seem that the Yorkists had the better of the archery duel and that their fire produced a reaction, provoking the Lancastrians into coming forward, at which point of course the archers on both sides would have stepped aside or back to allow their colleagues to move against the enemy. There can be little doubt that men towards the left of the Lancastrian line closed first, owing to the lie of the land.

Perhaps before the battle commenced some with scores to settle, or simply little commonsense, had been eager for such a confrontation. If so, few could have relished it when it occurred. The fighting was ferocious. Death soon came to some. Others, who successfully dispatched one opponent after another, found to their despair that new ones constantly appeared and sooner or later exhaustion would have drastically reduced their chances of survival. One way or another then, the number of dead and dying increased, and Vergil states that the 'dead bodies hindered those that fought'. Moreover, snow appears to have made things worse. Hearne's Fragment relates that 'all the while it snew', and the *Croyland Chronicle* comments that 'the snow covered the whole surface of the Earth'.

For some time neither side appears to have made much headway. But then, sooner or later, the outnumbered Yorkists began giving ground, having perhaps also been assailed from the left by the possible ambush party referred to earlier. According to a letter written on 7 April by a supporter of the Yorkist cause, the Bishop of Salisbury, after hard fighting the time came when the Yorkists despaired of victory, 'so great was the strength and dash of the Lancastrians'. Things must have looked bleak. The Yorkists were being driven towards the southern edge of the plateau and Edward and his lieutenants no doubt knew that if that point were reached resistance would surely disintegrate: they must have desperately awaited the arrival of the expected reinforcements under Norfolk. What on earth had happened? Would Norfolk's men arrive before it was too late?

Whether Norfolk made his way to Towton or remained at Pontefract is uncertain. What is clear is that his men duly arrived on the right of the embattled Yorkist army. Hearne's Fragment relates that at 'about noon [the] Duke of Norfolk, with a fresh band of good men of war came to the aid of...King Edward', while Vergil states that after protracted fighting it was 'espied' that the Yorkist force had increased in strength and that this led to the Lancastrians giving ground.

It is certainly reasonable to assume that the arrival of Norfolk's contingent was a turning point. Nonetheless, the Lancastrians had made good progress earlier in the day and many were presumably in no mood to let victory elude them. Bitter fighting must have continued. However, with their front extended somewhat by the arrival of Norfolk's men, the Yorkists were able to turn the Lancastrian left. Hence Lancastrian morale, if it had not already begun to do so, started ebbing away and the Yorkists began gaining ground. Consequently the mangled bodies of those who had fallen earlier in the day were joined by those of men whose blood was yet to congeal.

Back, and further back still, the Lancastrians were pushed until resistance collapsed and they were in full retreat. Many failed to escape, for they were pursued. The slaughter appears to have been particularly great on the low ground – Bloody Meadow – between the west end of the depression and the Cock Beck.

Fugitives perished elsewhere along the beck – which is frequently assumed to have been in flood – such as at a point known as the Bridge of Bodies, northwest of the battlefield on the old road to Tadcaster. The ground falls away steeply to the site of a crossing here, which is often said to have been a bridge but may have been a ford, and as Cyril Ransome has commented: 'No one who has seen the place can wonder at the disaster which followed'. Congestion soon became terrible as more and more men tried to make good their escape. Some lost their footing, for the ground was marshy, and were crushed to death. Others were pitched headlong into the icy water and were no doubt seized with terror as they were pushed under by the weight of their comrades, and soon ceased to know anything at all. It is said that the number of those who perished in the beck was so great that more fortunate individuals managed to make their way across the water by clambering over the bodies of the fallen. This may well have also been true of other points along the beck.

Those who made it across the stream were not necessarily safe, for Yorkists continued hounding them. For instance, the *Croyland Chronicle* states that Edward's army 'eagerly pursued' fleeing Lancastrians, cutting them down 'just like so many sheep for the slaughter', and thus 'made immense havoc among them for a distance of 10 miles as far as the city of York', while the Bishop of Exeter comments that the dead littered an area '6 miles long by 3 broad and about four furlongs'.

When Henry and Margaret heard of the disastrous defeat they rode out of York and headed for Scotland, accompanied by their son and a retinue which included the Dukes of Somerset and Exeter. They must have been greatly saddened by what had happened. It was only six weeks since the victory at St Albans: how the wheel of fortune had spun.

Casualties at Towton were exceedingly heavy, though contemporary claims such as that of 28,000 slain evidently reported in a widely circulated newsletter, can reasonably be rejected as too high. Instead, Ross has commented that the figure 'of 9,000 deaths, apparently on the Lancastrian side,' given by the *Annales Rerum Anglicarum* 'seems more plausible'. This is no doubt a more accurate figure, though it almost certainly errs on the low side bearing in mind that the battle was prolonged and that many Lancastrians perished while in flight. 12,000 Lancastrian dead is perhaps closer to the mark. Though heavy, Yorkist losses were undoubtedly lower than those of the vanquished.

Many Lancastrians of consequence were among the slain. Among such were the young Earl of Northumberland, Lord Wells and Willoughby, and Lord Dacre. Moreover, according to *Gregory's Chronicle* (which was written about ten years after Towton), 42 captured knights were executed immediately after the battle. The young Earl of Devon's turn to die came the following day when Edward rode into York and needed the earl's head to replace that of the Duke of York which had adorned the battlements of Micklegate since Wakefield. The only Yorkists of note slain at Towton were Sir Richard Jenney, and the Kentishman, Robert Horne, who had thrown in his lot with the Yorkists the previous summer.

Interestingly, Lord Dacre's tomb can be seen in the churchyard of All Saints', Saxton, with the worn inscription: 'Here lies Ralph, Lord of Dacre and Gilsland. A true soldier valiant in battle in the service of King Henry VI, who died on Palm Sunday March 29 1461, on whose soul may God have mercy'. According to tradition, Dacre was buried in an upright position alongside his horse and this appears to have been confirmed in the nineteenth century. Lesser victims of Towton were likewise buried in the churchyard, but not surprisingly most of the dead lie on the battlesite where a number of likely burial mounds can be seen.

Towton was by far the greatest battle of the Wars of the Roses. Indeed, it enjoys the distinction of being the greatest battle ever fought on British soil. It shattered, albeit temporarily, the power of the Lancastrian party and in the eyes of many gave evidence of divine approval for Edward Plantagenet.

The Bishop of Exeter mentioned with admiration the performance of Edward and his lieutenants at Towton, and no doubt they did indeed acquit themselves well. Edward must also receive commendation for the resolution shown by the Yorkists during the final stages of the campaign, resolution which owed much to his preference for offensive warfare.

Edward spent Easter in York and took measures to stamp out what remained of Lancastrian power in the north. He then travelled south for his coronation and was greeted with great acclaim as he did so. On 14 April an anonymous individual in London wrote: 'Words fail me to relate how well the commons love and adore him, as if he were their God'. Many hoped that it was the beginning of a peaceful new era. One such was the Bishop of Exeter, who declared: 'After so much sorrow and tribulation I hope that grateful tranquillity and quiet will ensue, and that after so many clouds we shall have a clear sky'.

However, Henry and Margaret were still at large, as were several of their diehard supporters. Hence the Milanese ambassador to Paris, Prospero di Camulio observed, if they remained so it seemed 'certain that in time fresh disturbances' would arise. He was not mistaken. Edward's supporters had not seen their last storm-clouds: the adherents of the Houses of York and Lancaster were to fight again.

13

BARNET
14 APRIL 1471

After the Yorkists' crushing victory at Towton on 29 March 1461, which had avenged their earlier defeats at Wakefield (30 December 1460) and the Second battle of St Albans (17 February 1461), their victorious commander, Edward Plantagenet, made his way to London and was crowned. In the years which followed the young king left governing the country largely in the hands of his cousin, Warwick, and in 1464 the earl was involved in delicate negotiations with the French – who had rendered assistance to the Lancastrian cause – with the aim of changing this by marrying Edward to a French princess. But in the midst of the negotiations he was suddenly informed that the king had secretly married a widow, Elizabeth Woodville, on 1 May. Warwick felt humiliated, and as time passed became increasingly estranged from Edward, his disenchantment largely being increased by the way the king showered favours upon the Woodvilles.

In 1469 Warwick finally rebelled. After a short campaign he captured Edward at Olney. However the king soon recovered his freedom, for Warwick found it too difficult to run the country with him imprisoned. Subsequently, though, the king declared Warwick a traitor and so the earl fled to France in the spring of 1470, accompanied by his son-in-law, the Duke of Clarence, Edward's brother. Warwick received the backing of Louis XI on condition that he became reconciled to the exiled Queen Margaret, whose husband Henry VI had been a prisoner in the Tower for some years by this date, having been captured in the north of England.

In September 1470 Warwick returned to England, intent on overthrowing Edward and restoring Henry. He was soon joined by Lancastrians and by men who deserted Edward in his hour of need. In such circumstances Edward fled to Burgundy and the sanctuary of his brother-in-law, Charles the Bold. His adversaries soon entered London in triumph and released Henry, who was now permanently mad.

However, in March 1471 Edward landed in Yorkshire at the head of a force financed by his brother-in-law. He was soon joined by many adherents, and by Clarence who deserted Warwick. On 11 April Edward entered London. The next day news arrived: Warwick was approaching with a large army. He was at St Albans, having marched south from Coventry. On the 13th Edward moved against him with about 9,000 men, and as night fell took up a position close to Warwick's larger host, which now occupied high ground just north of Barnet.

Battle was joined at dawn in mist so thick it was hard to 'judge one thing from another'. The armies were not directly aligned: the right wings overlapped the enemy's left somewhat. In the fighting Warwick's right under the Earl of Oxford routed the opposing wing, while on the other flank the Yorkists gained the upper hand, with the result that the battle line turned so that it lay almost parallel with the Barnet to St Albans road. Hence, when Oxford's men returned to the field, they were mistaken for Yorkists by their own side who fired upon them. Panic ensued, and Warwick's army disintegrated.

Barnet was a hard-fought battle which lasted three or more hours. Both sides sustained substantial losses. Warwick's brother, Lord Montagu, was one of the notables who perished, as was Warwick himself, for he was cut down while in flight.

14

TEWKESBURY
4 MAY 1471

Margaret of Anjou did not accompany Warwick when he returned to England in September 1470 (see Chapter 13, Barnet). She remained in France and this largely contributed to his downfall for several senior Lancastrians failed to support him: they were waiting for her return. Eventually, on 14 April, the very day Warwick perished at Barnet, she landed at Weymouth – contrary winds were partly responsible for her late return – and among those with her was her son, Edward Prince of Wales. She was soon joined by the Duke of Somerset and the Earl of Devon, two prominent Lancastrians.

It was decided to move west to recruit support. At Exeter Margaret was joined by a considerable force. She then moved to Bristol, via Taunton, Glastonbury, and Bath, arriving on 1 May at the head of a growing army and intent on linking up with forces in Wales under Jasper Tudor.

Meanwhile, Edward IV had commenced moving against her (he left Windsor on 24 April), and arrived at Malmesbury on 1 May at the head of an hastily assembled army. On the 2nd, Margaret marched towards Gloucester, intending to cross the Severn. News that she was making for Gloucester, and was beyond Berkeley, reached Edward in the early hours of the 3rd and he set out in pursuit. The Lancastrians arrived before Gloucester on the morning of 3 May only to find its gates shut. They thus pressed on to Tewkesbury, arriving that evening. With the army exhausted, and hotly pursued by Edward, it was decided to stand and fight. The Lancastrian commander, the Duke of Somerset, chose to do so on ground just to the south of Tewkesbury Abbey. His men then settled down for the night. Edward's did likewise at nearby Tredington.

On Saturday, 4 May, Edward moved against the Lancastrian army arrayed on 'marvaylows strong grownd...full difficult to be assayled' owing to trees, hedges, bushes and 'evell lanes, and depe dykes'. The Yorkists approached in three battles. The Duke of Gloucester led the van, Edward himself the centre, and Lord Hastings the rear. To guard against an ambush from Tewkesbury Park to his left, the king posted 200 spearmen 'in a plomp' to keep an eye on that quarter with orders to engage in the battle if the wood proved free of the enemy. Somerset led the Lancastrian right, Prince Edward the centre, and Devon the left wing.

The battle began when the Yorkist gunners and Gloucester's archers opened fire. The enemy responded in kind. Somerset then advanced, either because his men were 'sore annoyed' by the Yorkist fire or because he hoped to strike before the enemy were fully deployed. Fierce hand-to-hand fighting ensued between his battle and those of Gloucester and Edward. Unsupported by the rest of the Lancastrian army, and attacked on the flank by the 200 spearmen, Somerset's battle was pushed back, then broke and fled. Edward then soon routed in turn the demoralised Lancastrian centre and left.

The number of Lancastrian slain was heavy, and the most notable fatality was the Prince of Wales. Somerset sought sanctuary in Tewkesbury Abbey but was soon seized and executed. Margaret managed to escape but was subsequently taken and remained in confinement for four years until she was ransomed by the King of France. Her husband – who had been a captive in the Tower once again following Barnet – was murdered there when Edward returned to London in triumph.

15

BOSWORTH
22 AUGUST 1485

'The Cat, the Rat, and Lovell our Dog,
Rule all England under an Hog.'
—William Colingbourne

Edward IV died on 9 April 1483 at the palace of Westminster shortly before his 41st birthday. The first half of his reign had been beset by unrest which reached its height in 1469–71 when his erstwhile colleague, Warwick the Kingmaker, opposed him and threw in his lot with the Lancastrians. As we have seen, Edward had destroyed Warwick at Barnet in 1471 and soon after defeated another Lancastrian force at Tewkesbury, shortly after which he had had his captive kinsman, Henry VI, murdered.

Now Edward himself was dead and sensible people wondered whether his demise would be followed by renewed conflict, for his successor was a mere boy of twelve, his son, Edward V. Tension there certainly was. Between whom? And why? In 1464 Edward IV had married a widow, Elizabeth Woodville, a woman of good but not exalted birth, and had proceeded to reward her numerous relations with titles and marriages to important heiresses, a policy which alienated members of the old nobility (including Warwick) who came to hate the avaricious, overbearing, and in some cases unforgiving, newcomers.

One of those hostile to the Woodville group was the Duke of Buckingham, a descendant of Edward III and the possessor of vast estates, who had been almost entirely excluded from power by Edward IV. Another opponent of the queen and her kinsmen was Lord Hastings (who had been ennobled by Edward in 1461), the late king's right-hand man. Sir Thomas More states, in an account dating from c.1513, that Elizabeth hated Hastings because of the influence he had had with her husband. Moreover Hastings was on bad terms with her brother, Earl Rivers, whom he had supplanted as Captain of Calais in 1471, and more particularly with the Marquis of Dorset, Elizabeth's son by her first husband, for a contemporary Dominic Mancini declares that they had quarrelled 'over the mistresses whom they had abducted, or attempted to entice from one another'.

Edward IV's brother, Richard of Gloucester, is also often said to have been on bad terms with the queen and her relations. But whether this was so during Edward's lifetime is uncertain. It does seem likely that Richard's relationship with Elizabeth was strained: according to Mancini she was jealous of the influence he had with her husband. On the other hand there seems to have been no hostility between Gloucester and Rivers. Indeed, only a week or so before Edward's death the latter agreed to let Richard be the arbitrator of a dispute in which he was involved.

Edward's untimely and unexpected demise dramatically raised the political temperature and heightened whatever animosity and tension existed. The deeply unpopular Woodville clan was determined to retain as much power as possible (including control of the person of young Edward V), fearful that failure to do so would jeopardize their prosperity and safety by opening them up to attack by the many people who hated them; while for a number of reasons their enemies and critics wished to prevent a Woodville dominated minority. Furthermore, even if Richard's relations with the queen and her kin had been amicable hitherto, he also had reason for preventing them from gaining the ascendancy. If that occurred his position as the greatest subject in the realm would inevitably be compromised. Moreover, if Elizabeth did bear him enmity, then perhaps his very survival would be threatened.

It was the queen's party who initiated the power struggle. In the days immediately following Edward IV's death they seized the royal treasure in the Tower and in other ways prepared to maintain their position by force if required.

Additionally, in the council which most probably met following the late king's burial on 20 April, they sought to minimise the role Gloucester would play in the direction of affairs. Shortly before his death, Edward IV had added a codicil to his will stating that upon his demise Richard should become the Protector of his heir and the realm. The council, however, was not bound to accede to the wishes of the late monarch (though some councillors, most notably Hastings, pressed it to do so), and owing to Woodville opposition a compromise was reached. A very early coronation would be held, on 4 May, thereby obviating the need for a protectorate, after which the government of the realm would be conducted until Edward V was old enough to rule by a governing council of which Gloucester – who was in the north – would be the chief councillor.

Furthermore, it was agreed following vigorous protestations by Hastings (who feared that the Woodville group would attempt to achieve dominance by force), that the absent Rivers, Edward V's governor, would bring the youngster to London (from Ludlow) with a moderate retinue instead of the substantial force proposed by the queen.

Thus in the council, Elizabeth and her kin did not have everything their own way. Nonetheless they had achieved some of their objectives and Dorset at least, we are told, was in a cocksure mood.

Meanwhile, Richard had received the news of his brother's death and last wishes from Hastings, who advised him to come to London with a strong force. Gloucester first made for York (probably from his stronghold at Middleham) and there pledged loyalty to Edward V. He began moving south on the 20th. While doing so he received news from Hastings of the council's decisions and, according to Mancini, was advised to seize 'before they were alive to the danger' those in favour of minimising his role during the minority.

On the 24th, Rivers and the young king left Ludlow and headed towards Northampton in accordance with Richard's wish that the royal party rendezvous with him so that a stately joint procession to the capital could ensue. On the 29th Richard arrived at Northampton. He was welcomed by Rivers, who told him that the king and the rest of the royal party had pressed on fourteen miles to Stony Stratford.

Later in the day one of Richard's new allies, the Duke of Buckingham, arrived on the scene. As has been noted, he was no friend of the queen and her relations: Mancini tells us that he 'loathed her race'. Nonetheless, as More states, that night there was 'much friendly cheer' between the dukes and Rivers. Just what Richard was thinking at this time is uncertain. His mind may have been set on seizing the throne, or he may have been determined to secure the protectorate entrusted to him by his late brother. If he compromised and accepted the position of chief councillor, following Edward V's coronation there was a very real possibility that the council would veer in the direction of the Woodville group. For one thing, the young king's wishes could not be entirely ignored and he was much closer to the queen and her kin than to Richard.

After Rivers retired to bed, Gloucester discussed matters with his impulsive companion. Buckingham convinced him, if indeed he were not already convinced, that it was in his best interests to seize the initiative. And so, at dawn on 30 April, Rivers, whom Mancini describes as 'a kind, serious, and just man' in marked contrast to other members of the Woodville clan, was arrested and the road to Stony Stratford guarded so that news of the event could not reach the king's party.

Richard and Buckingham subsequently rode south to Stony Stratford and paid their respects to young Edward. Gloucester then stated that he had been obliged to arrest Rivers because he was plotting, with others of the Woodville group, to do away with him. Despite protestations by the king, Richard proceeded to arrest Edward's half-brother Sir Richard Grey and Sir Thomas Vaughan, the treasurer of the king's household, before dismissing the majority of the royal escort.

News of these events soon reached London. According to the contemporary *Croyland Chronicle*, two armed parties thus formed, 'some collected their forces at Westminster in the queen's name, others at London under the shadow of the Lord Hastings'. Upon failing to win sufficient support, and aware that the initiative now lay firmly in the hands of her enemies, Elizabeth hurriedly sought sanctuary in Westminster Abbey with Dorset, her youngest son the Duke of York, and her daughters. On 4 May Edward entered London with Gloucester and Buckingham (Rivers, Grey and Vaughan had been sent north to be incarcerated in Yorkshire), and in order to smear the Woodville faction, wagons full of weapons and armour bearing their devices were at the forefront of the procession and criers let it be known on Richard's behalf that the queen and her kin had intended to destroy him.

On 10 May, at a meeting of the council, a new date for the coronation, 24 June, (later altered to Sunday 22 June), was decided on. Moreover Richard was installed as Protector. His allies, Buckingham and Hastings, were naturally chosen to play a prominent part in the new government. The former in particular was lavishly rewarded. For instance, on 15 May he was made constable and steward of all the castles and lordships in Wales and the Marches at the disposal of the crown. As for Hastings, he retained both the office of lord chamberlain and the captaincy of Calais, and on the 20th was confirmed as Master of the Mint, a lucrative position he had likewise held under Edward IV. On the other hand, not surprisingly, Rivers, Dorset and other members of the Woodville group were stripped of their offices and grants. Nonetheless, Richard's administration was a broadly based one which included many former members of Edward IV's household. The prospects for political stability seemed fairly good.

However, in the second week of June whatever optimism there was gave way to widespread fear and suspicion. On Friday 13th, Hastings was accused of treason by Richard at a meeting of the council in the Tower and immediately executed on Tower Hill. Three other accused councillors, two of whom were prelates, were seized and imprisoned.

Just why Richard acted the way he did on the 13th is disputed. Some believe that Hastings had become disillusioned with Richard and jealous of Buckingham, and had thus become involved with the other councillors and the queen in a plot against the Protector. A plot was referred to by Richard on the 10 and 11 June in letters he sent to the north, his power-base, calling for military assistance against Elizabeth and her supporters who intended 'to murder and utterly destroy us and our cousyn the duc of Buckyngham'. Others, however, believe that Hastings was destroyed by Richard because the Protector knew that he would not support his planned usurpation of the throne: the charge of plotting against Richard is seen as a concoction to excuse moving against Hastings and other leading members of the council loyal to Edward V.

Apparently, prior to this Richard had for sometime hoped to secure the consent of the council and parliament – the latter had been summoned to meet on 25 June – to an extension of his protectorate until Edward came of age, which if the precedent of Henry VI were followed, would occur when the king was fifteen. However, by this date it appears that Richard was intent on seizing the throne in the belief that doing so was the best way of safeguarding his future.

On 16 June he surrounded the Westminster precinct with a strong force, determined on gaining possession of Edward's younger brother, York, on the grounds that he should be beside his brother at the forthcoming coronation. The Archbishop of Canterbury urged the queen to hand the youngster over and she agreed, realising that resistance was futile. He was led away to be lodged in the Tower with Edward. Writs were issued the following day cancelling the parliament called to meet on the 25th, and the coronation was put off until 9 November.

On 22 June, the day Edward was to have been crowned, Dr Ralph Shaw, at Richard's instigation, preached a sermon at St Paul's cross in which the Protector's claim to the throne was first put forward. He was declared to be the only legitimate heir of his father, the late Duke of York. As Charles Ross has stated: 'Precisely on what grounds Richard justified his claim to the throne in June 1483 has been the subject of lengthy debate'. It seems that Shaw stated that Edward IV had been conceived in adultery and was thus falsely said to be York's son, though some historians are of the opinion that he declared that Edward V and his young brother were bastards. The view that they were illegitimate was apparently repeated, or expressed for the first time, by Buckingham when addressing a meeting of the mayor and aldermen of London at the Guildhall two days later.

This accusation was based on a claim (told to Richard by the Bishop of Bath and Wells), that before his marriage to Elizabeth Woodville Edward IV had been secretly betrothed to Lady Eleanor Butler, a pre-contract which invalidated his subsequent marriage, thereby rendering the offspring of the union bastards.

Both the above allegations were highly dubious. Nonetheless on the 25th Buckingham evidently repeated the claim of the boys' illegitimacy when speaking to an assembly of lords and commons. Furthermore, it seems certain that he stated that Edward, the son of Richard's late brother, the Duke of Clarence, (who had been executed in 1478), was ineligible to succeed to the throne owing to his father's attainder. A petition was then assented to by the assembly, requesting that Gloucester should assume the crown. It is said that the assembly assented to the petition largely owing to fear of Richard and Buckingham 'whose power,' Mancini states, 'supported by a multitude of troops, would be hazardous and difficult to resist'.

The following day the petition was read in Richard's presence at Baynard's Castle, London. He assented to it, and then rode to Westminster Hall where he usurped the throne by sitting on the royal chair in the court of king's bench. As he sat at Westminster Richard knew that Rivers, Grey and Vaughan, were almost certainly dead for he had ordered their execution: instructions which were carried out at Pontefract on, or about, 25 June.

Richard was subsequently crowned on 6 July. It was a splendid occasion well attended by the nobility, and after it the new king began travelling about his realm to meet and impress his subjects.

And what of his nephews in the Tower? According to a contemporary source, the *Great Chronicle of London*, the boys had been seen 'shooting and playing in the garden by the Tower' but were then seen 'more rarely behind the bars and windows' until they were viewed no more. According to Mancini, by the time of Richard's coronation many Londoners believed that the boys were no longer in the realm of the living, or that if they still breathed, it would not be long before they ceased doing so.

Rumours that the boys were dead, or as good as, spread into the home counties and beyond and turned many people against Richard, who nonetheless enjoyed much support in the north where he had long served loyally as the lieutenant of his late brother. Thus in October, by which date Richard's nephews had very probably been done away with, most likely on his orders, the king heard that a serious revolt had broken out in the south with the intention of overthrowing him and installing a Lancastrian claimant to the throne, an exile by the name of Henry Tudor, a descendant of Edward III. At the rebellion's head was Buckingham, who had turned against Richard. However, the insurrection was suppressed, for magnates such as the Duke of Norfolk and Lord Stanley rallied to the king's cause. Buckingham was captured and executed on 2 November, by which date Tudor had made an abortive attempt to land in Dorset before returning to Brittany.

After the revolt Richard attainted many people. Their confiscated estates were granted to northerners 'to the disgrace and lasting sorrow of all the people of the south' states the *Croyland Chronicle*, 'who daily longed more and more for the return of their ancient rulers, rather than the present tyranny of these people'. As J. R. Lander has observed, Richard's government had 'contravened one of the most deeply rooted conventions of power, that local government should be the preserve of local families'.

Among the northerners who benefitted greatly from the king's largesse was Sir Richard Ratcliffe, one of the men referred to in the seditious rhyme dating from 1484 quoted at the beginning of this chapter. The other men with whom he was linked in the rhyme were William Catesby and Viscount Lovell, other prominent figures in the regime of Richard.

As noted, by now the hopes of diehard Lancastrians rested with Henry Tudor. They did so by default. In 1471 the House of Lancaster had become extinct when Henry VI was murdered shortly after his only son the Prince of Wales was slain at Tewkesbury where another Lancastrian, the last Beaufort Duke of Somerset, (a descendant of Edward III's fourth son, John of Gaunt), likewise perished.

Lancastrians were not the only ones now pinning their hopes on exiled Henry. So too were many Yorkists who had become disenchanted with Richard, for in the event of a successful invasion of England, Tudor had promised to marry Elizabeth of York, the eldest sister of the king's ill-fated young nephews: a promise he made at Rennes Cathedral on Christmas Day 1483.

Richard was well aware that Henry remained a threat despite the failure of the recent insurrection and so took steps to thwart his adversary. For example, early in 1484 he wrote to Elizabeth Woodville, who was still in sanctuary at Westminster, promising to guarantee her safety and that of her daughters and to give her an annuity of £700 if they left Westminster. The letter, witnessed by the lords spiritual and temporal and the mayor and aldermen of London, resulted in Elizabeth going to Richard's court where she reneged on the agreement made with Tudor – via intermediaries – that he marry Elizabeth of York.

Richard also moved directly against Henry. In June he made an agreement with the Duke of Brittany's treasurer (the duke was temporarily mentally deranged), whereby he would give Francis II the annual revenues of the earldom of Richmond if Tudor were handed over. However, Henry heard of this scheme and fled to the protection of the French court, as did English exiles who had gathered round him in Brittany. Moreover he was subsequently joined by others opposed to Richard, among whom was the Earl of Oxford, an experienced and able soldier.

By this date Richard had experienced a major personal setback. In April his only legitimate son, the young Prince of Wales, had died at Middleham in Yorkshire: a loss which devastated the king.

Then in March of the following year, 1485, Richard lost his wife Anne (a daughter of Warwick the Kingmaker), and rumours spread that he had poisoned her in order to marry his niece, Elizabeth of York. The king may have contemplated such a match. What is certain is that his close associates objected to such a move and Richard proceeded to publicly disown entertaining thoughts of marrying Elizabeth and denied, likely in good conscience, poisoning his wife for the rumour that he had done so had added to the repugnance many felt towards him and, significantly, had damaged his standing somewhat in the north.

To a large extent Richard must have felt an embattled and isolated figure. He seems to have longed to come to blows with Tudor, whom he well knew had for months been planning an invasion of England. To deal with such a threat, and aware that his opponent could land anywhere, the king made Nottingham Castle his headquarters for it was situated in the middle of England. Moreover, he established a system of mounted scouts so that news of an invasion could reach him quickly, while beacons were set up to signal such news from hill to hill across the land.

Aware that an invasion was imminent, Richard alerted his commissioners of array on 22 June. He ordered them to muster able-bodied men and commanded them to inform nobles and other persons of note that they were to put aside any quarrels they had and unite in a national effort so that Richard could deal effectively with the 'rebels and traitors...purposing the destruction of us, the subversion of this our realm and disinheriting of all our true subjects'.

Henry sailed from the mouth of the Seine on 1 August. His destination? Milford Haven, Pembrokeshire. On the afternoon of Sunday 7 August the splendid coastline of this Welsh county came into view, and at sunset the invaders entered Milford Haven and proceeded to come ashore.

Henry did not arrive at the head of a formidable army. With him were his uncle Jasper Tudor, Oxford, and a few hundred other exiles. The bulk of his following was a force of about 2,000 French mercenaries. Clearly he expected that people would rally to his cause once they heard that he had landed, and before embarking on the venture, had written to persons of consequence encouraging them to do just that.

After landing Henry made his way to Haverfordwest, and then pressed on into Cardiganshire. He made his way along the coast, then turned inland at Machynlleth. So far he had received little support and his progress was being flanked by a force under Rhys ap Thomas and Sir Walter Herbert. Therefore it must have been with a great sense of relief that he greeted the news that these two important men, upon whom Richard was relying, wished to join forces with him. They evidently did so before Tudor reached Welshpool.

On 15 August Henry crossed into England and demanded the surrender of Shrewsbury, which soon capitulated. He then moved on eastward at the head of a growing force towards Newport. Here he received his first significant English support for he was joined by Gilbert Talbot, the uncle of the young Earl of Shrewsbury, with a Shropshire contingent 500 strong. He then made for Stafford, where he arrived on the 17th and was joined by Sir William Stanley, the brother of Tudor's stepfather, Lord Stanley, a member of a powerful family in the north-west of England. Sir William stage-managed Henry's entry into Lichfield on the morning of the 19th and then, to Tudor's dismay, departed. Nonetheless, that afternoon Henry made for Tamworth. His army arrived there that evening, but the pretender only did so the following morning after becoming separated from his men and spending the night a short distance away with his bodyguard.

By now, of course, Richard had heard of Tudor's landing. He did so on the 11th and reacted promptly. Summonses were rapidly sent to the Duke of Norfolk and the Earl of Northumberland among others, instructing them to join him promptly with their men under pain of forfeiture and death. Richard then moved south to Leicester on the 20th, aware that men such as Rhys ap Thomas whom he had expected to oppose Tudor had in fact gone over to him. He arrived in Leicester late on the 20th, no doubt a bitter and anxious man.

Among those who evidently caused Richard concern was Lord Stanley, who was at the head of a strong force. He had been summoned to join the king but had failed to comply – excusing himself on grounds of illness – and by this date was in the country to the west of Leicester, most probably near Higham on the Hill. Though Stanley had not openly committed himself to the pretender (his son, Lord Strange, was a hostage in the royal camp), his behaviour was nevertheless not such as would be conducive to Richard's peace of mind.

On the evening of 20 August Henry arrived at Atherstone, a short distance north-west of Higham on the Hill. His army evidently encamped in the neighbourhood for he subsequently recompensed a local landowner, the Abbot of Merevale, for 'the destruccioun of his cornes and pastures'. Sir William Stanley had likewise moved south separately with his own force, and appears to have encamped for the night a short distance to the north of Atherstone.

The following day, Sunday 21st, Tudor and the Stanley brothers met at Atherstone or somewhere in its vicinity, and Henry was evidently assured that they would support him in the impending battle.

On the same day Richard moved west from Leicester at the head of a substantial army which included contingents brought to his side by the country's most powerful nobles, Norfolk and Northumberland, and according to Raphael Holinshed's chronicle (published in 1577), 'pitched his field on a hill called Anne Beame, refreshed hys Souldiours and tooke his rest'. The hill in question, Ambion Hill, is 11.5 miles west of Leicester and just to the west of Sutton Cheney.

Tudor now moved east towards the king and apparently encamped somewhere beyond Fenny Drayton, most probably along, or in close proximity to, a Roman road from Mancetter to Leicester. He subsequently compensated Atherstone, Witherley, Mancetter, Atterton and Fenny Drayton for the loss of corn and grain evidently taken by foraging parties prior to the army's setting up camp for the night.

On the other hand, Lord Stanley does not appear to have moved to a new encampment on the 21st. However it seems that Sir William did so, and that as a result was not far from his brother.

Thus the respective forces spent the night in fairly close proximity to each other. During the hours of darkness Richard's army was weakened somewhat by desertion for Sir John Savage junior, Sir Brian Sandford and Sir Simon Digby, slipped away with their men and defected to Tudor.

Reportedly, Richard slept badly. This may well have been the case but Henry, with a smaller army, uncertain allies, and himself a stranger to battle, probably did not sleep well either.

Before discussing the site of the ensuing engagement, and the course of battle, something needs to be said about the character and careers of the principal protagonists.

RICHARD III AND HENRY TUDOR

Many people are familiar with Shakespeare's portrayal of Richard as a man deformed in both body and mind, an ambitious monster with a string of heinous crimes to his discredit – a man whose hands were stained with blood. Others have maintained likewise, before and since. Conversely, Richard has been portrayed as one of England's noblest sons by those who have tried to exonerate him of all the crimes with which he has been associated. Then, again, some have viewed Richard with moderation. E. F. Jacob for instance, while acknowledging that he behaved ruthlessly after Edward IV's death, declared: 'That there was a sound constructive side to Richard III is undoubted. He was very far from being the distorted villain of tradition'.

Richard was born on 2 October 1452 at Fotheringhay, and was the youngest son of the Duke of York. His youth was marred by the Wars of the Roses. When only eight, for example, his father and one of his brothers were slain at Wakefield after which Richard and another brother, George, were sent abroad for their safety. They returned several months later after their elder brother, Edward, had secured the throne.

From 1465 until early 1469 Richard was a member of the household of Warwick and when the latter rebelled in 1469, he stood by Edward – in marked contrast to George – and thus accompanied Edward when he fled to the Low Countries in 1470. The following year, after returning, Richard helped Edward defeat Warwick at Barnet and fought courageously at Tewkesbury.

His consistent loyalty did not go unrewarded for, among other things, he was granted estates formerly held by Warwick. During the course of the 1470s Richard emerged as the principal figure in the north: a great landowner, and in effect, Edward's lieutenant in the region. Then, in early 1483, he had a palatinate created for him by parliament consisting of Cumberland and as much of adjacent Scotland as he could conquer.

Evidently Richard was slightly built, and as A. J. Pollard has said of his alleged physical abnormalities, 'no one in his lifetime thought a physical deformity was worth reporting'. Richard was able, courageous and ambitious. He loved music and jewels, was generous, and enjoyed the company of scholars. He was moreover very religious, was interested in the pursuit of justice, and showed concern for the lowly. Some maintain that such facets of his personality preclude the possibility that he could have behaved unwarrantably. This is not so. His concern for justice undoubtedly waned when his own interests were at stake. He had grown to manhood in a harsh and very uncertain world and had inevitably been affected by the spirit of the times.

And what of Henry Tudor? He was born at Pembroke in January 1457, shortly after the death of his father, the young Earl of Richmond. For a while he resided there with his mother, enjoying the protection of his Lancastrian uncle, Jasper Tudor, Earl of Pembroke. But after the latter was forced to flee abroad in 1461 Henry became a ward of a Yorkist, Lord Herbert, and became separated from his mother.

Through his mother, Margaret, the daughter and heiress of John Beaufort, Duke of Somerset, Henry was descended from Edward III's fourth son John of Gaunt, for the Beauforts sprang from an irregular union between the latter and Catherine Swinford. The three sons of this liaison (born at Beaufort in Champagne), were subsequently legitimised in 1397 and this was confirmed by their half-brother, Henry IV, in 1407 at which time however it was specified that they were barred from any claim to the throne. Though the Beauforts and their offspring had been barred from the succession this did not matter overmuch to staunch Lancastrians for in reality the crown was a prize to be fought for by those, such as Tudor, who had royal blood in their veins.

In 1470, following the revival of Lancastrian fortunes, Henry and his uncle enjoyed the favour of the government and were awarded the custody of Herbert's lands. But after the Yorkist victories of 1471 Henry fled abroad, accompanied by his mother and Pembroke.

They intended landing in France, but owing to misfortune, came ashore in Brittany where they were taken into custody by the duke. They remained in unfavourable circumstances for years but Henry then received Breton aid for his abortive expedition against Richard III in 1483. As stated earlier, the following year Henry had to flee to France and while there received the support which set him on the road to Bosworth.

Henry Tudor lacked panache and was certainly not over endowed with charisma. He was cool and judicious, a methodical man who did not love warfare. Indeed, as has been noted, he had never participated in battle. He was also untried in the field of government. Not surprisingly, then, many persons of consequence in England who had been alienated by Richard's regime thus remained aloof before Bosworth, unwilling to support the hazardous enterprise upon which the daring young man was engaged.

DESCRIPTION

The site of the battle of Bosworth has been fiercely debated in recent years. The traditional site is Ambion Hill and its immediate vicinity, just west of Sutton Cheney.

According to this view, as it is generally maintained, Richard deployed his army on the hill in three battles. Norfolk led the van, which crowned the western slope, Richard the centre, and Northumberland the rearguard further to the east. Henry closed with Richard after marching east and then veering north to avoid a marsh normally said by historians to have been just to the south or west of Ambion Hill and drained during the sixteenth century. Fierce fighting occurred between Norfolk and Henry's van under Oxford. Intent on slaying Henry, Richard then charged down the hill with his household troops and, after skirting the fighting, clashed with the isolated Tudor and his escort and was slain after Sir William Stanley rode to Henry's aid. According to the proclamation issued after the battle by Tudor, the place where Richard died was 'called Sandeford' and this has been identified as a crossing of the Sutton brook a short distance north-west of Ambion Hill. Shortly after Richard's charge, the resistance of his army as a whole collapsed. We are not told the direction of the ensuing flight, but some believe that the fugitives were chased south towards Dadlington and Stoke Golding.

However, in 1985 Colin Richmond argued against the traditional battlesite and suggested that Bosworth was fought on ground immediately overlooked by Dadlington a mile or so to the south of Ambion Hill: a position closer to Crown Hill (where according to tradition Henry was crowned after the battle), than is Ambion Hill. Among other things, Richmond cited the comment written early in the first half of the nineteenth century by the antiquary, John Nichols, that 'indented spaces of ground' he saw about Dadlington were 'probably the graves of the victims' of Bosworth.

It is moreover interesting to note that the ballad, *Bosworth Feilde*, (which apparently was initially composed within ten years of the battle by a member of the Stanley connection), states that Richard's host was deployed in a dale, and that in his account of Bosworth written c.1540, Edward Hall declares that on the morning of the engagement the king's men came 'oute of their camp into the plaine'. That the battle was fought on a plain is also mentioned by William Burton, the lord of the manor of Dadlington and Higham, who heard second-hand accounts of the encounter from local people who had known eyewitnesses of the event. In 1622 Burton wrote that the battle was 'fought in a large, flat,

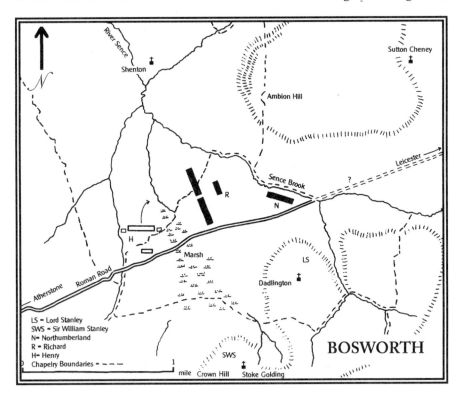

plaine, and spacious ground, three miles distant from [Market Bosworth] between the Towne of Shenton, Sutton, Dadlington, and Stoke [Golding].'

Furthermore, as M. J. Phillips has recently commented: 'The preponderant weight of archaeological evidence does seem to point to Dadlington and its environs as the location of certainly the majority of deaths due to battle'. For instance, the *Hinckley Parish Register, Village Advertiser and Local Church Register* of 1868, records that while a grave was being prepared in the churchyard at Dadlington 'a number of human bones was found about 2ft below the surface, amongst them as many as twenty skulls,' and notes that they were 'supposed to be the remains of some of those who fell in the battle of Bosworth'. Additionally, layers of compacted skeletons were unearthed in the churchyard when another grave was being dug in about 1950, a discovery which drew a crowd of onlookers. Reports of the discovery of skeletons believed to be the remains of men who perished in the battle have also come from the neighbouring parish of Stoke Golding. It is instructive to note that Burton relates that at the enclosure of Stoke Golding in about 1600 'divers peeces of armor, weapons and other warlike accoutrements' were unearthed.

As noted above, some historians have attempted to explain such discoveries by stating that the pursuit which occurred at the end of the battle was in the direction of Stoke Golding and Dadlington. However it is more reasonable to conclude that the traditional site for Bosworth is erroneous and that the battle was fought closer to Dadlington and Stoke Golding than hitherto thought.

This conclusion is reinforced by the fact that in 1511 the churchwardens of Dadlington received royal permission to collect contributions in the Midlands for 'the bielding of a chapell of sainte James standing upon a parcell of the grounde where Bosworth feld, otherwise called Dadlyngton feld...was done'. (It appears that the resulting building work entailed repairs and improvements to an existing chapel of St James rather than the construction of a new structure). Furthermore, a confraternity letter of indulgence printed shortly after the licence was issued is also significant. It states that 'ye bodyes or bones of the men sleyne in ye seyde feelde' had been brought and buried in the vicinity of Dadlington church.

The re-siting of the battle does not mean that Ambion Hill – which was first mentioned in connection with the engagement by Holinshed, and possesses a fine visitors' centre – need be viewed as of no consequence as far as the events of August 1485 are concerned. There is reason to believe that the royal army spent the night prior to the battle encamped on the hill. For one thing, as Peter J. Foss has commented: 'Such a vantage point, with its grass covered banks, vestigial closes [a deserted medieval hamlet had been situated on the hill], and ample fresh water, was an ideal place for a camp.' Furthermore tradition has it that Richard drank from a spring on Ambion Hill (a cairn was erected at the supposed spot in 1813), and additionally, the odd cannonball has been found on the hill. In short, it is reasonable to conclude that the statement in *Holinshed's Chronicle* that the royal army encamped on Ambion Hill on the eve of the battle was based on accurate information.

The earliest record of the battle – save for Tudor's proclamation – is in the *York House Book* B2-4 which contains an entry made on 23 August 1485. It refers to the engagement as 'the feld of Redemore'. The name 'Redemore,' like that of 'Sandeford,' has disappeared from the map. In part it refers to wetland and thus chimes with references to a marsh by writers such as Polydore Vergil – our principal source for Bosworth – a distinguished scholar who wrote his account of the battle in the early sixteenth century after talking to participants and evidently reading earlier material.

Where this marsh was situated has long been disputed. It is apparent that much of this part of Leicestershire was once marshy and this is certainly true of the chapelry of Dadlington. For example, a document dated 1283 refers to 'six roods of meadow in Redemor, in the fields of Dadlington'.

On geological grounds it has recently been argued that the most likely location for the marsh which featured in the events of 22 August 1485 was to the south-east of Ambion Hill and the north-east of Dadlington. That a marsh existed hereabouts is a reasonable deduction. On the other hand another recent writer, Foss, whose work *The Field of Redemore* is essential reading for anyone seriously interested in the Battle of Bosworth, argues that the marsh was to the west of Dadlington and to the north of Stoke Golding where there is 'a band of alluvial flatland subject to periodic flooding. This must once have remained open water or marsh for much of the year, fed by streams and springs emerging from the cleft of the hills between Dadlington and Stoke [Golding].'

It is reasonable to accept Foss' location for the marsh which features in accounts of the battle. For a start, Vergil states that the marsh was situated between the opposing armies, that is across Tudor's line of advance from the west on the 22nd. In view of this, the former of the two proposed sites just mentioned for the relevant marsh is surely too far east bearing in mind the finds, and reports of finds, referred to earlier associated with Bosworth in the Stoke Golding/Dadlington area. Furthermore Foss' site is close to Crown Hill near Stoke Golding, where as noted, tradition maintains that Henry was crowned immediately after the battle.

If, as is accepted here, Foss' site for the marsh is correct, then it is also reasonable to conclude that the 'Sandeford' mentioned in Tudor's proclamation was connected with it. An eminent philologist, Margaret Gelling, has stated that the suffix 'ford' has not only been employed in connection with crossings of rivers and streams, but also with causeways across marshland. Hence it is possible to assume that the 'Sandeford' in question referred to the area where the Roman road from Mancetter to Leicester crossed the alluvial land mentioned by Foss, an area where there are 'pockets of running sand below the soil surface'.

Like the location of the battlesite, the size of the armies at Bosworth is also a moot point. According to the act of attainder of November 1485 Richard's force had been 'a great host'. That it was stronger than Henry's is certain, though the wildly inflated figures given for its strength by some sources have to be rejected. The Castilian courtier Diego de Valera, for instance, (who wrote about Bosworth in 1486), relates that Richard had 'as many as 70,000 combatants'. We must reject too the statement dating from the same year in the *Croyland Chronicle* that the king had 'a greater number of soldiers than had ever been seen before in England assembled on one side'.

As mentioned earlier, Richard received the news of Henry's landing on 11 August and hurriedly sent instructions hither and thither for the assembly of an army 'in all haste'. For example, a Derbyshire gentleman, Sir Henry Vernon, was summoned to urgently 'come with such number as ye have promised ... sufficiently horsed and harnessed ... upon pain of forfeiture'.

As Charles Ross has highlighted, Richard's force at Bosworth 'must very largely' have consisted of men who had arrived on horseback, irrespective of whether they intended to fight mounted or not. Even allowing for this, there can be no doubt that not all of those who responded to the king's summonses were present at Bosworth owing to the speed with which he clashed with his adversary. Ross was thus of the opinion that Richard 'may have had no more than 8,000 men in his command, although 10,000 is by no means unlikely'. Some historians have given rather smaller or larger figures than these. A force of approximately 8,000 men is the figure accepted here.

And what of Tudor's army? It is generally said by historians to have numbered about 5,000 men, and as mentioned earlier, included a strong French contingent. As for the Stanleys, between them they may have had nearly 5,000 men.

Before discussing the events of Monday 22 August 1485, it is worth noting that the arms and armour of the men in the opposing armies had changed little, if at all, since the days of the Towton campaign in 1461. (See Chapter 12).

Sunrise on the 22nd occurred at 5.15am. Richard's camp must soon have been a hive of activity – indeed it may have already been so – as his army prepared to leave Ambion Hill (an unsuitable location for the effective deployment of his substantial force), aware that Tudor was no great distance away. It is said that confusion reigned in the royal camp. The *Croyland Chronicle*, for example, states: 'At dawn on Monday morning the chaplains were not ready to celebrate mass for King Richard nor was any breakfast ready with which to revive the king's flagging spirit'. Perhaps this was so. Recently, however, John Woods has expressed doubts on the matter and has plausibly suggested that the idea that Richard did not hear mass was probably invented to portray him as a villain foredoomed to disaster.

Before long the foremost units of the royal army must have been taking up positions on the lower ground to the south-west of Ambion Hill.

Henry's men had likewise been stirring. While preparing to move off, the pretender sent a messenger to Lord Stanley asking him to join forces with him. Stanley, who had avoided committing himself at several battles, did not comply. Vergil relates that he told his stepson that he 'should set his own men in line' and that he 'would be at hand with his army in proper array', a reply 'contrary to what was expected'.

However, according to *Bosworth Feilde*, on the morning of the battle Lord Stanley did augment Tudor's force with a contingent led by four knights, John Savage, Robert Tunstall, Hugh Pearsall and Humphrey Stanley. Furthermore, like *Ladye Bessiye* (another ballad which evidently contains material of an early date), *Bosworth Feilde* relates that after reinforcing his stepson Stanley took up a position on a hill to watch the expected clash of arms. It seems reasonable then to conclude that Henry's request met with partial success, and that before moving towards the enemy he was augmented by the reinforcements in question.

Lord Stanley appears to have already been on the move when he received Tudor's request – having as noted probably spent the night near Higham on the Hill – and he evidently proceeded to take up a position near Dadlington by which time, most likely, much of Richard's army had descended on to the plain. At this juncture Richard may well have still been on Ambion Hill for *Lady Bessiye* describes him 'hoving' on a 'mountaine', cognizant of the banner of the 'boulde Stanley'.

And what of Sir William Stanley? Where was he? Some are of the opinion that he was to the north of the battlefield. This idea is derived from a speech attributed to Henry by Hall in which the pretender states, 'before us be our enemies, and on either side of us such as I neither surely trust nor greatly believe'. But when the date of Hall's work is borne in mind it becomes clear that it is unwise to give much credence to what he says on this point. It is, moreover, sometimes said that Sir William was to the north of the battlefield because his intervention late in the proceedings led to the southward flight of the vanquished, but as we have seen none of the sources stipulate the direction of the flight and though some of the fugitives may indeed have fled southward most, if not all, of the material associated with Bosworth found in the Stoke Golding/Dadlington area can be explained as the debris of the battle itself.

On the whole, the evidence indicates that Sir William Stanley was on high ground to the south of the battlefield as was his brother. *Bosworth Feilde* states that Sir William was 'hindmost at the outsetting', and he was most probably in the vicinity of Stoke Golding.

As with so much else about Bosworth, uncertainty exists about the dispositions of Richard's army. Part of the royal host was commanded by Northumberland and of him the *Croyland Chronicle* notes: 'In the place where the Earl of Northumberland was posted, with a large company of reasonably good men, no engagement could be discerned, and no battle blows given or received'. This, and subsequent statements such as that of the chronicler Robert Fabyan (written early in the sixteenth century) that 'some stode hovynge a feere of tyll they sawe to whiche partye the victory fyll', have led some to conclude that Northumberland opted out of the conflict by remaining back on Ambion Hill.

On the other hand, however, Vergil relates that Richard 'drew his whole army out of their encampments' on the morning of the 22nd and proceeded to array his forces for the impending engagement. The resulting battle line 'extended at such a wonderful length', being composed of 'footmen and horsemen packed together in such a way that the mass of armed men struck terror in the hearts of the distant onlookers'. In the front, Richard 'placed the archers, like a most strong bulwark, appointing as their leader John, Duke of Norfolk'. The king was to the rear of the battle line 'with a select force of soldiers'.

Interestingly, though, the *Croyland Chronicle* states that Norfolk was with a 'wing' while, to add to the confusion, Jean Molinet (whose account dates from about 1490) comments that Richard's van, which he believed 'had 11,000 or 12,000 men altogether', was commanded by Norfolk and Sir Robert Brackenbury, the keeper of the Tower of London.

All in all, it seems likely that Richard intended drawing the bulk of his army up in the usual way – a line of three battles with the vanguard and rearguard taking up positions on the right and left respectively and with, less typically, himself and his household troops and perhaps a few peers to the rear. If so, it seems probable that this deployment was not entirely achieved, with the rearguard under Northumberland halting en route to take up its position, likely upon seeing Lord Stanley arrive in the vicinity of Dadlington.

If this interpretation is correct, we can envisage two battles in line, the king and his 'select troops' to the rear, and Northumberland further back still. As shall be seen, it is reasonable to conclude that Norfolk was in command of the northernmost of the two proposed foremost battles. It will be remembered, moreover, that Molinet was of the opinion that Brackenbury was in joint command of the 'vanguard' and it is thus perhaps safe to conclude that Brackenbury had been placed in command of the other battle. If so, this was a rather unusual occurrence in view of the fact that he was a commoner. The frequent references in later sources to Norfolk solely commanding a vanguard probably derive from the fact that his battle had evidently been the van on the march from Leicester and the fact that Bosworth commenced in earnest, following an exchange of fire, when Norfolk closed with the oncoming enemy.

The bulk of Tudor's army was evidently placed under the command of the Earl of Oxford, an experienced soldier who had distinguished himself when leading the Lancastrian left wing at Barnet and in other military ventures. Not for nothing did the Croyland chronicler describe him as 'a most valiant soldier'. Vergil relates that at Bosworth Oxford was protected by wings. That on the left was under Sir John Savage junior, while Gilbert Talbot was in command of that on the right. Tudor was to the rear of this 'vanguard' as it is sometimes called, with a company of horsemen and a few infantry.

Vergil states that between the two armies 'was a marsh...which Henry deliberately left on his right, to serve his men as a defensive wall', and that in so doing 'he simultaneously put the sun behind him'. Of this stage of the proceedings Molinet writes: 'The king had the artillery of his army fire on the earl of Richmond, and so the French...resolved, in order to avoid the fire [Molinet makes no mention of a marsh at this stage in his narrative], to mass their troops against the flank rather than the front of the king's battle'. *The Rose of England*, a ballad probably composed in or shortly after 1485, states: 'The right hand of them [the enemy] he [Oxford] took'. We can thus picture the pretender's host turning north or north-west from the Roman road near the marsh postulated by Foss and skirting the wetland under fire in order to close with Richard's right wing.

As Anthony Goodman has commented, Henry evidently had a penchant for remaining at a distance at military encounters, (he did so at Stoke in 1487, and at Blackheath in 1497), and it seems likely that on this occasion he remained in the vicinity of the Roman road near where it commenced crossing the marsh, and thus not far from the Stanleys upon whom he was relying for support.

Apparently, before the armies joined, Richard ordered the immediate execution of Lord Strange, having been angered by the behaviour of the man's father, Lord Stanley. For some reason the order was not carried out, most probably because the onset of fighting diverted the king's attention from ensuring that the deed was performed.

Vergil relates that as soon as the pretender's army had advanced past the marsh Richard's men raised 'a great shout', whereupon the archers in the royal ranks let fly their arrows after which their opponents 'in no wise holding back, returned the fire fiercely'. Fighting at close quarters followed. As Hall comments: 'The terrible shot once passed, the armies joined and came to hand strokes'.

Initially, at least, it appears that this clash was between Richard's northernmost battle – Norfolk's – and the men under Oxford. The latter may have been caught off balance by the assault launched against them. If so, their courage and discipline prevented the situation degenerating into a rout. Vergil states that they obeyed an order given by Oxford just before battle was joined that 'no soldier should go more than ten feet from the standards'. Their resolution seems to have unsettled their adversaries, many of whom Vergil relates were fighting under compulsion anyway, for Norfolk's men reportedly 'broke off from fighting for a little while'. The conflict resumed when Oxford's 'tightly grouped units' went into the attack, as did 'the others in the other part', the wings under Savage and Talbot, 'pressing together in wedge formation'. Hence fighting 'raged between the front lines in both sectors'. As Rosemary Horrox has commented: 'The course of the battle of Bosworth is notoriously controversial'. It does seem, however, from Vergil that the wings under Savage and Talbot had at some point coalesced – they were probably somewhat to the rear of Oxford to begin with. On the other hand, it may well be that the situation was more simple or complex than that portrayed by Vergil.

What is safe to conclude is this: the pretender's men gained the upper hand in the struggle and drove their adversaries back, likely in a south-east direction, and perhaps in some disarray. Sooner or later, then, it became apparent that the battle was not going Richard's way. According to Diego de Valera, a Spaniard in the king's service called Salazar 'went up to him and said: "Sire, take steps to put your person in safety, without expecting to have the victory in today's battle, owing to the manifest treason in your following"'. Vergil also records that the success of the pretender's men owed much to the lack of commitment to Richard's cause of some in the royal army. He states that the king's companions reportedly 'seeing from the very outset of the battle that the soldiers were wielding their arms feebly and sluggishly, and that some were secretly deserting, suspected treason, and urged him to fly'.

However, Richard had no intention of fleeing. De Valera states that he exclaimed: 'God forbid I yield one step. This day I will die as a king or win'. Hence, upon determining Henry's whereabouts, (Tudor had probably moved closer to the fighting in view of his men's success), he charged against him at the head of those with him. According to Vergil, the angry monarch rode against his adversary 'from the other side, beyond the battle-line' (presumably to the north of the fighting), 'wearing the royal crown, so that he might thereby make either a beginning or an end of his reign'. The sight of the king and those with him charging against the man who dared to claim the throne must have been awe-inspiring and the event has been described as 'the swan-song of medieval English chivalry'.

The moment of truth had arrived. It is reported by Vergil that in the resulting clash – in which it is likely that the pretender's men were initially driven back to some extent – Richard struck down William Brandon, Henry's standard-bearer, before coming to blows with the doughty John Cheney, a strong man 'of surpassing bravery' whom he nonetheless overcame, knocking him to the ground. All about the embittered and desperate king blows were being exchanged in what was undoubtedly a furious confrontation.

The situation was dramatically transformed by the arrival of Sir William Stanley who moved to the pretender's aid. Richard and those with him were thus thrown onto the defensive. Relentlessly their number was reduced as more and more were struck down, leaving their riderless mounts to add to the mayhem. Some of the king's men turned to flee, but Richard fought on, striking at those closing in for the kill. Eventually, it seems, he was pushed back into the marshy ground mentioned earlier, at which point his horse became immobile. Then, according to Molinet, a Welshman 'struck him dead with a halberd [a

weapon combining a spear and a battleaxe]' and so Richard 'ended his days iniq-
uitously and filthily in the dirt and the mire'.

Meanwhile, in the main encounter, Oxford and his associates had by now put
to flight their adversaries, and according to Vergil many of the latter were cut
down in the rout. Some members of the royal army who had remained aloof
from the battle managed to depart unhindered while others stayed on the field
and submitted to Tudor following Richard's death. Vergil states that one such
was Northumberland.

Henry Tudor must have wiped his brow and smiled with relief and satisfac-
tion at the battle's outcome. Barring a future reverse, his years of exile and
despair were over.

Owing to the rather short duration of the battle – Vergil states that it lasted
over two hours, though it may have been an even quicker affair – casualties were
evidently not particularly heavy. Indeed, Molinet states that only 300 were slain
on either side, whilst Vergil was of the opinion that about a thousand members
of the royal army perished in contrast to 'scarcely a hundred soldiers' from
Tudor's host.

Richard's army undoubtedly suffered the greater losses, though the ratio is
unlikely to have been as disproportionate as Vergil comments, and among the
men of rank who fell were the Duke of Norfolk, Lord Ferrers of Chartley, Sir
Robert Brackenbury, Sir Richard Ratcliffe and Sir Robert Percy. In contrast,
William Brandon was the only notable fatality on the winning side.

Among prominent Ricardians made captive were the Earl of Surrey (Norfolk's son) and William Catesby. The Earl of Lincoln may likewise have been
captured though it is possible he managed to escape from the field, something
which Viscount Lovell certainly did.

Immediately after the battle Henry thanked God for the victory and con-
gratulated his men for their sterling services. Then, after moving to the nearest
hill, one of the Stanley brothers, most probably Sir William, placed Richard's
crown on Tudor's brow amid the acclaim of his supporters. As has been noted
tradition has it that this occurred on Crown Hill near Stoke Golding. The site
has been known as Crown Hill since at least 1605 and it is reasonable to believe
that it is indeed where this emotionally charged event occurred.

The outcome of Bosworth is often attributed to the treachery and indiffer-
ence of many of Richard's men, individuals who either had little or no love for
the king or whose morale had been undermined by rumours that there were traitors in their ranks and by the fact that the Stanleys could not be relied on. This
is reasonable.

Northumberland is often severely censured for his performance, or rather the
lack of it, and it may have been the case that he did indeed prove false. It is
interesting to note, however, that he was imprisoned following the battle and
remained captive until late in the year when he was released under surety. As A.

Above: The battlefield at Hastings looking towards the English position. (Shaun Dodds)

Below: Norman knights and archers depicted on the Bayeux tapestry. (With the special permission of the town of Bayeux)

Left: Robert the Bruce in personal combat on the eve of Bannockburn. (Courtesy of Ladybird Books Ltd)

Left: English knights charging at Bannockburn. (Courtesy of Ladybird Books Ltd)

Right: A scene showing the Prince of Wales wounded at Shrewsbury. (Courtesy of Ladybird Books Ltd)

Right: Edward IV. (Courtesy of the Society of Antiquaries of London)

Left: The Battle of Towton. (Courtesy of Ladybird Books Ltd)

Below: Lord Dacre's tomb, Saxton. Dacre was killed at the Battle of Towton, which took place nearby on Palm Sunday, 1461. (Gavin Dodds)

Right: The Towton memorial cross. (Gavin Dodds)

Below: Middleham Castle. (Shaun Dodds)

Below: The Tower of London where Richard III's nephews were murdered.

Right: Henry VII: painted after 1504. (Courtesy of the Society of Antiquaries of London)

Below: The chapel of St. James, Dadlington. (Shaun Dodds)

Left: The Richard III Memorial Stone, Bosworth. (Shaun Dodds)

Right: Twizel Bridge, which was crossed by the English *en route* to Flodden. (Gavin Dodds)

Left: Norham Castle, captured by James IV during the Flodden campaign. (Gavin Dodds)

Right: Flodden Field from Branxton Hill. (Gavin Dodds)

Above: Charles I on the eve of the battle of Edgehill, 22 October 1642. (Courtesy of the Mansell Collection)

Left: Prince Rupert. From a 1637 portrait by Van Dyck. (Courtesy of the Mansell Collection)

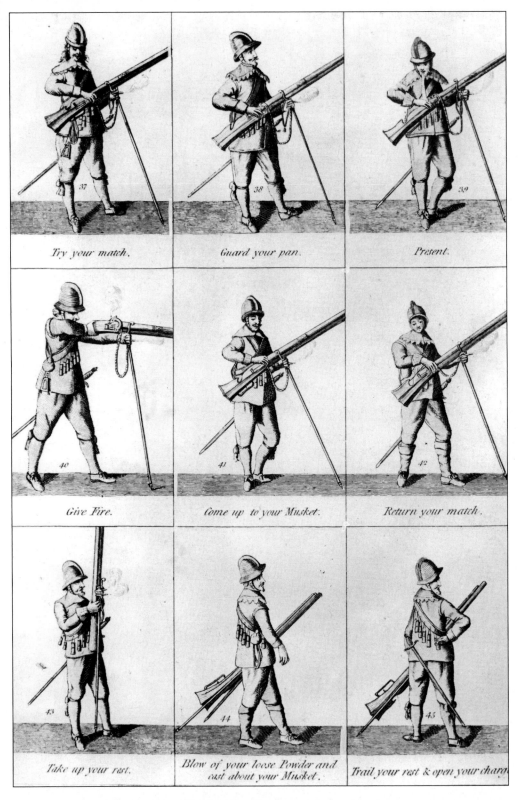

Above: 17th century musket drill. (Courtesy of the Mansell Collection)

Left: The Battle of Marston Moor. (Courtesy of Ladybird Books Ltd)

Below: Marston Moor. (Gavin Dodds)

Right: Oliver Cromwell in his early fifties, from a painting by Samuel Cooper. (Courtesy of the Birmingham Museum and Art Gallery)

Below: Skipton Castle, a Royalist stronghold which endured a lengthy siege during the Civil War. (Shaun Dodds)

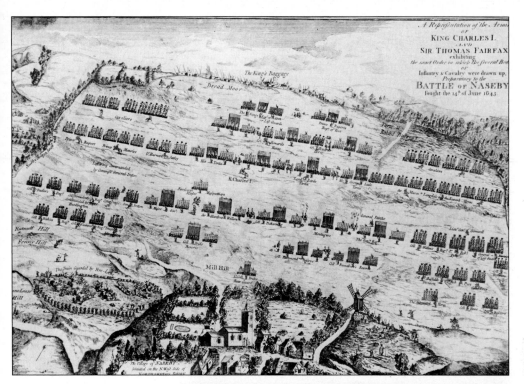

Opposite page top: Prince Rupert summoning the garrison of Leicester to surrender to the army of Charles I, 30 May 1645. (Courtesy of the Mansell Collection)

Opposite page, bottom: Charles I, from a painting by Van Dyck. (Courtesy of the Mansell Collection)

Above: A representation of the Battle of Naseby, 14 June 1645. (Courtesy of the Mansell Collection)

Right: The 2nd Duke of Argyll, from a painting by William Aikman. (Courtesy of the Scottish National Portrait Gallery)

Above: The entry
of Prince Charles
into Edinburgh.
(Courtesy of the
Mansell
Collection)

Right: Charging
clansmen at
Culloden.
(Courtesy of
Ladybird Books
Ltd)

J. Pollard has commented, this does not suggest that Henry regarded Northumberland's performance as one of 'masterly inactivity' and it is reasonable to conclude that the earl's behaviour was more ambivalent than is often supposed.

Richard has likewise been censured. His charge against Tudor is said to have been the rash act of a tense and impulsive man. That the king was anxious need not be doubted. However, it is wrong to view the charge as a tactical blunder. It is clear from the sources that it occurred after the battle had turned in Henry's favour. In such circumstances Richard could either flee or set out to destroy his adversary, something which if achieved would mean that the victory was his. The attempt failed, but Richard's courage deserves respect. As John Rous wrote some years later, 'to his credit...he bore himself like a gallant knight and acted with distinction as his own champion until his last breath'.

The performance of Richard's army must not be allowed to detract from the achievement of Henry Tudor and his men. They could not be sure that the Stanleys would assist them, but had nonetheless marched against the Plantagenet's big battalions. Moreover, at Bosworth they fought bravely. Furthermore it is apparent that there was a high degree of discipline in their ranks. Oxford in particular is worthy of commendation. Had the 'vanguard' been commanded by a less able man the outcome of the battle may very well have been different.

Following the battlefield celebrations, the victors began making their way towards Leicester which they entered late on the 22nd. According to the *Great Chronicle of London*, Henry was 'received with all honour and gladness' by the inhabitants, many of whom, as the cavalcade made its way through the streets, would have caught sight of Richard's naked body slung over a humble steed and 'all besprung with mire and filth'.

His body lay on public display for two days before being unceremoniously buried at the Franciscan Friary in Leicester. It is often said that the king's remains were thrown into the River Soar at the time of the Dissolution of the Monasteries but this is uncertain: they may still lie in the heart of Leicester.

From Leicester, Henry slowly moved towards London, which he entered in style on 3 September. Some weeks later, on 7 November, soon after a splendid coronation, he presided at the opening of parliament and emphasised that his right to the throne had been vindicated 'by the true judgement of God'. Richard's downfall at Bosworth – the engagement gradually acquired the name of the principal settlement near the battlefield – was believed due to the Almighty and gave Tudor a kind of divine right.

Shortly after Bosworth, Catesby and two relatively minor royal agents were executed, while a number of other Ricardians were later attainted. On the whole however it is clear that Henry wished to build bridges: reconciliation and widening his power-base were uppermost in his mind. Englishmen of all ranks were tired of discord and hoped that the inexperienced newcomer would return England to an even keel. His marriage to Richard III's niece, Elizabeth of York, in

January 1486 was part of this process and was understandably well received in many quarters.

Nonetheless, the country had not seen the last of unrest. Several attempts were made to oust Henry. In 1487, for instance, Lovell and Lincoln invaded from Ireland only to be defeated at Stoke. Such attempts made Henry an increasingly suspicious character whose determination to retain the throne and safeguard the future of his dynasty made him arbitrary, avaricious and unloved. Vergil observed, Henry 'began to treat his people with more harshness and severity than had been his custom in order...to ensure that they remained more thoroughly and entirely in obedience to him'. Ironically, then, many of those who had rejoiced when they heard the news of Richard's death at Bosworth must have come to believe that the battle had not resulted in a new and lasting political atmosphere, but rather, had led to the replacement of one tyrant by another.

16

FLODDEN
9 SEPTEMBER 1513

'The Flowers of the Forest are a' wede away'
—Scottish Lament

9 September 1513 was a cold and miserable day for thousands of men who had assembled to do battle in the vicinity of Branxton in the North East of England, and for a considerable number of them it was to prove a fatal one. Among those present, was James IV of Scotland who had led a formidable army into England on a campaign which was to reach its climax here, a short distance from the border, in one of the bloodiest battles in British history.

As he gazed towards the English before the commencement of hostilities, James may have reflected on the events which had led him to invade the realm of his brother-in-law, Henry VIII. Indeed, perhaps he even briefly cast his mind further back to the days when Anglo-Scottish relations had been strained in the mid-1490s. Then, when England was ruled by Henry VII, the youthful Scottish king had invaded England in 1496 and 1497, on the first occasion in support of a claimant to the English throne, Perkin Warbeck, from whom he principally hoped to receive the town and castle of Berwick if the campaign were a success – it was not – and on the second occasion to capture the strategically important castle of Norham. Again, the campaign had terminated without success.

Friendly relations between Scotland and England had been subsequently established (a Treaty of Perpetual Peace was concluded in 1502), and amicable relations continued following Henry's death in 1509. In 1511, however, one of James' favourite sea-captains, Andrew Barton, a merchant and privateer, was intercepted by English vessels which had been ordered to deal with him after he had plundered a number of English ships. In a bitter encounter Barton was mortally wounded.

Barton's death infuriated James. According to the Treaty of Perpetual Peace – which Henry VIII had himself confirmed in 1509 – Henry should have first asked James for redress instead of ordering the Lord Admiral of England to act. Tense relations thus returned and were imperilled even further later in the year when Henry joined a formidable coalition – the Holy League – ranged against Louis XII of France, the monarch of a land with which Scotland had enjoyed friendly relations for generations. Louis needed all the friends he could muster and in 1512 the 'auld alliance' between France and Scotland was renewed following certain concessions to James.

In June of the following year Henry VIII crossed the Channel to wage war in France. James had promised to invade England if Henry moved against Louis and had been preparing for war, preparations for which had indeed commenced before the renewal of the auld alliance. Records reveal that since 1507 guns had been manufactured at the castles of Stirling and Edinburgh, and in 1511 the scale of work had increased when a group of French craftsmen set to work at Edinburgh making cannon, gunpowder and other military equipment. Now, following Henry's invasion, final preparations were made. Moreover, on 25 July a fleet consisting of at least nine vessels sailed down the Firth of Forth from Leith en route to France with the aim of combining with a French fleet (and perhaps Danish vessels), and gaining control of the English Channel, thereby preventing Henry from returning home safely. The following day James sent a herald, Lyon King of Arms, to the English king, who was encamped outside Thérouanne, to inform him that he would advance into England if Henry did not desist from attacking Louis.

In a reply of 12 August – which James never received – Henry made it clear that he had no intention of halting his campaign. He insulted James, whom he accused of dishonourably wishing to attack England when its king was out of the country. In fact, however, Henry had not left England defenceless. He had appointed the Earl of Surrey Lord Lieutenant of the North with the duty of defending the country in the event of a Scottish invasion.

The invasion came on or about 23 August when James entered England by crossing the Tweed at or near Coldstream with a formidable army which had assembled at Ellem some days before. (Summonses for the campaign had been issued on 24 July). There was, moreover, an impressive artillery train drawn by 400 oxen. James moved downstream into Norhamshire, an outlying part of the bishopric of Durham, where he besieged Norham Castle, a stronghold belonging to the bishop and situated in a commanding position on the south bank of the Tweed.

Norham was a formidable and strategic castle which had been the target of generally unsuccessful Scottish aggression – in 1318 they had fruitlessly spent almost a year before its walls – and as noted earlier, it had been attacked by James in 1497, who used artillery against it for the first time. For two weeks he had pounded its walls without success. Now he was back, no doubt more determined to succeed. For some days the assault continued until much of the walling had been destroyed by his guns and on 28 or 29 August the castle surrendered. James then headed south towards another castle, Etal, and captured it before progressing a few miles south-east to Ford Castle which was capitulated to him by Lady Heron.

And what of Surrey? He had issued orders for a general levy of the northern counties. On 30 August he was at Durham where he heard mass in the splendid cathedral and received the banner of St Cuthbert from the prior of Durham.

St Cuthbert was the north's premier saint and the banner was venerated in the region by people who believed that its presence would no doubt bring about a victory over the Scots. Others had felt likewise. In the 1290s Edward I had required Durham monks to carry the banner on his expeditions to Scotland, and his successors Edward II and Edward III did likewise in 1307 and in the 1330s. Moreover, the banner featured in the Battle of Neville's Cross in 1346, and was used again in 1400 when Henry IV invaded Scotland.

From Durham, Surrey proceeded to Newcastle upon Tyne where the bulk of the forces mustered had assembled. Then, on 3 September, he arrived at Alnwick where he was joined the following day by his eldest son, Thomas Howard, the Lord Admiral, who had sailed from France, bringing about 1,000 men.

On 4 September Surrey sent a herald, Rouge Croix, to James at Ford stating that he was resolved to do battle with him in view of his invasion. Two days later, in response, a Scottish herald, Islay, made his way to the English army (which was now encamped at Bolton in Glendale, to the west of Alnwick), to inform Surrey that James had accepted the challenge. According to a contemporary tract, *The Trewe Encountre* by Richard Faques, Surrey replied that he would 'gyve the sayde Kynge batayle by frydaye next at the furthest'. Moreover, according to another contemporary source, the *Articles of Battle*, (which may have been written by the Lord Admiral) James promised to 'abide' at Ford 'till Friday at noon'.

However, James did not remain at Ford. After burning down the castle he took up a very strong defensive position at Flodden Hill a few miles to the west. Consequently on 7 September, after having advanced to Wooler on the 6th, Surrey wrote indignantly to James stating his surprise that 'it hath pleased you to chaunge your said promyse and putte your self into a grounde more like a fortresse or a campe...'. Furthermore he suggested that James should behave chivalrously and descend to the plain of Milfield where battle could be joined on neutral ground the following day. According to another source, *Hall's Chronicle*, (which dates from c.1540), James replied by stating 'that it besemed not an earle' to 'handle a Kynge' in such a manner, and that he had no intention of doing as Surrey wished. Surrey and his advisers were thus faced with this question: should they attack James on Flodden Hill or attempt to dislodge him somehow before engaging him as promised? To do the former would be to invite disaster, and so not surprisingly this alternative was rejected.

Instead, at dawn on the 8th, the English left Wooler and marched north with the aim, states the *Trewe Encountre*, of luring James from his position by threatening to cut off his line of retreat. They marched through driving rain and encamped for the night beside Barmoor Wood, about four miles north-east of Flodden Hill. But James failed to move, and so following a reconnaissance the

Lord Admiral suggested that he should be attacked from the rear, that is the north. At about 5.00am on the morning of the 9th the march resumed to do just that. Surrey had divided the army into two divisions, each of which reportedly had two wings. The foremost division was under the Lord Admiral, while the earl commanded that to the rear.

According to the *Articles of Battle*, 'at 11 of the clock' on the 9th the Lord Admiral 'passed over the bridge of Twizel with the vaward and artillery'. The bridge is still extant. It has a span of 90ft and is 40ft high, an impressive monument to medieval engineering. Where Surrey crossed the Till is not stated. Some are of the opinion that he followed in his son's footsteps and therefore likewise crossed at Twizel Bridge. Others have suggested that his less encumbered division (it had no artillery) forded the river instead. This seems more probable. It would have been a time consuming undertaking for the entire army to cross via the fairly narrow bridge and hence would have been more reasonable for Surrey to cross elsewhere. Several places have been suggested. The most likely, it seems, is Castle Heaton a mile upstream. Once across the river the contingents of the army were marshalled into battle formation and then the advance resumed.

And what of James? How did he react to the daring manoeuvres of the English army? As has been stated, at first he did nothing. No doubt he did not wish to forsake his strong position until he was sure of Surrey's intentions. This was not to the liking of all his nobles. In a council of war the old Earl of Angus argued that they should withdraw to their homeland, believing that Surrey intended invading Scotland. According to George Buchanan, (whose account was published in 1582), James replied curtly: 'Douglas, if you are afraid, you may go home'. The earl – who was not on good terms with the king – did just that.

It was not until James was informed by his scouts that the English were crossing the Till that he gave orders to abandon Flodden Hill. His destination? Branxton Hill, one mile to the north and almost as strong a position as the one he was leaving, and a position he understandably wished to deny to the enemy.

Thus at about midday the Scots began moving north after setting fire to refuse, including straw which had served as bedding. At about 1.00pm the foremost Scots began taking up positions on Branxton Hill which at its highest point is 500ft above sea level.

Meanwhile, the English were of course marching to engage James. For most of the campaign the weather had been unpleasant and the 9th was no exception. A letter written in late September by the Bishop of Durham, Thomas Ruthal, to Cardinal Wolsey, states that as the English advanced wind and rain blew into their faces, something which must have hampered their progress. Moreover another contemporary letter, written by a royal clerk called Brian Tuke, tells us that the English had to negotiate marshy terrain. This evidently refers to the valley of the Pallin's burn not far to the north of Branxton Hill. The burn, flowing eastward towards the Till, was no great obstacle, 'but a man's step over' states

Hall. But the valley itself was an impediment to quick progress for it was largely a morass. The bog was about a mile from east to west, and in places about a quarter of a mile wide. There were two crossing points. One crossed its centre and consisted of a causeway leading to Branx Brig, a bridge across the burn. The other was near Sandyford, not far from where the Pallins' burn joins the Till.

A local guide directed the English to the former, (it is sometimes held that the artillery could not cross via Branx Brig and had to be sent east towards Sandyford instead). Upon emerging from the Pallin's burn valley in the vicinity of a village called Branxton, the foremost troops caught sight of the Scots drawn up on Branxton Hill about half a mile to the south. At seeing this himself, the Lord Admiral was greatly alarmed. He took the Agnus Dei, a medallion which hung on his breast, and sent it to his father urging him to come up in support as quickly as possible. Surrey did as his son wished, and his men hurriedly drew up alongside the Lord Admiral's and prepared for battle. The English had done an arduous journey of approximately eight miles. Ruthal refers to 'the mervelous grete payn and laboure that they toke in going 8 myles that day on fote'.

JAMES AND HIS ARMY

James was born in 1473 and ascended the throne in June 1488 after his father, James III, had been murdered following his defeat by rebels in battle at Sauchieburn. As James IV had been on the side of the disaffected barons, he reportedly henceforth always wore an iron chain around his waist as an act of penance.

James was an adventurous, high-spirited character who loved hunting, hawking and womanising. But there was more to him than this, much more. He was an able and popular king. He improved the administration of justice and furthered Scotland's commerce, patronised art and science and founded a navy. Norman MacDougall has observed: 'A review of widely varying source material... leaves no room for doubt that James IV was a ruler of great ability'.

According to Don Pedro de Ayala, Spain's ambassador to Scotland in 1496-7, James was 'of noble stature, neither tall nor short, and as handsome in complexion and shape as a man can be'. He also relates that the king was a martial figure who did 'not think it right to begin any warlike undertaking without being himself the first in danger'.

Don Pedro de Ayala was not the only person to write well of James. The noted scholar, Erasmus, for example, did likewise. He states that the king 'had a wonderful intellectual power, an astonishing knowledge of everything; an unconquerable magnanimity, and the most abundant generosity'. It would, of course, be wrong to conclude without mentioning his foibles. James was, for instance, prone to obstinacy and extravagance. Arrogance and overconfidence also manifested themselves.

The size of the Scottish army is uncertain. The *Articles of Battle* states that James had 80,000 men at Flodden. A streak of cynicism is not required to view such a figure as suspect. Other inflated figures are given by some sources. Hall, for instance, states that James had entered England with an army 100,000 strong. In contrast, the Venetian Ambassador to London relates that James crossed the border with 24,000 men, while several modern historians have given the figure of approximately 40,000 for the strength of the army at the commencement of the campaign. Irrespective of the initial figure, losses had undoubtedly sapped its strength, especially through desertion which had begun on a significant scale during the siege of Norham. Enough deserters had arrived in Edinburgh by 5 September for the fact to be noted with displeasure by the Burgh Council! Despite such losses, James may have had about 25,000 men at Flodden: a higher figure seems unlikely.

James' host was a disparate one comprising English speaking men from the Borders and Lowlands, and Gaelic speakers from the Highlands and Isles. There was also a French contingent under the Count d'Aussi. It was, moreover, a well equipped one for by law periodic musters of men between the ages of sixteen and sixty were held in Scotland and at these 'wapenshaws' sheriffs and other officials were empowered to fine men who had failed to provide themselves with suitable military equipment.

In general the Scots were thus well-equipped. Men of rank of course possessed suits of plate armour which would have varied both in terms of quality and date of manufacture, for while some no doubt had expensive harnesses of a high calibre made on the continent in the latest fashion, most probably had to make do with less prestigious older armour. Many lesser folk also had armour, either suits of light armour 'Almayn [German] rivets', or body armour of other kinds.

The Scots possessed various weapons but the principal arm was the 18ft long Swiss pike. The King of France had sent a party of officers under d'Aussi to Scotland to instruct the Scots in its use. To be effective, it had to be used en masse by phalanxes operating on ground which would make a steady advance possible.

As has been noted earlier, James had an impressive artillery train, for he was interested in ordnance and had amassed a fine collection of cannon. Indeed at Flodden he had seventeen guns of which five were 'great curtals' capable of throwing shot weighing as much as 60lbs. The Bishop of Durham was to describe the Scottish cannon as 'the fairest and best that lately hath been seen'.

SURREY AND HIS ARMY

Thomas Howard, Earl of Surrey, was an able man, tough, resourceful, tried and tested, courageous and sagacious. He was born in 1443, and thus of advanced

years at Flodden. He had fought on behalf of Edward IV against Warwick the
Kingmaker at Barnet in 1471, and in 1483, the year after being created Earl of
Surrey, had supported the usurpation of Richard of Gloucester. In fact, he carried the sword of state at Richard's coronation. Two years later he fought at
Bosworth and was among prominent Ricardians taken captive. He was incarcerated in the Tower of London until 1489 but following his release became a
loyal servant of Henry VII.

As such, he moved against James at the head of a powerful army in 1497
when the king was besieging Norham Castle. Alarmed by his approach, James
abandoned the siege and Surrey proceeded to cross the border and conduct a
punitive raid in the neighbourhood of Berwick. A battle with James threatened,
but the king decided against it and after a few days Surrey withdrew to Berwick
at the head of an army whose morale had begun to collapse owing to continual
rain and cold weather.

In 1503 Surrey entered Scotland again in happier circumstances following an
improvement in Anglo-Scottish relations which resulted in James marrying
Henry VII's daughter, Margaret Tudor. Surrey escorted her north, an event
which not surprisingly was surrounded by much pomp and ceremony.

The strength of Surrey's army is uncertain. The *Trewe Encountre* gives the
only comprehensively precise figures for its strength. It states that the English
approached the battlesite in two divisions. The Admiral's was 9,000 strong, Surrey's 5,000. Moreover, each division had two wings, both 3,000 strong, giving a
total of 26,000 men. This figure also appears in a later work, Hall's, and is
accepted by some modern historians. On the other hand, W. M. MacKenzie has
highlighted that the figures given in the *Trewe Encountre* are at variance with
what can be gleaned from other early material such as the *Articles of Battle*. He
thus estimates that Surrey had 13/15,000 men, and that he was not significantly
outnumbered. Another student of the campaign, Robert MacKie, has likewise
rejected the figure of 26,000 men, but has concluded that the English army was
just under 20,000 strong and this view is accepted here.

Part of Surrey's army consisted of his own men – a force 500 strong – but
the bulk were northern levies, many of whom were accustomed to bearing arms
and using them in the feuds which were a characteristic feature of life in the
border region. Inevitably, all classes of society were represented. Persons of rank
were encased in plate armour, but at least some of the rank and file no doubt also
wore plate armour, mostly of low quality and primarily intended to protect the
torso and arms, though humbler armour such as brigandines and jacks (the latter consisting of several layers of stout fabric stuffed with soft material secured
in place by stitched quilting) must have been more commonplace.

As normal, the men-at-arms carried various weapons such as swords,
poleaxes, maces and battleaxes. The longbow was still a popular weapon in
England (Flodden was to be the last major engagement in which it was used),

and would have been the chief weapon of many of the rank and file. A novel feature of this period was the widespread use of quivers. It seems that they were suspended from the waist by 'girdles'. Some archers would also have possessed swords, though for most a dagger would have had to suffice as a secondary weapon. To use the longbow effectively required a great deal of practice. This was not true of another traditional weapon, the bill, (which resembled the agricultural scythe), and was 8ft long with a heavy jagged blade suitable for cutting or slashing, and there can be little doubt that the majority of the men in Surrey's army were billmen. Many such would also have carried swords or daggers.

Finally, like James, Surrey had an artillery train. It was rather larger than that of his opponent though the guns were not as impressive.

Description

The Scottish army on Branxton Hill was arrayed in four divisions (with a fifth in support) and we are told by the *Articles of Battle* that a bow shot – probably around 200 yards – separated each division from the next. The cannon were placed in the intervals. The division on the left comprised High-

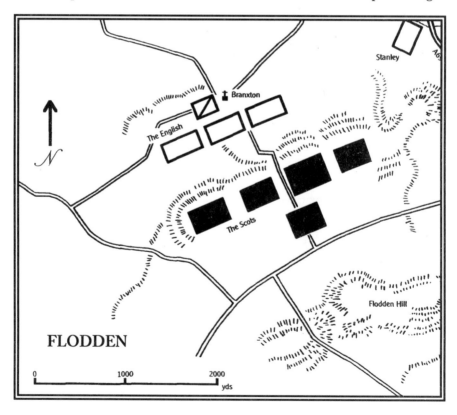

landers and Borderers under Lord Home and the Earl of Huntly. Then came a division commanded by the Earls of Crawford and Montrose. The king's division, the largest, was next in line, while the fourth comprised Highlanders under the Earls of Argyll and Lennox. The reserve was led by the Earl of Bothwell. According to the *Trewe Encountre* the Scots discarded their shoes to fight in the vamps of their hose to gain a greater footing on the muddy ground.

The army was well-fed. Provisions were abundant and included beef, mutton, cheese and good quality beer. This, coupled with the fact that the Scots were well-rested and occupied a strong position, no doubt indicates that morale was high.

The English deployed on a ridge, the highest point of which is known as Piper's Hill, just to the south of Branxton village. With the exception of the western side of the battlefield, the ground in front of the English position (which was lower than that of the Scots) sloped down to what was perhaps rather boggy terrain before rising steeply toward the commanding position occupied by the enemy.

Edmund Howard, one of Surrey's sons, commanded the division on the right. The next division was under the Lord Admiral. Then came that of Surrey himself, while somewhere to the left was a division under Sir Edward Stanley, which all things considered, seems to have only appeared on the scene after battle was joined. Lord Dacre may have been stationed just to the rear of the line to give 'succour when need should seem to appear' as *Holinshed's Chronicle* (published in 1577) states. Some are of the opinion, however, that Dacre was in line with the rest of the army having been posted with Edmund Howard. The cannon were placed between the divisions along the line.

Unlike the Scots, the English must have been rather tired. They had, after all, been far more active, and to make things worse, had eaten little or nothing during their march owing to the failure of the commissariat. Indeed, they had been on short rations for a couple of days or so. Moreover, the Bishop of Durham tells us that they had run out of beer and for three days had had nothing to drink other than water. Nonetheless the performance of Surrey's men in general during the subsequent engagement indicates that the army was not unduly dispirited. Morale was no doubt buoyed up by an event which had occurred in mid August just prior to James' invasion. A large Scottish raiding force had been intercepted and routed nearby by Sir William Bulmer, an event known to the Scots as the 'Ill-Raid'. Knowledge of this incident must have been a source of encouragement to many in Surrey's ranks, including Bulmer himself who was now once again to come to grips with the enemy.

According to the *Articles of Battle* and the *Trewe Encountre*, the battle began between 4.00 and 5.00pm. The weather had remained unsettled, a southerly wind still blew in the faces of the English and there was intermittent rain.

The battle opened with a cannonade. According to Tuke this was ineffectual: the guns 'were of little use'. However there is reason to believe that the cannonade was more significant than Tuke believed. Dacre subsequently stated in a letter to Henry VIII that 'at the first shot of the Scottish guns' some of his command, levies from Tynemouth and Bamburghshire, panicked and fled. On the whole, though, it seems that the English had the best of the contest. James, it is true, had the superior cannon but the crews were generally inexperienced – he had sent his best gunners with the fleet to France – and consequently most, if not all, the Scottish shot flew over the heads of the English. On the other hand the English guns inflicted some fairly significant damage. We hear, for example, in the *Trewe Encountre* that 'our gonnes did so breake and constreyn the Scottisshe great army, that some part of thaim wer enforsed to come doune [Branxton Hill] towards our army'.

It was Home and Huntly's division on the Scottish left which came to blows first. Likely, the division managed to maintain the momentum of its assault right up until the point of impact for the English right flank under Edmund Howard was stationed on virtually level ground. If so, little momentum was required. Doughty resistance was not encountered. Far from it: Howard's men performed lamentably. The *Articles of Battle* states that 'the Cheshire and Lancashire men never abode stroke, and few of the gentlemen of Yorkshire abode, but fled'. Edmund's command simply collapsed and thus Howard and some of his men decided, or were compelled, to make for the Lord Admiral's division. Whether they would make it was touch and go. Howard was felled to the ground on three occasions but survived to tell the tale. His standard-bearer was less fortunate for he was slain. The standard itself was hewn in pieces.

Howard's survival was likely due to intervention by Dacre, who restored the situation on this flank. Tuke comments that Dacre came to Howard's relief with 1,500 horsemen. Other sources also refer to action by Dacre. For example, an account by Paolo Giovio published in 1553 refers to Dacre's 'blast of horsemen' against the victorious Scots. Some have challenged whether Dacre's men were mounted. Whether they were or not is rather incidental (on the whole it seems likely they were). What really matters is that Dacre's intervention prevented Home and Huntly from moving against the Admiral's division with at least part of their command – some of their men had resorted to plundering the dead – and indeed drove them back somewhat. A stand-off ensued. In fact Dacre and his opponents were to remain inactive for the rest of the battle, something which besmirched their reputations. Hall, for example, erroneously believed that: 'The Lord Dacre with his company stood still all day unfoughten with all'. Rumours that Dacre had behaved ignobly moved Bishop Ruthal, who sympathised with him, to suggest to Wolsey that the king should send him a letter of encouragement.

And what of the rest of the Scottish army? It is sometimes maintained that the other divisions – evidently with the exception of that under Argyll and

Lennox – only began descending Branxton Hill upon seeing the initial success of Home and Huntly and in the belief that the victorious division would move against the Lord Admiral, thereby providing an opportunity to roll up the enemy. Such a view is at variance with Hall, who relates that although contact was first made on the left of the Scottish line all the divisions were soon engaged. That the other divisions came to blows shortly after the Scottish left clashed with Edmund Howard is no doubt correct. Moreover, although Home and Huntly's division clashed first this does not automatically mean – as many have assumed – that it advanced before the other divisions. The nature of the terrain has to be borne in mind. As has been noted, the approach towards the English position for the Scottish left was not as arduous as it was elsewhere. Hence if the divisions had begun advancing in unison, or at least at about the same time, contact would inevitably have first been made by Home and Huntly.

Owing to the lie of the land, the divisions in question were unable to maintain the momentum of their assault to the same degree as did their colleagues on the left, and their laborious approach was rendered more difficult by continued cannon fire from the English guns and arrows sent against them. Fortunately for the Scots, however, they were generally well protected – this is said to have been especially true of the king's division – and thus did not suffer as severely as they would have done otherwise. As the *Trewe Encountre* states, the Scots were 'as well appointed as was possible at all points with armour and harness, so that few of them were slain with arrows'. Finally, and no doubt with a sense of relief on the part of some, they came to grips with the enemy.

Determined, bloody conflict resulted. The division under the earls was evidently soon brought to a standstill but the king's – which was supported by the reserve under Bothwell – seems to have done rather better, managing to drive Surrey back somewhat before likewise being halted.

Meanwhile, what was happening on the right of the Scottish line? The evidence is conflicting and has resulted in some confusion. George Buchanan's account, for example, states that Argyll and Lennox rushed down the hill in a disorderly fashion after being encouraged by the success of the Scottish left and were attacked in the rear by a body of English soldiers with disastrous consequences. In general, however, it is believed that Argyll and Lennox remained on Branxton Hill and it is said that they did so because Sir Edward's Stanley's division – with which they clashed – had not quite arrived on the scene, likely owing to a possible bottleneck caused while the English had crossed the Pallin's burn. Hall declares that Stanley's division 'was the last that fought', becoming engaged shortly after battle was joined elsewhere. The contemporary *Trewe Encountre* states clearly that, unlike the other Scottish divisions which advanced to attack the English, that under Argyll and Lennox was attacked by Stanley, who 'coragiously and like a lusty and an hardy knyght, did sett upon' it when it was preparing to advance to assist the 'King of Scottes batell'.

All things considered, it thus seems reasonable to conclude that as Stanley approached the field he observed Argyll and Lennox's inactive division and decided to move against it by advancing up the east slope of Branxton Hill with the aim of conducting a flank attack. We are told that his men removed their footwear to gain a better grip as they ascended the slippery ground. Their approach was unnoticed by the Scots whose attention was no doubt focused on the battle raging below. Indeed, it seems likely, as the *Trewe Encountre* states, that Argyll and Lennox were on the point of moving to assist James against Surrey when Stanley fell upon their right flank. The surprised Scots were subjected to a rain of arrows. Chaos soon reigned; the division rapidly disintegrated and those that could began to flee. The *Trewe Encountre* gives no details about their flight. Hall, however, relates that Stanley chased the Scots 'over that place where the King's battle joined...and the said Sir Edward...followed them over the same ground...and found there the Scots, who were by [Surrey's] battle slain before...and fell a-spoiling'.

Is Hall correct in saying that by now the king's division had been destroyed? It seems not. An account of the battle by Bishop Leslie (which dates from 1578) tells us that Stanley attacked the king from the rear. That Stanley proceeded to attack James' division after routing the men under Argyll and Lennox seems more reasonable than what we read in Hall. After all, the battle continued until nightfall, about 6.00pm and if, as Hall states, Stanley was in action not long after the other English divisions acceptance of his statement that Stanley chased the fleeing Scots over ground covered with the wreckage of James' division would mean that Surrey had soon overcome the most powerful and best equipped component of the Scottish army. It could of course be maintained that Stanley clashed with Argyll and Lennox later than Hall believed. But this again is unlikely – it is improbable that the earls would have stood idle for any significant length of time while their king was engaged in a ferocious encounter with Surrey. In short, a number of modern historians believe that after overcoming Argyll and Lennox, Stanley closed in for the kill against the division of the Scottish king and this view is accepted here.

If so, it appears that Stanley's men were not the only ones to assist Surrey. Apparently, the Lord Admiral did so with at least part of his command after destroying Crawford and Montrose's division in, as Hall states, 'a great conflict'. (The rest of his men may have been in pursuit). Hence, as Leslie comments, likely with a degree of exaggeration, the king was 'surrounded on every side'.

Like the division of Crawford and Montrose, the Scots under the king and Bothwell put up a good fight, 'determyned outher to wynne the ffelde or to dye' says the *Trewe Encountre*. But it was a fight they could not win, for in common with the men under Crawford and Montrose, they fought at a disadvantage. It soon became apparent that their long spears were not as effective – as deadly – as the bills of many of their adversaries. The tips of the spears were chopped off and when the Scots had recourse to their secondary weapons they found themselves again at a disadvantage for they were outreached by their assailants. Nonetheless they continued fighting stubbornly. As Ruthal states, 'the Scots faght sore and valiauntlye with their swerdes'.

The conflict degenerated into a one-sided affair. The Scots' formation began to disintegrate. More and more of them were slaughtered as English soldiers penetrated their ranks wielding their bills to deadly effect. It is said that some of the Scots tried to surrender but received no mercy. The *Trewe Encountre* relates that because the Scots 'wer soe vengeable and cruell in their feightyng...when Englisshmen had the better of thaim they wold not save thaim'.

At some point, perhaps quite soon in the bloodbath, King James was himself cut down. We are told that he had fought bravely, something which need not be doubted. Indeed, according to the *Articles of Battle* he got to within a spear's length of Surrey when he fell, struck by an arrow and gashed by a bill. For sometime after his death resistance continued to be given, but such an uneven contest could not go on for very long and by about 6.00pm it was all over.

Some of the English soldiers pursued fleeing Scots far from the field, but others fell to plundering. Ruthal comments: 'King, bishops, lordes, knightes and nobles, and others were not so soon slain but forwith despoiled out of thair harnais and array and lefte lying naked in the felde'.

Ruthal further relates that the abundant supplies of food and drink found by the victors provided sustenance, to their 'great refreshying', which is not surprising considering the privations they had endured.

Surrey's tired but exultant men spent the night on the field they had won. The following morning a body of Scottish horsemen appeared on the skyline before them but departed after a few rounds of cannon fire from the English guns. The rest of the day was spent sorting out the dead and preparing for their burial.

The legend subsequently developed that King James had survived the slaughter. As Adam Abell, a friar of Jedburgh, noted in 1533: 'Of him diverss is opinion; ane is at he wes nocht slane in that feid of flowdone....Ane odir is at he wes slane in the feild'. It is, however, certain that James did perish at Flodden for his body was identified by Lord Dacre (who knew him well), and by the king's captured secretary Sir William Scott. It was subsequently transported south to the Carthusian monastery of Sheen near London – an establishment founded by another warrior-king, Henry V – and was later taken to London and buried with royal honours at St Paul's.

The king was not the only exalted Scot who perished at Flodden. Many others also fell. One such was James' bastard son, the 23-year-old Archbishop of St Andrew's who, according to Erasmus, was so short-sighted he 'could not read without holding his book to the very end of his nose'. One bishop also perished, as did nine earls (Huntly, Home and Marischal were the only ones who survived), and fourteen barons. As William Seymour has observed: 'The chronicles of calamity have few precedents for the extinction in battle of almost a complete generation of a country's nobility'. Just how many lesser Scots died is uncertain, but that they died in significant numbers is undoubted. The English put the figure at 10,000, while the most moderate contemporary estimate (by a Scot), is 5,000. No doubt the former is closer to the truth.

English losses were lower, much lower. Contemporary estimates range from 400 to not more than 1,500 men, with the latter figure likely being the more accurate. Moreover, few persons of high rank were among the slain.

Of King James' performance at Flodden, Hall wrote: 'O what a noble and triumphaunt courage was thys for a kyng to fyghte in a battayll as a meane souldier'. That James was valiant – and went down fighting manfully – is accepted by modern writers. But what of his conduct of the Flodden campaign? On this matter opinion not unnaturally differs. James is sometimes portrayed as an individual whose courage surpassed his sagacity, a quixotic figure whose campaign was an ill-considered affair which inevitably ended in disaster. This is wrong. For a start, the army he led south was a formidable one, the largest and best equipped ever led into England by a Scottish monarch: a fact which testifies to his popularity and the quality of his preparations.

Some believe that James displayed indecision during the campaign. He has been criticised for not advancing further into England instead of, it is maintained, dithering on the border. This criticism is unwarranted. James' objectives were to secure Norham Castle – a fortress which the Scots had long wished to capture – and to honour his pledge to Louis XII by advancing across the border at the head of an army. Hence he did not have to move far into England: he could await Surrey with a rested and well positioned army instead.

James has also been censured for not opposing Surrey's crossing of the Till on the morning of the 9th. This again, as some historians have pointed out, is unreasonable. Time was against such a manoeuvre. If upon hearing that the English were crossing the Till, James had abandoned his strong position and moved against them he would have been unable to arrive in time to oppose the crossing.

He is also criticised for not attacking the section of the English army under the Lord Admiral which arrived in the vicinity of Branxton while Surrey was still some distance away: it has been maintained that if he had done so he may have been able to defeat the two sections of the English army in detail. This is a rather more valid criticism. But James' decision to remain on Branxton Hill is nonetheless understandable in the circumstances. He reasonably believed that he did not have to resort to such action to win the day, likely intending to use his cannon to soften up the English army as it approached his position before advancing with his formidable host to sweep it from the field.

In the event, the performance of the Scottish artillery at Flodden proved lamentable. James thus deserves to be censured for sending his best gunners with the fleet to France. Undoubtedly it was a blunder.

Nevertheless, on the whole the late Colonel Burne's comment, 'I can see no blatant military faults committed by the King of Scotland in the campaign of Flodden' is a reasonable one.

The disaster which befell the Scots at Flodden can be primarily attributed to their use of the pike. As has been noted, the cumbersome pikes were chopped into pieces by the bills of their adversaries and the Scots were thus forced to fight at a disadvantage with their secondary weapons. Not for nothing did Bishop Ruthal write: 'Our bills...did more goode that day thenne bowes for they shortely disapointed the Scotes of their long speres wherin was their greatest truste and whenne they came to hande strocke...they coude not resiste the billes that lighted so thicke and sore upon thaym'. The same point is made elsewhere, such as in the *Trewe Encountre*, 'the billes did beat and hew thaim downe', it says.

Nonetheless, Surrey could be justly proud of his conduct of the campaign which culminated in the epic engagement which is his chief memorial. Despite his advanced years, he had behaved with courage and resolution and had sensibly refrained from attacking James on Flodden Hill, preferring to execute the unusual march which brought his army to the vicinity of Branxton Hill, caused concern in the Scottish camp, and led James to abandon his well-nigh impregnable initial position.

Surrey's commendable performance did not go unrewarded. In February 1514 King Henry reinstated to him the family title, Duke of Norfolk, a title which had been forfeited through his father's support of Richard III at Bosworth.

And what of Scotland? Flodden left the country like a battered ship bereft of a popular and able captain and devoid of much of its crew; a vessel ill-equipped to meet whatever storms might lie ahead. The new king, James V, was little more than a baby (he was born at Linlithgow in April 1512), and consequently in accordance with James IV's will, the youngster's mother, Margaret, became regent and a council of ecclesiastics and nobles was appointed without whose consent she was unable to act.

Margaret soon lost the regency (upon her marriage to the Earl of Angus), and in July 1515 the Duke of Albany was proclaimed in a parliament at Edinburgh Protector and governor of Scotland until James became eighteen. The subsequent period, however, was far from harmonious. For a start, the young king's mother was compelled to hand him over to guardians after being besieged in Stirling Castle, and in the years which followed James was a pawn in the power game as factions endeavoured to secure his person and gain supremacy.

When James finally became king in more than name he had to deal with significant lawlessness, conspiracies to destroy him, and English interference. As Norman MacDougall has commented, as a result of Flodden 'the purpose, drive, and unanimity which [James IV] had instilled in the political community were shattered, and Scottish national self-confidence was lost for the remainder of the century'. In view of this, and the losses sustained at Flodden, it is not surprising that the battle ingrained itself on the national psyche. It is not for nothing that pipers still play the haunting lament: 'The Flowers of the Forest are a 'wede away'.

17

PINKIE
10 SEPTEMBER 1547

In January 1547 England's king, Henry VIII, was succeeded by his young son Edward VI, and it was soon agreed that the Duke of Somerset would serve as Protector during Edward's minority. At this date Scotland's monarch, Mary, was likewise a minor. She had ascended the throne in 1542 when only a few weeks old, and the Earl of Arran was regent. In treaties of 1543 intended to improve relations between the hitherto hostile countries, and later nullified by the Scots, it was agreed that Mary would marry Edward. The Scots' volte face had angered Henry, who sent punitive raids north. Though he was now dead, the Protector was likewise determined to ensure that Mary would marry Edward Tudor.

Military preparations commenced in the spring of 1547. On 1 September, following the failure of talks, Somerset crossed the border with 16,000 men, of whom 4,000 were cavalry. In support was the English fleet, under Lord Clinton, sailing parallel to the army as it advanced up Scotland's east coast. On 8 September Somerset arrived in the vicinity of Prestonpans and proceeded to deploy his forces on Fawside Hill and Carberry Hill, from where he had good views westward to where Arran had stationed his army on the far side of the River Esk. The infantry was in the centre, with cavalry on the wings.

Arran had about 25,000 men, and thus although weaker in cavalry, was numerically stronger overall. The left wing was under the Earl of Huntly, then came 3,000 Highlanders under the Earl of Argyll. Arran led the centre. To his right were more infantry under another earl, Angus, and then came the cavalry under the Earl of Home.

On the morning of the 9th, Home's men crossed the Esk and carried out provocative manoeuvres intended to draw the English from their position. The move misfired, and misfired badly. At an opportune time, when the Scots were off balance, they were assailed by the heavy English cavalry and routed. Those that could, fled back across the river.

At about 8.00am the following day Somerset advanced, intent on securing Inveresk Hill in close proximity to a bridge across the Esk and towards the left of the Scottish line. From here the English guns could dominate much of the Scottish position. As Somerset advanced the Scots began crossing the Esk, though what was left of Home's horse held aloof. As Argyll's Highlanders made their way across the river they came under fire from Clinton's fleet off Musselburgh and fled. In contrast, Huntly's men pressed on. Once across the Esk, the Scots formed a massive phalanx of pikemen and continued moving forward.

Then, as they momentarily halted, the bulk of the English cavalry attacked them. They repelled the assault, only to be attacked again. As before, they held. But the attacks allowed Somerset to bring his guns to bear and they now began pounding the densely packed Scots, who were also shot at by mounted Spanish troops (serving in the English army) who were armed with handguns and rode along their flanks firing as they did so. Arran's hard-pressed men were then attacked by Somerset's infantry. Finally, when the cavalry came forward again the Scots broke and fled, suffering numerous casualties as they did so. In all, Scottish losses may have approached 10,000 men. Reportedly, English losses numbered about 500.

Nevertheless, despite his great victory, Somerset failed to secure possession of Mary, and in 1548 she was spirited away to France where she married the heir of Henry II.

18

EDGEHILL
23 OCTOBER 1642

In 1642 hostility between Charles I and parliament was such that both began preparing for civil war. (For the background to the war see Chapter 21). Charles raised his standard at Nottingham on 22 August. The force at his disposal was small and thus on 13 September he left Nottingham and made for Shrewsbury believing rightly that he would receive much support in the west. He arrived at Shrewsbury on 20 September.

Parliament's army was at Northampton when its commander, the Earl of Essex, heard that Charles was making for Shrewsbury. He thus also moved west and occupied Worcester just after the king's nephew, Prince Rupert, had routed an advanced detachment of his army at Powicke Bridge on the 23rd. On 12 October, the king, who had now raised a substantial army, began marching towards London and proceeded to bypass Essex. When aware of this, the earl set off in pursuit.

On the evening of Saturday 22nd Charles was at Edgecote: Essex at Kineton. On the following day, at the suggestion of Rupert, the king moved to Edgehill and deployed, having decided to engage the Parliamentarian army. When it became clear that Essex would not attack uphill, Charles descended Edgehill and took up a position just below it to the north of Radway. His army numbered about 14,500 men and Lord Forth was placed in command. Charles' nephew, Prince Rupert, led the horse on the right, Sir Jacob Astley the foot in the centre, and Lord Wilmot the horse on the left.

Essex deployed a short distance to the north of the Royalists. He had about 14,900 men and also had more cannon than the king. Sir James Ramsey led the cavalry on the left of the army. The infantry in the centre was under Philip Skippon and was arrayed in three brigades – in contrast to the five of the Royalist foot – and to the rear of the right brigade were two regiments of horse, one led by Sir William Balfour, the other, by Sir Philip Stapleton. The cavalry on the right of the army was under Lord Feilding.

The battle began at about 3.00pm with an ineffective artillery duel. The Royalists then advanced. Rupert's wing quickly routed the opposing cavalry and swept on to Kineton two miles away and proceeded to plunder the enemy baggage train. Wilmot likewise achieved success, and many of his men also went plundering in Kineton.

In the centre, a fierce struggle occurred between the infantry with the Roundhead foot receiving valuable assistance from Balfour and Stapleton. The Royalists were slowly driven back. Charles' son, the Duke of York, was to recall that his father rode forward to encourage the hard-pressed infantry and that as he did so 'one of his footmen was shot in the face by his horse's side; after which [Charles] continued in the rear of the foot, till the battle was ended by night'. The victorious Royalist cavalry had returned to the field as darkness was falling, but they were not in a fit state to charge and thus held aloof as the fighting died down.

It is estimated that about 1,000 Roundheads perished at Edgehill and that Royalist losses were approximately 500 strong. On the following day the Royalists stood firm, but Essex decided not to renew hostilities and withdrew 'in great disorder to Warwick', leaving Charles to all intents and purposes the victor: the road to London was open.

19

THE FIRST BATTLE OF NEWBURY
20 SEPTEMBER 1643

After the Battle of Edgehill Charles delayed moving against London until it was too late. When he did so, he was confronted by 24,000 men at Turnham Green on 14 November 1642 and thus withdrew to Reading. Nonetheless, in subsequent months the Royalists generally had the better of things. Then, on 10 August 1643, Charles invested Gloucester, an important Parliamentarian outpost. On the 26th Essex set out from London to relieve its garrison. His approach led Charles to raise the siege on 5 September and withdraw to Sudeley Castle near Winchcombe.

On the 8th Essex entered Gloucester. He soon headed north to Tewkesbury and thus the king moved to Evesham to keep in touch, partly expecting Essex to make for Worcester. On the 15th Essex left Tewkesbury. His destination? – London. Charles therefore set off in pursuit and reached Newbury on the 19th before his adversary. The way to the capital was blocked and so Essex determined to fight.

The battle was fought just to the south-west of the town by forces which both probably numbered about 14,000 men. The Royalists faced west towards their opponents who had managed to secure Round Hill, a feature of tactical importance. The hill was in the centre of Essex's line, and upon it he placed infantry and cannon.

The battle commenced at about 7.00am on the 20th. The task of dislodging the Parliamentarians from Round Hill chiefly fell to Sir John Byron and his brother Sir Nicholas Byron, who led a brigade of horse and foot respectively. The latter attacked first, but encountered stiff resistance and so asked for cavalry support. However, the terrain was not suited to horse. The ground before the hill was enclosed and as Sir John's troopers advanced they found their way barred by a high hedge with a gap just wide enough for one horse to pass through at a time. Before the gap could be widened, Lord Falkland, 'more gallantly than advisedly', spurred his mount through it and was instantly killed. As soon as the hedge had been rendered passable, Byron's men charged only to be repulsed. The Royalists later repeatedly tried to drive their opponents from the hill, but again failed.

Meanwhile, on the south flank, where much of the ground was open, Prince Rupert charged and recharged the enemy, primarily Sir Philip Stapleton's cavalry wing, which answered in kind. Eventually Stapleton was driven off, but Rupert then failed to achieve similar success against foot stationed among small enclosed fields. On the north flank, fierce fighting evidently also occurred, but neither side gained the ascendancy. As the day progressed a fierce artillery duel commenced between the Roundhead gunners on Round Hill and their counterparts firing from near tumuli on Wash Common to the east. Fighting continued until about 7.00pm. During the course of the night Charles began withdrawing to Oxford. Essex resumed marching toward London the day after the battle, of which he can rightly be viewed the victor.

Perhaps 3,500 men perished in the fighting. Clarendon wrote the following about the most notable fatality: 'In this unhappy battle was slain the lord viscount Falkland; a person of...inimitable sweetness and delight in conversation, of so flowing and obliging a humanity and goodness...that if there were no other brand upon this...accursed civil war than that single loss it must be most infamous and execrable to all posterity'.

20

CHERITON
29 MARCH 1644

Shortly after retiring to Oxford following the First Battle of Newbury (20 September 1643), which checked the progress of the Royalist war effort, Charles and his council of war decided to raise an army to clear Dorset, Wiltshire and Hampshire of the enemy.

The man chosen to command the new force was Lord Hopton. Though eager to conduct operations in the intended theatre, Hopton was soon lured into Sussex where he proceeded to capture Arundel Castle in early December 1643. However, it did not remain in Royalist hands for long. Sir William Waller, the commander of a Parliamentarian army, retook the castle and Hopton retired to Winchester unwilling to continue campaigning during the winter months against numerically superior forces, especially in view of significant losses sustained in a clash with Waller at Alton on 13 December.

In March 1644 Charles sent Hopton reinforcements. With them came the elderly and gout-ridden Lord Forth, a higher ranking officer who was to take command, though in reality he allowed Hopton a great say in conducting the ensuing campaign and battle.

Waller, who had also been reinforced, proceeded to march west towards Winchester. On 28 March he encamped in and around Hinton Ampner, three miles south of Alresford. Meanwhile, the Royalists had marched east to confront their opponents and spent the night a short distance to the north.

The battle was fought the following day on ground just to the north of Hinton Ampner, and between the village of Cheriton to the west and Cheriton Wood to the east. The armies were marshalled on two ridges with the Parliamentarians facing their adversaries to the north. Moreover, Waller stationed 1,000 musketeers in the wood to threaten the Royalist left flank. His army numbered about 10,000 men of whom 3,500 were cavalry. The Royalists were some 6,000 strong of whom 2,500 were horse. They were also inferior in cannon.

Fighting commenced when Hopton ordered Colonel Appleyard to clear the wood with 1,000 musketeers. A fierce fire-fight ensued and Hopton committed more musketeers to the struggle, thereby securing the position.

Hopton wished to follow up this success by attacking Waller's right wing. However, Forth preferred to hold back and let the enemy commit themselves to an assault. But this decision was soon overturned by Sir Henry Bard on the right of the Royalist line. At about 11.00am he charged towards the opposing horse under Sir Arthur Hazlerigg, acting 'with more youthfull courage then souldier-like discretion'. His regiment was soon overwhelmed and heavy casualties were inflicted on regiments which rode to its assistance.

Fighting now became general and very confused. When it became clear that the day was lost, certain Royalist regiments courageously fought a delaying action while their comrades withdrew towards Tichborne Down. From there the defeated army pressed on to Basing House where it arrived that night. It then retreated to Oxford. On the other hand the victors made for Winchester, which surrendered to Waller on 30 March, and he was soon in control of the whole of Hampshire.

According to a Parliamentarian, Captain Robert Harley, the Roundheads lost about 60 men and the Royalists 300 at Cheriton, but these figures are almost certainly too low. What is undoubted is that the battle was an important triumph for the king's enemies. It was their first clear-cut victory and as the Royalist, Sir Edward Walker noted, 'marked a watershed in the war'.

21

MARSTON MOOR
2 JULY 1644

'I see, all my birds have flown'
— Charles I

The king uttered these memorable words on 4 January 1642 in the House of Commons where he had gone at the head of armed men to arrest five of his opponents. The MPs, however, had received news of his intent and had resorted to flight. Charles' action had dire political consequences and within months the realm was torn apart by civil war. But, before coming to the melancholy tale of armed conflict, and in particular the Marston Moor campaign, it will be profitable to briefly discuss the events which led to the commencement of hostilities.

Charles, whom the nineteenth century historian Lord Macaulay aptly described as having 'an incurable propensity to dark and crooked ways', ascended the throne in 1625, a shy, reserved young man, and an ardent believer in the divine right of kings. He was, moreover, greatly influenced by his favourite, the Duke of Buckingham. They soon adopted an unrealistic foreign policy by entering the European conflict known as the Thirty Years' War and Buckingham's inept performance against Spain resulted in his being censured by parliament in 1626. Indeed, the assembly refused to vote further taxation unless he were removed. In response, Charles dissolved parliament and resorted to levying forced loans from the upper-classes with which to finance the war effort.

Following Buckingham's subsequent failure against French forces, Charles summoned another parliament. This met in 1628 and in return for subsidies the king reluctantly accepted the Petition of Right which forbade arbitrary imprisonment and the raising of taxes not authorised by parliament. An attempt was also made to impeach Buckingham – who was later assassinated by a Puritan fanatic during an adjournment of the national assembly. His death did not result in a permanent reduction in tension between Charles and parliament. Things came to a head following parliament's reassembly in early 1629, with the king's infractions of the Petition of Right and his religious policies being causes of conflict. Once more, therefore, parliament was dissolved.

Why was Charles' religious stance a source of discord? The problem was this: shortly after the commencement of his reign he openly aligned himself with the right wing of the Church of England, a reactionary group which wished among other things to introduce more ritual into religious services and beautify churches. Disenchantment with the king's religious views increased during the 1630s for in 1633 Charles, whose wife was a Catholic, appointed William Laud Archbishop of Canterbury, and under him like-minded clergymen received promotion, Puritans were persecuted, and steps taken to restore the power and authority of the episcopate. Hence an increasing number of people came to believe that the king and archbishop were crypto-Catholics spearheading a campaign to undermine the Reformation.

Laud was appointed Archbishop of Canterbury during the period when Charles ruled without parliament, a period sometimes termed the 'Eleven Years' Tyranny' or the 'Personal Rule'. The latter is more appropriate. It is certainly true that he behaved high-handedly during this era, imprisoning for instance, several MPs who had offended him in 1629, but it would be wrong to envisage Charles as a cruel and utterly arbitrary monarch whose actions inflicted abject misery on his subjects: the number of political and religious prisoners was small. On the whole, in fact, life was peaceful and more prosperous than it had been, for inflation, which had marred the early decades of the century, had become less acute.

Opposition to Charles' rule only became serious in the late 1630s. The principal cause of the unrest was an attempt to introduce religious reforms in Scotland similar to those implemented in England. The Scots were outraged, and a National Covenant pledging resistance to reform was drawn up and signed in February 1638.

Charles decided to use force against the Scots in order to impose his will and restore his authority. However, although his financial resources, the customs being one, were adequate for peacetime needs, they were insufficient to wage war successfully and so he failed to achieve his objectives in the First Bishops' War of 1639. Nevertheless, Charles soon set to work planning another war against the Scots (whose cause was widely viewed with sympathy in England), and to gain adequate funds resorted to summoning a parliament. In the event, the 'Short Parliament', which assembled in April 1640, refused to grant subsidies until its grievances against the king's rule had been addressed. It was thus soon dissolved.

One of the grievances was 'ship money'. This was an annual charge, first raised in Elizabethan times, for the refitting and enhancement of the navy, which Charles reintroduced in 1634 and extended from coastal counties to inland ones the following year. Initially 'ship money' had an impressive yield but by the close of the decade resistance to it among the king's subjects was strong and widespread making it harder and harder to collect.

In the summer of 1640, soon after the dissolution of the 'Short Parliament', Charles became involved in the Second Bishops' War. Unlike the first, this witnessed some serious fighting and not surprisingly in view of the king's limited resources, things went badly for him. In fact, the Scots occupied England north of the River Tees. In the ensuing Treaty of Ripon Charles agreed, among other things, to summon a new parliament which would ratify a permanent settlement and pay the Scots to return home.

Thus, on 3 November, the 'Long Parliament' assembled. The vast majority of those who attended were critical of the king and the leaders of the Commons were in no hurry to see the Scots return north, for they were well aware that the Scots' presence in England strengthened their hand.

Parliament soon moved against Charles' 'evil counsellors', the foremost being his right-hand man, the Earl of Strafford, and Archbishop Laud. They were impeached and sent to the Tower. In March 1641 the former was put on trial, accused of treason, and through a bill of attainder, executed in May. (Laud was to suffer the same fate in 1645).

By the time of Strafford's death, Charles had conceded to the Triennial Act under which parliaments would be held every three years, and to a bill which stipulated that the existing parliament could only be dissolved by its own consent, a major encroachment on the royal prerogative.

During the course of the summer a series of reforming bills passed into law and resulted, inter alia, in the abolition of 'ship money' and the prerogative courts such as Star Chamber and the ecclesiastical Court of High Commission, which were instruments of arbitrary rule. By late summer enough money had been raised to pay off the Scots. In view of this, and the programme of reform, some people felt sanguine about the future. John Pym, the leader of the Commons, was not one of them. He rightly believed that Charles would seek to reverse his concessions, and passionately believed that Protestantism was threatened by a popish plot to which the king and queen were party.

Marked tension revived in late 1641. News of a Catholic uprising in Ireland involving the massacre of Protestant British settlers arrived, and the rebels claimed to be acting in the king's name. As G. E. Aylmer has observed of the rebellion: 'In Ireland it was overwhelmingly an ethnic and religious conflict: an abortive war of national liberation. In England it was seen as a bloody papalistic rebellion, a horrifying manifestation of the work of AntiChrist.'

Control of the army which needed to be raised to crush the revolt (and of the militia at home), now became a major political issue, for the king's opponents such as Pym believed that he would use force to achieve his objectives here instead. (Plots to forcibly dissolve parliament had been uncovered earlier in the year). Thus parliament raised money by voluntary subscription to send its own forces to deal with the rebels.

Mistrust between Charles and his adversaries was now profound. He believed that they wished to end monarchical authority: they, that he had absolutist and papalistic designs. Polarisation was taking place at an increasing level. For instance, some of the king's former critics were now going over to his side believing that constitutional reform had gone far enough and that Puritan measures to reform the Church, such as the proposed abolition of episcopacy, were too extreme.

Emboldened by his growing support, and alarmed by rumours that the queen was to be impeached for supposedly encouraging the Irish rebels, Charles went to parliament on 4 January 1642 to arrest the five MPs referred to earlier. Following this unprecedented breach of parliamentary privilege, Charles left Whitehall and subsequently headed north. Both sides now began preparing for civil war. For several months the king's position was weak. His behaviour on 4 January had cost him support. Aware of its strength, parliament sent commissioners to York in June with peace terms, 'the nineteen propositions', which demanded among other things that Charles accept parliament's claim to appoint ministers and control the militia and castles. Not surprisingly, Charles refused to become a mere figurehead and once again his support began to increase. As John Kenyon has commented: 'Parliament's intransigence, its insistence on terms which no man of honour would accept, began working against it'.

So preparation for war continued, with both sides endeavouring to gain control of the militia. It had always been the monarch's right to control the militia (through lords lieutenant of counties and their deputies), but in March the Commons had passed a militia bill as an ordinance and by means of it the king's opponents had replaced the majority of lieutenants with men they trusted. Initially, the new lords lieutenant did not call the trained bands to arms, but in early June they had commenced doing so. In response, Charles now resorted to the archaic practice of issuing commissions of array to groups of Royalist gentlemen, including expelled lords lieutenant, empowering them to summon the militia. Thus both sides tried to rally the militia to their cause, (parliament already enjoyed the support of the London trained bands, some 8,000 men in all), but in general the response was poor due to political divisions within the trained bands and a widespread desire to remain neutral. Hence both parties resorted to issuing commissions to individuals instead and so men of substance began recruiting volunteers for the cause they had espoused. Furthermore, others did likewise on their own initiative.

Though more peers rallied to the king than to parliament, it would be wrong to view the Civil War as primarily a class war for the most numerous section of the upper-class, the gentry, was about evenly divided (slightly more gentry may have supported the king than parliament), and inevitably the stance of landowners affected that of their tenantry. In short, as Maurice Ashley has commented: 'Serious work that has been completed on county histories shows that no clear-cut picture is to be found of class conflict.'

On the other hand, marked regional divisions did exist. In general the north, Wales, and western counties of England, were areas where Royalist sympathies were dominant while the parliamentary cause was more highly favoured in the rest of the country, including its wealthiest regions.

Finally, and not surprisingly, religious divisions also existed. Catholics and Anglicans mainly supported the king, whereas Puritans and other nonconformists generally favoured parliament.

Though Charles unfurled his standard at Nottingham on 22 August 1642 his forces were too weak to confront those of parliament and so he moved to Shrewsbury to augment his strength before marching towards London. Thus the first battle of the Civil War, Edgehill, was fought several weeks after the king's standard had been raised. Both sides had expected the engagement of 23 October to be decisive. It was not, and so the war dragged on. During the following year the Royalists generally had the better of things and consequently, in September 1643, parliament secured Scottish assistance.

An army over 21,000 men strong, under the Earl of Leven, duly crossed the Tweed at Berwick on 19 January 1644. The commander of the Royalist forces in Northumberland, Sir Thomas Glemham, fell back to Newcastle upon Tyne from Alnwick before the formidable host. On 2 February the king's commander-in-chief in the north, the Marquis of Newcastle, joined Glemham after hastening up from Yorkshire with part of his army. The following day Leven appeared on the scene and proceeded to invest the city.

Later in the month, however, Leven decided to head south to effect a junction with Parliamentarian forces. On the 28th he crossed into County Durham, leaving six regiments north of the Tyne, and moved towards the port of Sunderland, 'the fittest place for receiving of Intelligence, and supplying our Army' as one of his soldiers observed. Sunderland was occupied on 4 March.

Newcastle followed with his numerically weaker forces and some fighting ensued in the vicinity of Sunderland. The most serious clash occurred in the Hylton/Boldon area on the 24th. It began at about 5.00pm and continued until around midnight and one contemporary source, *The Taking of the Fort at South Shields* (the fort had been captured by the Scots on the 20th) relates that: 'Many officers, who have been old souldiers did affirm they had never seen so long and hot service in the night time...the number of [Royalists] slane did very farre exceed ours, as wee understood by the dead bodies we found the next day.'

Then, on 12 April, when Newcastle was at Durham he received dreadful news from Yorkshire. The previous day the forces he had left there to hold what had been won in 1643 had been soundly defeated at Selby by a Parliamentarian army led by Lord Fairfax and his son, Sir Thomas. Upon hearing this, Newcastle decided to return post haste to prevent York – widely considered the second city in the land – from falling into enemy hands. On 14/15 April he entered York.

The Scots likewise moved south, though with less dispatch. On the 16th they occupied Thornaby on Tees before moving on to Wetherby where they linked up with the Fairfaxes. On 22 April the combined armies invested York. Initially the city was only partially besieged. The situation worsened for the Royalists when the allies were joined by the Earl of Manchester and the army of the Eastern Association (drawn from East Anglia) on 3 June.

In view of York's importance, and what remained of the Marquis of Newcastle's army to the Royalist cause, it was deemed vital that the city be relieved. On

22 March the king's nephew, Prince Rupert, had brilliantly relieved the strategically important town of Newark and thus the task of saving York fell to him. In general the state of the Royalist war effort had taken a turn for the worse, and on 25 April Rupert attended a council of war at Oxford in which he successfully proposed a sensible defensive strategy for Charles, based on the ring of fortified garrisons protecting that city: something which he hoped would prove sufficient to defend the Royalist capital while he dealt with the situation in the north.

On 6 May Rupert arrived back at his own headquarters at Shrewsbury, and a few days later began marching towards Lancashire with his army of 2,000 horse and 6,000 foot. There were a number of reasons why he made for Lancashire. For one thing the county was on the whole sympathetic to the king and Rupert wished to gain men, money and supplies. Furthermore he was anxious to strike at the Parliamentary forces in Lancashire, aware that they could otherwise conduct serious raids into Cheshire and Wales while he moved to the relief of York.

A Parliamentarian force was routed at Garstang on 14 May, Stockport was subsequently secured, and Bolton stormed. Rupert then moved to Bury where he was joined on the 30th by Lord Goring and Sir Charles Lucas at the head of horse and 800 foot. The cavalry, numbering 5,000 according to one source, although they were probably not quite that strong, belonged to the Northern Horse and had been sent to Newark by Newcastle upon his arrival at York rather than have them pent up in a soon-to-be beleaguered city. After entering Wigan, where the streets were strewn with flowers for his arrival, Rupert laid siege to Liverpool on 7 June and entered it on the 11th.

Within a week or so of taking Liverpool Rupert received a letter from his uncle, the king, written at Tickenhall on 14 June. Since Rupert had left Shrewsbury, Charles' position at Oxford had been threatened by the armies of the Earl of Essex and Sir William Waller, closing in from the east and west. In the face of such a strong threat the king had hurriedly left the city on 2 June with a small army and had hastened to the west midlands with the Parliamentarians in pursuit. By the time Charles wrote to Rupert the situation had eased somewhat because Essex, after ordering Waller to continue pursuing the king, had marched off to relieve Lyme and recover lost ground in the west. Even so, Charles' letter had an urgent tone. In part it reads:

'If Yorke be lost I shall esteeme my Crown little lesse, [than lost] unlesse supported by your suddaine Marche to me, & a Miraculious Conquest in the South before the effects of the northern power can be found here; but if Yorke be relieved, & you beate the Rebelles Armies of both kingdoms, which ar before it, then...I may possiblie...spinn out tyme, untill you come to assist mee; Wherefor I command and conjure you...(all new enterpryses laid aside) with all your force to the relief of York...'

Shortly after receiving the letter Rupert set out across the Pennines at the head of a force which had been augmented by levies from Lancashire, Cumberland and Derbyshire. He first made for Preston and then headed up the Ribble valley towards Skipton, where he arrived on 26 June. Here he halted for three days, partly no doubt to prepare his new recruits for battle. He then marched via Otley to Knaresborough which he reached on the 30th. He was just fourteen miles from York.

By now the commanders of the allied army besieging the city were well aware of his approach. Hitherto they had rejected messages from the Committee of Both Kingdoms that they should send a strong force to intercept him in Lancashire, for they wished to maintain the pressure on York. Now however, they rightly felt obliged to oppose Rupert's advance. They held the mistaken view that his army numbered around 18,000 men (it was not that strong), and so on the 30th they reluctantly abandoned the siege and marched six miles west to the vicinity of Long Marston with their more powerful army to bar the approach from Knaresborough. The position also blocked any advance via Wetherby.

It was a wise move. But unfortunately for the allies Rupert had other plans. After sending out a cavalry screen to deceive them, he moved north on 1 July and crossed the Ure at Boroughbridge before pressing on to Thornton Bridge where he crossed the Swale. He then moved south-east and scattered a force of dragoons guarding a bridge of boats over the Ouse to Poppleton near York, thereby securing the crossing after a brilliant day's march of 22 miles.

The prince's army quartered for the night in the vicinity. Rupert was determined to confront the allies as soon as possible with the combined Royalist armies. Hence he sent a message to Newcastle ordering him to have his men ready to march by 4.00am the next day. Furthermore, he sent some horse across the bridge of boats to reconnoitre the enemy position. For his part, the marquis sent Rupert a congratulatory letter which stated: 'You are welcome, Sir, so many several ways, as it is beyond my arithmetic to number, but this I know, you are the Redeemer of the North and the Saviour of the Crown...I am made of nothing but thankfulness and obedience to your Highness's commands.'

And what of the allies? How did they react to the relief of York? They had been completely outmanoeuvred and left in the cold and so at a council of war (in which a proposal to give battle was overruled), it was decided to march via Tadcaster to Cawood and Selby to secure crossings of the Ouse, thereby barring Rupert's route south and cutting off supplies from the East and West Ridings.

Early the next morning the allies began moving towards Tadcaster, led by the Scottish infantry. The rearguard, which comprised 'three thousand Horse and Dragooners' according to the Parliamentarian Scoutmaster-General, Lionel Watson, remained in the vicinity of Long Marston to cover the retreat. But at about 'nine of the clocke' Royalist horse arrived in strength on Marston Moor (some had appeared earlier but had then ridden off out of sight), and this changed everything. It was clear that Rupert was intent on giving battle. The allied generals' dispatch records that the van of their army was 'within a mile' of reaching Tadcaster when 'notice was sent us by our horsemen...that the Prince's army...was ready to fall upon them'. The senior allied general, Leven, gave the order to about-face and the march back to the vicinity of Long Marston commenced.

Following the arrival of the Royalist van at about 9.00am – the hour is not only mentioned by Watson – conflict occurred between the allied and Royalist horse, for the latter were intent on securing the ridge to the south of the Long Marston/Tockwith road. This they failed to do and so Rupert was forced to deploy on Marston Moor to the north of the road, leaving the allies to form up on the higher ground, and no doubt anxious for Newcastle's army to arrive soon.

The Marquis of Newcastle was against giving battle and made this clear when he met Rupert. Just where and when the two generals met is uncertain. According to *The Life of... William Cavendish, Duke of Newcastle*, (written in later years by Newcastle's wife under his direction), upon Rupert's relief of York the marquis had 'immediately sent some persons of quality to attend his Highness, and to invite him into the city to consult with him'. It seems that Rupert declined the invitation, for Newcastle 'went himself the next day in person to wait on his Highness' and urged him 'not to attempt anything as yet upon the enemy; for he had intelligence that there was some discontent between them, and that they were resolved to divide themselves'. Moreover, the marquis expected the arrival of Sir Robert Clavering 'within two days...with above three thousand men out of the North, and two thousand drawn out of several garrisons'. However, Rupert replied that he had a letter from the king 'with a positive and absolute command to fight...which he was bound to perform', and upon hearing this Newcastle stated that he was prepared 'to obey his Highness in all things'.

Some believe that this discussion actually took place on the evening of the 1st. Others hold that it occurred when Newcastle arrived at Marston Moor and that he did so at about 9.00am on the 2nd, the time Sir Hugh Cholmeley (who heard eye-witness accounts of events within a day or two of the battle) gives for the marquis' arrival in his *Memorials touching the battle* – written some years after Marston Moor.

However, according to an account written shortly after Marston Moor by a participant, Sir Henry Slingsby, and another Royalist source, the *Diary*, which seems to date from after the Restoration and be the work of someone who had been with Rupert during the Civil War, the prince had to send for Newcastle following his own arrival on Marston Moor urging him to come with all speed. Admittedly, neither source mentions when Rupert arrived on Marston Moor. When it is borne in mind, though, that the Parliamentarian accounts of Watson and Thomas Stockdale – written shortly after the battle – relate that the prince's men began arriving in strength on the moor at about 9.00am it seems reasonable to conclude that Newcastle arrived later than Cholmeley believed, for as noted, both Slingsby and the *Diary* show that some time elapsed between Rupert's arrival and that of the marquis. Cholmeley himself records that this was so. He wrote that upon Newcastle's arrival on the moor with his Lifeguard, which consisted of 'all the gentlemen of quality which were in York' (including Slingsby), Rupert commented, 'my Lord, I wish you had come sooner with your forces, but I hope we shall yet have a glorious day'.

All things considered, its appears that Newcastle arrived when the morning was well advanced (by which time much of the allied army must have been back from its abortive march), and it is thus reasonable to conclude that Newcastle advised Rupert against seeking battle at an earlier hour elsewhere.

Though Newcastle did not have a penchant for exertion he could behave with promptitude when occasion demanded, and it seems likely that at about dawn on the 2nd he rode out of York 'to wait on his Highness' and argue against acting hastily. Then, upon hearing that Rupert had orders to engage the enemy, returned to rally his forces before setting out for Marston Moor with his Lifeguard later in the morning leaving Lord Eythin, a veteran soldier, to bring on the foot. A seemingly garbled reminiscence of such a meeting was recorded by the Royalist historian Lord Clarendon in later years. He was informed that Newcastle caught up with Rupert en route to Marston Moor and that after both alighted and exchanged salutations, they 'went again to horse' after which the prince commented, 'My Lord, I hope we shall have a glorious day'. Whereupon, Newcastle asked Rupert whether he was intent on giving battle, and after hearing that he was, 'urged many reasons against' doing so.

What is certain is that not all was well with Newcastle's army, a fact which no doubt contributed to his decision to counsel against an engagement. Cholmeley relates that on the evening of the 1st the marquis had received orders via Lord Goring to have his forces ready to march by 4.00am the next day. Newcastle gave orders to this effect 'and accordingly all the foot were at 2 o'clock that night' drawn up in readiness to march but then 'quit their colours' and dispersed, unwilling to march until they received their pay. Cholmeley continues by stating that other informants told him that 'there was not half the foot, for many of them being plundering in the enemy's [abandoned] trenches...could not be drawn together so soon'.

Moreover, reportedly several senior figures in Newcastle's army were opposed to giving battle. Eythin was one such. According to one of Cholmeley's sources Eythin was responsible for the dispersal of the assembled foot, something which he himself denied. Furthermore, Sir Francis Cobbe, who served as the commander of Clifford's Tower during the siege of York, informs us that Eythin told Newcastle not to commit all his forces to Rupert's intended confrontation with the allies.

Upon arriving at Marston Moor, the marquis told Rupert that he had left Eythin to bring on the foot as soon as possible. At this, according to Cholmeley, the prince stated that he would attack without them (thereby attempting to take advantage of the disordered state of the allies), but was persuaded by Newcastle to await Eythin.

It is now time to discuss the character and career of Prince Rupert and the senior allied commander, Leven, and to discuss the composition, weaponry and tactics of the opposing armies.

THE COMMANDERS AND THEIR ARMIES

Prince Rupert was born in Prague on 17 December 1619, the third son of Charles I's sister, Elizabeth, and her husband Frederick of Bohemia, the 'Protestant Champion of Europe'. Within a year of Rupert's birth, his father lost his kingdom at the beginning of the Thirty Years War and the family was forced to flee, receiving sanctuary in the United Provinces. After initially residing at the Hague, they moved to Leiden in 1623, a place where Rupert found much of interest. For one thing, he soon became fascinated by ships and spent much time talking to sailors about their tasks and adventures.

Rupert soon demonstrated an aptitude for war. It is said, for example, that by the age of eight he had mastered the pikeman's eighteen postures and the musketeer's thirty-four. He was moreover keenly interested in the progress of the Thirty Years War.

In 1633, at the age of thirteen, he was invited by Prince Frederick Henry, the Stadholder of the United Provinces, to participate in the siege of Rheinberg (which was to fall in October) and hence had his first taste of campaigning. In later years one of Rupert's strengths was besieging towns, and no doubt serving with Frederick Henry, a master of siegecraft, laid the basis of his skill in this field.

In 1635 Rupert participated in a larger campaign than that of the Rheinberg siege – the invasion of Brabant – and did so as a volunteer in Frederick Henry's Lifeguard. The prince was in the thick of the fighting and displayed conspicuous bravery. He subsequently participated in the successful siege of Breda in 1637, and was captured the following year after an army in which he commanded a regiment was defeated at the Battle of Vlotho in Germany. He spent the next three years incarcerated at Linz on the Danube, save for occasional brief periods of parole.

Rupert regained his freedom at the end of 1641. In July of the following year – as England was descending into civil war – he landed at Tynemouth and made his way to join Charles at Nottingham to serve on his behalf in the impending conflict. The tall, elegant young prince, who held the post of General of the Horse, his first major command, distinguished himself from the beginning of hostilities for he was decisive, inspiring, knowledgeable and able. Sir Thomas Roe observed, 'whatsoever he undertakes he doth it vigorously and seriously' being 'full of spirit and action'. A string of successes rapidly won him the reputation of being the best Royalist commander: he was on the way to becoming a legend. Although Rupert's faults included tactlessness, a degree of impetuosity, as well as over sensitivity to criticism and at times lack of judgement, he was overall a very able operational commander.

An interesting and enigmatic man of wide interests (he was among other things a gifted scientific experimenter), Rupert lived until 1682 and was buried in Westminster Abbey.

Alexander Leslie, first Earl of Leven, was born in Scotland in around 1580 and was the illegitimate son of the Captain of Blair Castle and a 'wench in Rannoch'. An experienced soldier, Leven had entered the Swedish army in 1605 and had fought with distinction under the command of Charles IX and his redoubtable successor Gustavus Adolphus, the Lion of the North, during wars with Poland, Denmark and Russia. Indeed, his successful defence of Stralsund against Wallenstein in 1628 made him a soldier of repute. He fought at Lützen in 1642, where Adolphus was killed, and some years later returned to his homeland where he was prevailed upon to lead the Covenanters in the Bishops' Wars. Though a soldier of ability and experience, he seems to have been past his best by the time of Marston Moor.

Theoretically, most Royalist regiments of horse comprised six troops (each 70 strong), thus totalling 420 men plus officers. In practice regiments were usually below full strength, often well below, and this was certainly the case on 2 July 1644. On the other hand, Rupert's regiment of horse comprised ten troops and was probably nearly 500 strong at Marston Moor.

Throughout the Civil War Royalist regiments of horse usually had three field officers, a colonel, lieutenant-colonel and major, all of whom were troop commanders, though in practice the colonel's troop was led by his captain-lieutenant. The other troops were led by captains.

Though the regiments at Marston Moor varied in quality and experience, on the whole the Royalist horse had an excellent reputation. At Edgehill, for instance, they had easily swept all before them. They were mostly of gentle birth, possessed fine mounts, and had a high degree of horsemanship. However, lack of discipline was a problem. This was noted by Lord Clarendon, who wrote that although they usually 'prevailed in the charge' they 'seldom rallied themselves in order'.

In Parliamentarian regiments of horse the theoretical strength of a troop was 71 men plus officers, and many of the regiments had six troops. Again, the strength of the regiments varied greatly. Some were well below 426 men strong while others exceeded this figure substantially and contained more than six troops. The majority of regiments did not have a lieutenant-colonel (they only did so if they were very strong), and the colonel and major both served as troop commanders. The other troops were led by captains.

In the early stages of the Civil War the Roundhead horse had been inferior to that of the Royalists. Cromwell noted this at Edgehill and subsequently told his cousin, John Hampden: 'Your troopers are most of them old decayed serving men and tapsters, and such kind of fellows....Do you think that the spirits of such base and mean fellows will ever be able to encounter gentlemen that have honour, courage and resolution in them? You must get men of a spirit that is like to go as far as gentlemen will go.'

Cromwell practised what he preached and raised a formidable cavalry regiment composed in the main of East Anglian yeomen, godly 'men of spirit' who were staunchly committed to the cause they had espoused. Cromwell and his regiment were in the ranks of the allied army at Marston Moor. On the other hand, as with the Royalists, some of the other Parliamentarian regiments of horse present had had little experience of serious fighting.

There were six Scottish cavalry regiments in the allied army, and like the majority of Royalist regiments of horse they had lieutenant-colonels. In general the troopers rode inferior mounts to those of their English counterparts, for they rode 'little light Scotch nags'. Moreover, although the majority of field officers had seen service abroad the troopers were rather inexperienced.

Troopers on both sides usually carried a heavy sword. Many also had a pair of pistols which in some cases was supplemented by a wheel or flintlock carbine. Furthermore, it is interesting to note that some of the Scottish troopers used the lance, a weapon not employed by their southern counterparts.

Many troopers wore back and breast plates over a buff leather coat, though by this stage of the Civil War many had forsaken armour in favour of a thick buff coat which was full skirted, frequently sleeved, and offered a high degree of protection as well as easier movement. Helmets were commonplace. The most popular was the 'lobster-tailed pot', which had a round skull with attached earguards, neckguard, and faceguard of one or three bars dropping vertically from the peak. Finally, many troopers wore high heavy leather boots which afforded additional protection.

At the start of the Civil War Prince Rupert introduced a tactic pioneered by Gustavus Adolphus, one in marked contrast to the accepted Dutch practice in which horse trotted forward at least five ranks deep, halted close to the enemy and fired, before advancing again to engage in hand-to-hand combat. Rupert preferred to move forward with his cavalry three ranks deep and then charge home at the gallop sword in hand, reserving fire until contact had been made. This approach proved successful and some Parliamentarian officers, Cromwell for one, soon adopted the tactic themselves.

Turning from cavalry to dragoons, it should be noted that although the latter rode to battle, they usually dismounted to fight. Among other things they were used to hold key points such as bridges, while on the battlefield they were sometimes used to line hedges or were stationed among the horse to serve as musketeers. They were armed with swords and muskets, though some officers also had pistols. They wore no armour and often did not have buff coats or helmets either. Their general appearance was much like that of the foot.

Infantry regiments theoretically had ten companies. The colonel's was 200 men strong, the lieutenant-colonel's 160 and the major's 140. The remaining companies were commanded by captains and were 100 strong. In practice, how-ever, regiments were usually well below full strength owing to battle casualties, sickness and desertion, and varied in the number of companies they had.

In theory, companies had a ratio of two musketeers for every pikeman. In actuality the number of musketeers was often more or less equal to that of the pikemen and this seems to have been especially true of the Royalists.

Musketeers basically fought in everyday clothing, and the vast majority were armed with matchlock muskets. These were often 5ft long and weighed as much as 20lbs. Because of their weight they were frequently supported in the firing position by a rest, a wooden pole with a steel fork at the top. They were very unreliable weapons, for they were inaccurate and in inclement weather the smouldering match used to fire them was easily extinguished. Although the matchlock had a range of up to 400 yards it was only really effective at up to about 60. Furthermore, its rate of fire was slow. A good musketeer could prob-ably manage to fire two or three times a minute.

Musketeers had a bandolier from which hung twelve or more small powder containers, a priming flask and bullet-bag. The match, a length of cord soaked in saltpetre, usually hung from the belt. Moreover, many musketeers had short swords. English foot soldiers often ruined their swords by using them instead of axes to chop wood, and preferred to use the butts of their muskets when fight-ing at close quarters.

Musketeers were taught 'fire by introduction' and 'fire by extraduction', both of which resulted in rolling fire. In the former, the front rank fired, then the rearmost moved forward between the files and did likewise, followed by the next rank and so on, thereby making a steady advance. In the latter the process was reversed. After firing, the front rank moved to the rear and so on, a technique which made for an orderly withdrawal. For a more concentrated volley muske-teers were formed three ranks deep instead of six, the rear standing, the second stooping, the front kneeling, and fired a salvo in unison.

Pikemen had to be strong to use their principal weapon effectively, for pikes were heavy and unwieldy. Officially they were 18ft long, but they were often a couple of feet or so less than this for the men were prone to cut off part of the shaft to render the weapon lighter and more manageable. The shaft was usually of ash and had a slim steel head and cheeks, which were strips of steel riveted to the shaft below the head to prevent it being hacked off by an opponent. Apart from the pike, 'the queen of weapons', many pike-men carried short swords, though these were frequently of poor quality. For protection a fully equipped pikeman had a steel helmet, back and breast plates, a gorget, which protected the throat, and long tassets which covered the thighs.

To be effective pikemen had to fight en masse, and a regiment drawn up for action would have its pikemen in the centre and the musketeers on the flanks.

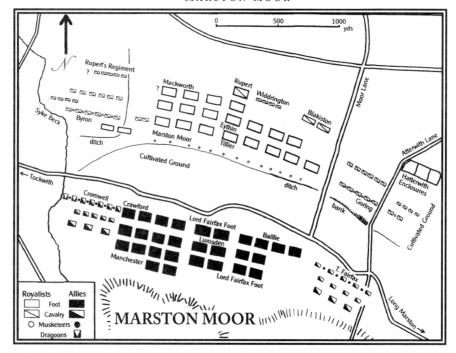

When moving forward to engage the enemy pikemen often held their pikes horizontally and at shoulder height. To oppose a cavalry charge infantry formed a circle with the pikemen inside, holding their pikes at an angle of 30 degrees with the butt against the instep of the right foot, thereby affording protection to themselves and the musketeers who crouched before them under the pikes.

Although officers, and to a lesser extent sergeants, dressed much as they wished, the rank and file on both sides were more uniformly dressed. For instance, the Earl of Manchester's regiment of foot had coats of green cloth lined with red, and some of Newcastle's regiments of foot wore white coats. The same basic colours were used by both sides and in order to avoid confusion on the battlefield distinguishing scarves were often worn (crimson for the Royalists and orange-tawny for the Roundheads), as were field signs. At Marston Moor, for example, the Parliamentarians had white handkerchiefs or pieces of paper stuck in their hats.

As for artillery, the heaviest gun used at Marston Moor was evidently the culverin. This weighed 4,000lbs, had a calibre of 5in and fired shot of 15lbs. Its point blank range was 460 yards but at an elevation of ten degrees this was extended to 2,650 yards. More common was the saker, a mid-sized gun weighing 2,500lbs with a calibre of 3.5in. It fired shot of approximately 5 to 6lbs and its point blank range was 360 yards, while at an elevation of ten degrees shot could be fired over 2,000 yards. Lighter cannon such as minions and falcons were no doubt also present.

DESCRIPTION

By the late afternoon of Tuesday 2 July 1644 both armies were deployed for battle. They were drawn up in the conventional manner with the infantry in the centre and horse on the flanks.

According to the Royalist, Sir Bernard de Gomme, Rupert's force comprised 6,500 cavalry and 11,000 foot, figures which are undoubtedly approximately correct. It was marshalled to the north of the Long Marston/Tockwith road on ground which was mainly moorland. Running north from the road were two lanes, Moor Lane and Atterwith Lane, and between these, separating the moorland from cultivated ground to the south, was a bank which was evidently partly lined by a hedge. The bank was more pronounced at the Atterwith Lane end where it may have dropped as much as 6ft to the moorland.

To the west of Moor Lane, and on the same line as the obstacle referred to, was a small ditch which seems to have had a hedge running along it, probably on its north side, and again this obstacle separated the moorland from cultivated ground. It has been generally held that the ditch ran virtually parallel to the Long Marston/Tockwith road as far as in front of the Royalist right wing to the west. But as Peter Newman has highlighted it petered out at a point where the moorland and arable converged, forming 'a plain' devoid of obstacles, according to Captain Stewart, who was on the allied right wing. Finally, further to the west was another ditch.

Rupert lined the obstacles with musketeers whose task it was to disrupt an advance by the enemy before falling back to join the main body of the army drawn up to the north, and presumably musketeers were also stationed to the fore elsewhere to do likewise. Hence in view of the manned obstacles, the Parliamentarian, Simeon Ashe, observed: 'Our souldiers could not assault [the Royalists] without very great apparent prejudice.'

The Royalist right wing was commanded by Lord Byron and comprised at least 2,600 horse and some 500 musketeers. The latter were stationed in bodies between the squadrons of the front line. Behind, and somewhat to the right of the line, was the Duke of York's regiment under Colonel Samuel Tuke. It was divided into four squadrons and had the task of protecting the flank. Further back was the second line proper led by young Viscount Molyneux. Rupert's regiment of horse was probably to the rear. If not, it would have been to the left of Molyneux.

The wing was drawn up to the north of the westernmost of the ditches referred to above, and this obstacle was partly manned by musketeers and pikemen under Colonel Thomas Napier. Behind, and to their left, was a regiment of horse led by Marcus Trevor.

The centre numbered about 10,000 men. The front line evidently comprised six regiments drawn up in eight bodies under Major-General Henry Tillier. The regiments belonged to Rupert's army. The second line (which presumably was commanded by Eythin) included two regiments which likewise belonged to Rupert's army. The rest of the line consisted of all, or at least some, of the 3,000 or so foot who arrived on the scene at about 4.00pm after being brought from York. There may have been a smaller third line containing infantry belonging to Newcastle's army under Sir Francis Mackworth, though this seems highly unlikely. To the rear of the foot was Rupert's Lifeguard, as well as two cavalry brigades commanded by Sir Edward Widdrington and Sir William Blakiston.

The left wing was commanded by Lord Goring, a flamboyant figure, and probably consisted of some 2,100 horse and 500 musketeers interposed among the squadrons of the front line. To the rear of the left of this line was Colonel Francis Carnaby's regiment, which was divided into four squadrons, and had the task of protecting the flank. Further back came the second line proper, with Sir Charles Lucas and Sir Richard Dacre leading the right and left of the line respectively.

Though a plan drawn up on the morning of the 2nd by de Gomme shows that the Royalists had sixteen guns, others were brought to the field later in the day, and in all the Royalists had 25 cannon. These were mostly placed between the bodies of foot in the centre, but some were placed along the line of the ditch. Furthermore, there was a small battery on a slight hummock before Byron's position.

The allied army, which is generally believed to have been about 27,000 strong, was deployed 'in a large field of Rie', according to Simeon Ashe, on the north slope of the ridge to the south of the Long Marston/Tockwith road. Watson recorded that at: 'About two of the clock we had indifferently well formed our army' and this time was also mentioned by Thomas Stockdale who wrote that the allies 'were all putt into order for a feight...by 2 a clocke'. Stragglers though, no doubt continued to arrive for some time after this.

The left wing was commanded by Oliver Cromwell, Manchester's lieutenant-general of horse, and was drawn up in three lines. The first contained units of Eastern Association cavalry between which were bodies of musketeers, while the left of the line was made up of Scottish dragoons under Colonel Hugh Fraser. The second line comprised Eastern Association cavalry, while the third was made up of Scottish regiments under David Leslie. The wing numbered about 4,700 horse, 500 dragoons and around 600 foot.

The centre was also marshalled in three lines and consisted of about 17,300 foot. The left of the front line comprised brigades of Manchester's army under Major-General Lawrence Crawford. Then came a brigade of Lord Fairfax's foot, while the right of the line was made up of Scottish brigades under Lieutenant-General William Baillie. The second line comprised Scottish brigades under Major-General Sir James Lumsden, while the third had, from left to right, brigades belonging to Manchester's army, that of the Scots, and Lord Fairfax. To the rear were two Scottish units in reserve.

The right wing was led by Sir Thomas Fairfax. Though drawn up in three lines it was not as strong as Cromwell's, for it consisted of about 3,300 horse and some 600 foot. Again, musketeers were interposed among the bodies of horse in the front line. The second line was under Colonel John Lambert and, like the first, was made up of the horse of Lord Fairfax's army. The third line consisted of Scottish regiments under the Earl of Eglinton.

The allies had between 30 and 40 guns. Most were probably stationed between the infantry units in the front line.

Watson informs us that at about 'two of the clock, [i.e., before the arrival of the bulk of Newcastle's men], the great Ordnance of both sides began to play' and this is supported by other primary accounts. The cannonade seems to have continued in a desultory fashion for an hour or so and no great damage was done, though some fatalities did occur. One such was Thomas Danby, a middle-aged Roman Catholic gentleman cut down on the Royalist left wing.

After the firing ceased, the allies began singing Psalms. Then, according to Watson, at 'about five of the clock' a general silence ensued on both sides, at which hour stragglers, in particular members of Newcastle's army, were perhaps still arriving on the scene. As time slowly passed neither side resumed hostilities. Most probably towards 7.00pm Rupert, who had decided not to attack until the next day and believed Leven felt likewise, allowed the Royalists to relax. Newcastle retired to rest in his coach. His relaxation was brief for according to *The Life of... William Cavendish, Duke of Newcastle*, he soon 'heard a great noise and thunder of shooting, which gave him notice of the armies being engaged'. Leven had seized the opportunity presented by Rupert and had given the order to advance. Thus the surprised Royalists looked up and saw the enemy army bearing down on them, which 'in its several parts' states Ashe, 'was like unto so many thick clouds'.

Fraser's dragoons, on Cromwell's wing, moved against Napier and according to Captain Stewart 'acted their part so well, that at the first assault they beate the enemy from the ditch', thereby facilitating the advance of the horse under Cromwell. Hence as Watson, who was on this wing, recorded: 'In a moment we were past the ditch into the Moore, upon equall grounds with the enemy'.

Byron moved forward to engage Cromwell. In so doing, he masked the fire of his musketeers and perhaps contributed to the discomfiture of Napier's men. Indeed, by advancing he may have disobeyed an order from Prince Rupert, for according to a late source, the *Life of James II*, he had been ordered 'not to quit his ground' but to 'recieve there the charge of the enemy'. If given, the order – which harmonises with other evidence that Rupert wished to fight a defensive battle – was intended to force the allied left wing to come to grips with Byron after being disordered and softened up somewhat by crossing the ditch and being subjected to heavy Royalist fire.

In the resulting clash, Byron came off worst and his line soon broke. But while Cromwell seems to have withdrawn temporarily to have a wound tended, leaving Leslie in command, his wing encountered stiff resistance from the Royalist second line, or at least part of it, under Molyneux. The latter received support from Rupert who hurried to the aid of the Royalist right wing with his Lifeguard and, presumably, Widdrington's brigade. According to Cholmeley, as the prince did so he encountered 'his own regiment turning their backs to the enemy which was a thing so strange and unusual he said, "Swounds, do you run, follow me."' In so doing, he managed to rally at least some of the troopers who had been affected by the panic which had swept through part of the right wing. Others though, no doubt continued their flight, as did troopers from other regiments, and the Duchess of Newcastle was to record that some of them slew fellow Royalists who tried to stop them.

Assisted by Rupert, Molyneux's men continued fighting resolutely. A Parliamentarian, Lord Saye and Sele, relates: 'The Enemies Horse, being many of them, if not the greatest part, Gentlemen, stood very firm a long time...standing like an Iron Wall, so that they were not easily broken.' According to Watson, 'Cromwell's own division had a hard pull of it: for they were charged by Rupert's bravest men, both in Front and Flank: they stood at the swords point a pretty while, hacking one another, but at last (it so pleased God) he brake through them, scattering them before him like a little dust. At the same instant the rest of our horse of that Wing, had wholly broken all Prince Ruperts horse.'

In part, the allies' success can be attributed to numerical superiority. But discipline no doubt also contributed to their success, and is certainly manifest in the aftermath for instead of pursuing the enemy Cromwell's men were held in check by their commander.

Meanwhile, ferocious fighting had taken place, and indeed was still taking place, in the centre. An anonymous source, W. H., notes, 'the main bodies joyning, made such a noise with shot and clamour of shouts that we lost our eares, and the smoke of powder was so thick that we saw no light but what proceeded from the mouth of gunnes'.

On the allied left, Crawford, with no obstacle between him and the enemy, did well. Some of his men assisted Fraser's dragoons against Napier before aiding their fellows against the foot on the right of the Royalist centre, (exactly what happened to Trevor's cavalry regiment is uncertain), who were driven back and had their flank turned somewhat. In due course Cromwell was able to assist Crawford and this resulted in the right flank of the Royalist centre being turned so that the axis of advance for the bulk of the allies in this sector was west to east instead of south to north.

So far one could be forgiven for thinking that the allies had gained the upper hand in the battle. But had they? How were they faring elsewhere on the field?

Here things were different, very different. Initially, it is true, Lord Fairfax's foot in the centre of the allied front line drove back the opposing soldiers under Colonel Robert Broughton. However, they were forced to give ground when the

Royalists received reinforcements from the second line. Then, to make matters worse, Sir William Blakiston's cavalry, perhaps at the instigation of Newcastle, charged the Fairfax foot and at least some of the Scots to their right, and succeeded in driving them and many of the men stationed to their rear, from the field. It is reported that at some stage in the battle, and most probably now, Newcastle charged with his Lifeguard and personally killed three members of a Scottish regiment of foot.

Captain Stewart relates that Blakiston charged as far as the top of the ridge. There he halted while panic-stricken allied soldiers ran on as fast as their legs would carry them. It was not just the rank and file who fled. The allied generals, Leven, Lord Fairfax, and perhaps Manchester, did likewise. The departure of the latter however, if it occurred, was only temporary. On the other hand Leven and Fairfax quit the field for good believing that the day was lost. According to the account of Lieutenant-Colonel James Somerville, Leven 'never drew bridle' until he arrived at Leeds.

Fortunately for the allies, some of the foot in the sector in question stood firm, most notably a brigade led by Lord Crawford-Lindsay on the right of the front line. Initially these infantry had made progress against the opposing Royalist foot but had then been held. Nonetheless, they continued fighting doggedly. As Lumsden records: 'They that faucht stood extraordinare weill'. This is undoubtedly true, for they were not only attacked by foot from the front – and no doubt the left flank – but were also assailed by horse under Sir Charles Lucas from Goring's wing. According to Stewart, Lucas 'assaulted the Scottish foot upon their...Flanks so that they had the foot upon their front and the...Cavalry of the enemies left wing to fight with, whom they encountered with so much courage.' Furthermore, he states that Baillie and Lumsden, 'perceiving the greatest weight of the battell to lye sore upon the Earl of Linsies, and Lord Maitelands regiment, sent up a reserve for their assistance'. Thus reinforced by men from the second line, the embattled regiments began to gain ground again.

Success was also achieved against Blakiston. According to Ashe, he was attacked on the ridge by a 'regiment of the Earl of Manchester's foot' stationed in the allied third line, which 'did wheele on the right hand upon' Blakiston's horse 'and gave them so hot a charge that they were forced to flie back disbanded unto the moore'.

Before continuing with events in the centre, let us turn to a discussion of the conflict between the allied right wing under Sir Thomas Fairfax and the opposing Royalist horse under Goring.

At the commencement of the battle Fairfax moved forward to engage his adversary. Some of the ground between Fairfax and Goring was crossed by the bank referred to earlier, running west from Atterwith Lane and evidently crowned for at least part of its length by a hedge. It seems, moreover, that there was some form of obstacle for some distance to the east of the lane for Captain

Stewart (who as noted earlier was on the allied right wing), relates that 'there was no passage' for Fairfax's men to come to grips with the enemy 'but at a narrow lane', that is, Atterwith Lane. As the troopers moved forward, they suffered from Royalist musket fire and sustained severe losses as they tried to make their way 'in threes and foures' along the lane onto the ground beyond the obstacles. When the bank was levelled in the 1960s hundreds of musket balls were discovered, a fact which testifies to the intensity of the fire Fairfax's cavalry encountered in this area. Not for nothing did Fairfax recall: 'Musketeers...did us much hurt with their shot'.

In view of this, it is reasonable to conclude that chaos soon reigned in the ranks of the horse attempting to gain the ground beyond, via the lane. As the front ranks, which consisted of a newly raised regiment, were shot up it would have become increasingly difficult for those behind to make their way past the dead and dying, riderless mounts, and those recoiling from the fray.

When one notes that Stewart himself comments that 'five or six Troopes' of horse subsequently managed to 'charge through the enemy', it thus becomes hard to imagine that all Fairfax's cavalry attempted to attack the Royalist left wing via Atterwith Lane. At Edgehill, Royalist cavalry had jumped over hedges barring their way and it seems apparent that whatever obstacles existed between Fairfax's wing and that of Goring likewise did not prove insuperable.

Once beyond, many of the troopers found themselves on the moorland where clumps of gorse bushes rendered orderly progress difficult. The horse on the right of the wing did not have to make their way onto the moor, for the opposing cavalry was drawn up on cultivated ground to the east of Atterwith Lane.

The troopers who had progressed this far proceeded to charge Goring, who counterattacked. Some of the Roundheads reportedly did very well, for as noted, Stewart relates that five or six troops managed to charge through their opponents. Fairfax recalled that 'with much difficulty I could get but 5 Troops' [i.e., 'a body of 400 horse'] 'in order: with which I charged the Enemy's Left Wing'. A fierce struggle ensued: 'We were a long time engaged one with another; but at last we routed that part of their Wing...and pursued them a good way towards York'.

It seems that the routed troopers had belonged to the left of Goring's wing. The bulk of his command, however, fared better, much better. They successfully dealt with the disordered troopers who came against them. Only Eglinton's Scottish regiment managed to partly halt the progress of the 'Cavalier-like assault' (W. H.), but after some hard fighting they too were driven off.

Many of the musketeers posted in support of the allied horse must have been cut down by the enemy or been trampled under foot. It is moreover recorded that in their haste to get away some of the broken horse overrode men on the right of the allied centre. As for Goring's victorious troopers, they pursued the fugitives as far as the crest of the ridge. Indeed, some continued the chase far beyond.

The collapse of the allied right wing seems to have occurred at about the same time as Blakiston's charge, for Cholmeley and the Parliamentarian, Edmund Ludlow, link Goring's success with the flight of the allied generals, and it is reasonable to suppose that they would have only quit the field if the allied centre seemed to be collapsing as well.

Certainly, by this stage of the battle widespread confusion reigned. As has been noted, the Royalist right wing had been routed, and the right flank of the Royalist centre had been turned. The allied right wing had, on the whole collapsed, and in so doing had caused some disorder on the right of the allied centre where many of the infantry took to flight, as did other allied foot attacked by Blakiston.

It is thus easy to imagine the scene which confronted a gentleman approaching the field with dispatches for Prince Rupert. His name was Arthur Trevor and he later recalled, 'in the fire, smoke and confusion of that day, I knew not for my soul wither to incline. The runaways on both sides were so many, so breathless, so speechless, and so full of fears, that I should not have taken them for men'.

It is evident that when the bulk of Fairfax's wing faltered Royalist horse of Goring's second line under Sir Charles Lucas moved against the exposed right flank of the allied centre, an action referred to earlier, and clashed with a Scottish brigade comprising the regiments of Lord Crawford-Lindsay and Lord Maitland. As Peter Newman has commented of this encounter: 'The fight between Lucas's cavalry and the Scottish regiments was a classic of infantry–cavalry fighting'. Twice Lucas charged against the foot (who it will be remembered were also assailed by Royalist infantry), but on both occasions the hedgehog of pikes prevented him from breaking the doughty Scots. Then the latter, as noted earlier, received reinforcements. Once again, though, Lucas came against them only to fail for the third time. Indeed, on this occasion he was captured and what remained of his dispirited horse gave up the struggle.

By now Cromwell was approaching, after circling the moor with elements of Crawford's foot in support, and cutting down Royalists unfortunate enough to get in the way. With Cromwell was Sir Thomas Fairfax who had returned from pursuing that part of Goring's wing he had routed. Fairfax tells us that he returned alone to the field to meet up with the men he had left behind, bearing a cut to his cheek. Upon finding that they had been put to flight, and that he was among bodies of enemy horse, he removed the field sign from his hat and made his way across to join Cromwell.

Interestingly, Captain Stewart makes no mention of a pursuit. He relates that upon charging through Goring's wing with five or six troops Fairfax and the cavalry with him 'went to the left wing of horse' that is, to join Cromwell, and that two squadrons of Balgonie's regiment (which had been stationed in Fairfax's third line), subsequently did likewise. One did so after clashing with a Royalist regiment of foot and putting it 'wholly to the rout', while the other, 'by another way', also joined Manchester's lieutenant-general of horse. In short it seems that though a pursuit of part of Goring's wing did take place, Fairfax was not the only one from his wing to make his way across to join Cromwell at some time or other.

As Cromwell and those with him drew near Atterwith Lane they came under fire from the Marquis of Newcastle's regiment commanded by Sir William Lambton, which may, as Newman maintains, have taken up a position in one or more of the Hatterwith enclosures just to the east of the lane. Cromwell moved against the regiment (which had been raised in north Durham and about Newcastle upon Tyne in 1642), but failed to make any significant headway. Hence he pressed on, leaving Fraser's dragoons and Leslie's horse to deal with the isolated infantry regiment.

Cromwell and his Eastern Association horse proceeded to engage what remained of Goring's wing. Cholmeley records that many of the Royalist commander's men were 'dispersed in pursuit' of fleeing allied soldiers, and he was therefore greatly outnumbered in this action, of which Watson wrote: 'And here came the business of the day'. Watson continues:

'The enemy [i.e., the Royalists], seeing us to come in such a gallant posture to charge them...began to thinke that they must fight again for that victory which they thought had been already got. They marching down the Hill upon us, from our Carriages, so that they fought upon the same ground, and with the same Front that our right wing had before stood to receive their charge; and we stood in the same ground, and with the same Front which they had when they began the charge'.

According to Sir Richard Bulstrode, Goring was 'without dispute as good an officer as any who served the King and the most dexterous in any emergency that I have ever seen'. This was no doubt the case now. Though outnumbered, Goring and the Cavaliers with him evidently fought resolutely and many of them paid with their lives. Among those who were killed or mortally wounded were Colonel Sir Richard Dacre, Colonel William Eure and Major Francis Salvin. Eventually, the Royalists who were able to do so, abandoned the struggle they could not win and made good their escape.

Meanwhile, the regiment under Lambton had been destroyed. Of the gallant soldiers in question, William Lilly (whose informant Captain Camby fought against them) wrote, 'by mere valour, for one whole hour, [they] kept the troops of horse from entering among them....When the horse did enter, they would have no quarter, but fought it out till there was not thirty of them living.' Camby, who was one of the first to enter among them 'protested he never in all the fights he was in, met with such resolute brave fellows'. Others too were impressed by what they saw or heard of this action. The Duchess of Newcastle wrote that her husband's 'White Coats showed such an extraordinary valour and courage...that they were killed in rank and file'. The performance of the doughty foot under Lambton, who was among the slain, was undoubtedly remarkable and has evoked admiration to this day.

By the time Lambton's regiment was destroyed the battle was almost over. Some of Leslie's horse and Fraser's dragoons may now have gone to the assistance of the allied foot engaged against what remained of the Royalist centre – if indeed any resistance were still being offered – while at least some of Leslie's troopers assisted Cromwell by carrying out a flank attack on Goring.

According to Watson the battle was over and the field cleared of the enemy by about 9.00pm. However, it is likely that the fighting continued for some time after this. Moreover a motley body of Royalist cavalry, said to have been 2,000 strong and apparently primarily composed of troopers of Goring's wing who had returned too late from pursuing fleeing allied soldiers to fight against Cromwell, or had refrained from doing so, remained on the ridge until about midnight. The troopers then rode off towards York, leaving the exhausted allies in possession of the field. Manchester was among the latter, and Ashe tells us that he rode around thanking the soldiers 'for the exceeding good service which they had done for the kingdom'.

During the course of 3 and 4 July the dead were buried. Ashe relates that the countrymen commanded to perform the task calculated that they buried 4,150 bodies. But more persons who fought at Marston Moor lost their lives than this, for many were slain in flight. Watson, for instance, states that fugitives were cut down to within a mile of York. Furthermore many individuals must have perished in the days and weeks to come from wounds they had sustained. It has been estimated that at least 6,000 men, all told, died as a result of Marston Moor and this figure seems reasonable.

The majority of the fatalities were Royalist, and included a significant number of officers. In addition, at least 1,500 of the vanquished were captured. The Royalists also lost their entire artillery train, a great quantity of arms, (10,000 according to the allied generals' dispatch), powder, ammunition, baggage, and about 100 colours.

And what of the allies? The *Despatch* states: 'Our loss is not very great, being only one lieut-colonel, a few captains, and 200 or 300 common soldiers'. It is reasonable, however, to conclude that allied losses were greater than this. After all, they had encountered stiff resistance from much of the Royalist army. Fairfax, for example, recalled of his charge which routed part of Goring's wing that 'few of us came off without dangerous wounds; and many were mortal'. In short, probably about one-third of the total number of those who perished at, or as a result of, Marston Moor were allied soldiers.

It is recorded that Prince Rupert (whose actions during the battle following the rout of the Royalist right wing are, to say the least, uncertain), arrived at York at about 11pm on the 2nd. There he met, or was joined by, Eythin. They were later joined by Newcastle who had remained on the field longer than either. According to Cholmeley, the following morning Rupert wished to attempt 'something upon the enemy' but was persuaded against doing so by Eythin.

On the 3rd Newcastle made for Scarborough – where the governor of the castle was Cholmeley – intent on going into exile, likely in the belief that he would be made a scapegoat for the defeat. He sailed to Hamburg. At Marston Moor much of his army had been destroyed and the bulk of his general staff, including Eythin, likewise sailed from Scarborough rather than continue the fight against the king's enemies.

On the other hand, Rupert left York on the 3rd at the head of about 3,500 men, mostly horse, and proceeded to recross the Pennines, no doubt with a rather heavy heart considering the outcome of Marston Moor; the loss of several personal friends in the battle, including his dog, Boy, a companion since his days of incarceration at Linz; and Newcastle's decision to give up the struggle for the marquis had expended a fortune in the king's service and was the man to whom the Royalists in the north naturally looked for leadership. On 5 August Rupert arrived back at Shrewsbury.

Meanwhile, the allies had soon resumed besieging York after Marston Moor. Within days of them doing so, its governor, Sir Thomas Glemham, had come to terms with the allied generals. Thus on 16 July he marched out of the city at the head of those members of its garrison who did not wish to lay down arms, and headed towards Knaresborough. Slingsby records that some of the soldiers then headed for Carlisle with Glemham whereas members of Rupert's army who had been left at York after Marston Moor 'took the nearest way to go to the Prince'.

Shortly after the capitulation of York the allied army split up. Manchester moved south; Lord Fairfax commenced reducing the remaining Royalists garrisons in Yorkshire (Skipton was the last to fall, some eighteen months later); while Leven moved north and captured Newcastle upon Tyne on 22 October.

It only remains to assess the performance of the senior figures at Marston Moor and the battle's importance. As has been noted, apart from his decision to commence the battle at an opportune time, Leven did not distinguish himself, and Somerville tells us that when the general received news of the 'most glorious victory' he 'knocked upon his breast' and stated: 'I would to God that I had died upon the place'. Lord Fairfax likewise rejoined the allied army under a cloud.

On the other hand Manchester, Crawford, Baillie, Lumsden and Sir Thomas Fairfax, conducted themselves creditably. The same can be said of Cromwell, who was ably seconded by Leslie. Indeed, he was the chief architect of the allied victory. As Peter Newman has commented: 'Cromwell's initial triumph was crucial to the outcome of the battle, for he was able, with his strong cavalry well in hand, to move across the battlefield taking the enemy in flank and rear, undermining their resolve...much of the honour won by the Allies on July 2nd 1644 is rightfully Cromwell's.'

Rupert's conduct of the campaign and battle is worthy of both commendation and censure. His actions in the north-west in May and June before making for York were sensible, for instead of acting precipitously he built up the strength of his army and took steps to reduce the likelihood of Parliamentary raids during his absence from the region. Moreover, his subsequent march from Knaresborough to York via Boroughbridge and Thornton Bridge was a classic manoeuvre. Furthermore, his deployment of the Royalist forces at Marston Moor showed some sound tactical thinking. For instance, good use was made of the natural obstacles of the battlefield; Napier's men were well placed to support Byron; and Blakiston's brigade was unusually placed to support the weak centre.

On the other hand, Rupert has been criticised for a number of reasons. The principal complaint is that he committed his numerically weaker forces to battle with the allies – yes, he had to save York if possible, but he did not have to follow up his success by confronting the allies, especially in view of the likelihood that the allied army would have soon fragmented. It will perhaps be remembered that Newcastle thought such a development likely. That 'irreconcilable differences and jealousies', to quote Clarendon, existed 'between the officers and the nations' may have been the case, but the prince believed that he could not afford to wait and see whether this would prove true. Unaware of a recent victory by his uncle at Cropredy Bridge on 29 June, he wished to conclude the northern campaign as soon as possible so that he could go to the king's assistance. Moreover, if he had not decided to resolve matters by battle the allies could simply have turned their attention to York once again after he had marched off. Furthermore, it has to be borne in mind that on the evening of 1 July Rupert did not know that the allies would decide against fighting. Hence one can understand why, after carrying out a brilliant outflanking manoeuvre and throwing the enemy off balance, he was eager to press home his advantage. True, the decision was a daring one and asked much of his men who had just undergone a strenuous march, and of Newcastle's army, which had experienced the rigours of a lengthy siege, but whether it was a wrong one is less clear cut.

The general consensus is that it was a mistake: the impetuous prince got carried away and threw commonsense out the window, thereby squandering many lives in a disastrous battle. In contrast, General Sir Frank Kitson has recently commented, 'it is surprising that historians have been so slow to recognise the tactical imperatives that drove Rupert on', and that 'Rupert was correct in...engaging the enemy as soon as possible'. On balance, it seems Kitson is right. It is certainly worth bearing in mind how close Rupert came to success at Marston Moor: the allied victory was certainly not easily won.

Rupert has also been censured for allowing his men to relax on the evening of the 2nd when several hours of daylight remained. The criticism is sound.

Although it was unusual for an army to attack at such a time, it was nonetheless unwise of the prince to let his men rest when such a large enemy force was overlooking his position. Perhaps his decision resulted from tiredness and despondency caused by the attitudes and actions of subordinates, most notably Eythin.

And what of Newcastle and Eythin? Though the former believed that Rupert was acting precipitously in bringing the allies to battle on the 2nd, he fought bravely, exhorted others to do likewise, and was the last of the Royalist generals to quit the field. Eythin's behaviour, though, deserves censure. He had a long-standing grudge against Rupert (whom he blamed for losing the battle of Vlotho, and for whose capture there he had been blamed), and his late arrival at Marston Moor was more probably due to tardiness and lack of confidence in the prince than anything else. Furthermore, upon his arrival he rudely stated upon being shown a plan of battle by Rupert: 'By God, sir, it is very fine in the paper, but there is no such thing in the field'. It seems fair to conclude that Eythin was more of a hindrance than an asset.

Lord Byron has likewise been censured by historians. At the very least, he moved against Cromwell prematurely, and at worst, in so doing disobeyed orders. What is undoubted is that the failure of Byron's wing enabled Cromwell to support Crawford in turning the right flank of the Royalist centre, and then carry out the manoeuvre which made it wellnigh impossible for the Royalists to win the battle.

In the centre, Major-General Henry Tillier, who was considered a resolute fellow, seems to have performed creditably. The same can be said of Goring. Indeed, his performance is praiseworthy. He led his wing in a well-timed counterattack against Sir Thomas Fairfax, and then gallantly confronted Cromwell in a stubborn contest in which the latter held the advantages and thus not surprisingly was victorious.

Marston Moor was the greatest battle of the Civil War. It was also one of the most important. It destroyed Prince Rupert's legend of invincibility, brought Cromwell more into the limelight, and to all intents and purposes lost the north for the king. The psychological impact of the defeat on the Royalist party was such that in the months which followed the engagement it failed to respond positively to the challenge which faced it in the region, and thus allowed the enemy to gain control of a part of England which, in the main, had been a valuable recruiting ground and source of contributions to the Royalist war effort.

Oliver Cromwell attributed the allied victory at Marston Moor to divine intervention. Immediately after the battle he wrote to his brother-in-law, Valentine Walton, stating: 'Truely England and the Church of God hath had a great favour from the Lord, in this great victory given to us, such as the like never was since this war began'. A 'great victory' it certainly was, but it did not end the Civil War, and in similar circumstances in the future Cromwell was to have reason to praise the Almighty again.

22

AULDEARN
9 MAY 1645

In 1638 a committee of Scottish nobles and divines drew up the National Covenant, which called for the defence of Presbyterianism against the 'papist' policies pursued by Charles I and his supporters. Opposition to the king was such that a large Scottish army subsequently crossed the border (January 1644) to fight on behalf of parliament during the Civil War.

However, some Scots were Royalists. The most notable was James Graham, first Marquis of Montrose. He had signed the Covenant but had become disenchanted by the extremism of fellow influential Covenanters. In August 1644 he crossed into his homeland, having received the king's commission at Oxford to secure Scotland for the Royalist cause. He entered the country with only two companions, but soon received a degree of support, and on the 28th raised the royal standard in Atholl.

Montrose was a friendly, courteous man, and Gordon of Ruthven relates that he 'quickly made a conquesse of the hearts of all his followers'. What is more, he soon showed that he was a man of military ability. He won an engagement at Tippermuir (1 September) and proceeded to beat other numerically superior Covenanter forces. For example, on 2 February 1645 he inflicted a crushing defeat at Inverlochy on the Campbell clansmen of the most important Covenanter of them all, the Marquis of Argyll.

Montrose thus greatly angered the Covenanters and caused consternation in their ranks. This was a situation one of them, Colonel John Hurry, was determined to rectify. He decided to lure the marquis into country hostile to the Royalist cause and engage him there in advantageous circumstances at the head of the army under his command.

Consequently, when Montrose advanced towards Elgin from Skene on 2 May, Hurry fell back west to Forres and then to Inverness where he received reinforcements. On the night of Thursday 8 May Montrose encamped at Auldearn, a small village on a low ridge two miles east of Nairn. Hurry moved against him, conducting a rapid night march from Inverness. Thus on the 9th, with his opponent closing in, Montrose prepared for battle. He placed part of his army of nearly 3,000 men just to the north of the village under Alasdair MacDonald. The bulk of his men he stationed to the south of Auldearn, on the reverse slope of the ridge. The royal standard was with MacDonald and Montrose hoped that Hurry would attack Alasdair in the belief that he was engaging the entire army, thereby allowing Montrose himself to fall upon Hurry's right flank.

As the Covenanter army of 400 horse and 3,500 foot made its way across marshy ground to the west, MacDonald disobeyed orders to remain where he was and charged down to engage the enemy. Fierce fighting ensued and Alasdair's outnumbered men were pushed back towards their original position. As Montrose prepared to move to their assistance Hurry, who was now aware of the marquis' position, ordered Captain Drummond to turn his horse to the right to face the threat, but the order was misheard and Drummond turned left instead. Not surprisingly, his troopers were soon routed by cavalry sent against them. Simultaneously, Royalist horse hitherto inactive on Alasdair's right, attacked Hurry's left flank. MacDonald was then joined by Montrose and they began pushing back the enemy centre. The battle soon became a rout, and at least 2,000 Covenanters perished in all. Montrose's reputation was going from strength to strength – a legend was in the making.

23

NASEBY
14 JUNE 1645

*'Our victories, the price of blood invaluable, so gallantly gotten and,
which is more pity, so graciously bestowed, seem to have been put in a bag with
holes; what we won one time, we lost another. The treasure is exhausted; the country
is wasted. A summer's victory has proved but a winter's story.... Men's hearts have
failed them with the observation of these things.'*
—A Parliamentarian

The above words date from December 1644 and clearly reflect the despondency felt by many of those opposed to King Charles. Despite their great victory at Marston Moor earlier in the year, they had failed to truly capitalise on their success, thereby prolonging the Civil War. Indeed, they had suffered a number of setbacks. At Lostwithiel, on 2 September, for instance, General Skippon had been forced to surrender at the head of over 6,000 men, while on 27 October a large Parliamentarian army had failed to defeat a numerically inferior Royalist force at the Second Battle of Newbury. Furthermore, by this date the Marquis of Montrose had two victories to his credit in Scotland, where he had recently commenced campaigning on behalf of the king.

Thus the closing months of 1644 found the Parliamentarians in an acrimonious mood. Leading figures quarrelled and blamed each other for not bringing the war to a successful conclusion. But some did more. They discussed ways of improving military efficiency and the quality of their forces.

In common with their opponents, the Parliamentarian generals had a number of problems to contend with. One such was the difficulty of maintaining the strength of their armies. For a variety of reasons, including arrears of pay and an unwillingness on the part of many men to serve away from their own locality, especially for long periods, desertion was commonplace.

The situation warranted the formation of an army which would serve wherever it was needed and for as long as circumstances required: a force which would receive regular pay and whose commander, instead of desiring a negotiated peace, as was the case with some Parliamentarian generals, would be determined to prosecute the war until victory was attained.

Consequently, on 19 November, the Commons ordered the Committee of Both Kingdoms to conduct an examination of the state of all Parliamentarian armies and, some days later, instructed it to put forward 'a Frame or Model of a New Militia' with which the war could be won. On 9 December the committee held a full-scale debate on the reformation of the entire military system. Then, on 9 January 1645, its proposal that a force of 8,000 horse, 1,500 dragoons and 16,000 foot should be established, was submitted to the Commons. Two days later the size of the planned New Model Army, which was to be formed by merging three Parliamentarian armies: that of the Earl of Essex, and those of the Eastern Association and Sir William Waller, was reduced by votes to 6,000 horse (later increased to 6,600) 1,000 dragoons and 14,400 foot.

On 21 January the Commons voted in favour of Sir Thomas Fairfax being appointed commander-in-chief of the proposed New Model Army. Furthermore, on the 28th it passed an ordinance for the creation of the New Model which was then sent to the Lords. After much debate, and some compromise, (the Commons for instance conceded that the peers could have a say in the selection of officers), the Lords reluctantly passed the ordinance on 15 February.

Fairfax was an able soldier. Significantly, moreover, he was not a politician. By this date there was a strong feeling that politicians should no longer exercise military command. Indeed, on 9 December Cromwell had stated in the Commons that people were saying that 'the members of both Houses had got great places and commands' and would 'perpetually continue themselves in grandeur and not permit the war to speedily end lest their own power would determine [end] with it'. Zouch Tate had then proposed that 'during the time of this war, no member of either house shall have or execute any office or command, granted or conferred by both or either of the Houses...and that an ordinance be brought in accordingly'. After some debating the resultant bill was passed by the Commons on 19 December.

The Lords however did not share their enthusiasm. Among other things, the ordinance would after all deprive peers of their historic function as military leaders. Thus in early January they rejected the Self-Denying Ordinance and it was not until 3 April that they accepted a modified version which obliged members of parliament to lay down their commands within 40 days, but did not prohibit their reappointment.

By this date a vigorous recruitment campaign was underway. The merging of the three armies referred to above had not provided enough men to fill the ranks of the New Model. Furthermore, at about this time supplies for the force began arriving at the army stores at Reading, for contracts had been made with about 200 suppliers to provide arms and equipment. Money to pay for the supplies and the soldiers' wages came from a variety of sources: most notably a loan from the City of London and a monthly assessment totalling £53,436 levied on the counties under parliament's control which had commenced on 1 February.

And what of the king? In the early spring of 1645 he was at Oxford, the Royalist capital, in sanguine mood. He believed the war could still be won despite recent reverses, (the most important being the loss of Shrewsbury on 22 February), and the formation of the New Model. On 27 March he stated in a letter to his wife, Henriette Marie, who was in France, 'the general face of my affairs...begins to mend...Montrose daily prospering, my Western business mending apace, and hopeful of all the rest'.

Charles' nephew, Prince Rupert, who had been appointed commander of the king's forces the previous November in succession to the Earl of Brentford, was in the west of England, attempting to restore Royalist fortunes following the loss of Shrewsbury which had served as a vital link between Oxford and areas such as Cheshire and North Wales. On 31 March Rupert was at Hereford. From there he sent a letter to Oxford to the effect that Charles should take the field. But the king did not act with any alacrity, and thus played into the hands of his enemies.

It was undoubtedly in the best interests of Charles' opponents to prevent him from taking the field during the critical period of the formation of the New Model, and so on 20 April the Committee of Both Kingdoms sent orders to Cromwell instructing him to prevent the king from joining Rupert and the Royalist forces in Herefordshire and Worcestershire. Among other things, he was ordered to 'take all advantages you can against the enemy for the public good'. He was to do so very successfully at the head of a brigade of horse.

On 24 April, for instance, he routed a Royalist force led by the dashing young Earl of Northampton near Islip Bridge and in so doing captured 200 men and many horses. Cromwell then moved against Bletchingdon House, a short distance north of Oxford. The Royalist governor was Lieutenant-Colonel Francis Windebanke, and although as Cromwell himself said, the house was 'strong and well manned', Windebanke surrendered without a shot being fired. It is said that his decision was due to the presence of his young wife and several other ladies. Whatever the reason, Windebanke, who had fought courageously at Cheriton, was subsequently court-martialled and shot on 3 May.

Following the capture of Bletchingdon Cromwell moved west. While doing so he encountered a Royalist force of some 350 foot at Bampton-in-the-Bush, and after some fighting forced it to capitulate. He then moved against Faringdon Castle. On 29 April he summoned it to surrender. The summons was refused. By now Cromwell had been reinforced by between 500 and 600 foot from Abingdon, and on the following day he attempted to storm the castle. The assault failed, and a few days later, on Saturday 3 May, as the diary of the Royalist Richard Symonds records, 'Cromwell's forces removed from before Farringdon'.

Nonetheless Cromwell's activities had been largely successful, so successful in fact that the king remained in Oxford for he found himself without the requisite number of draught horses to move his guns, owing to Cromwell's seizure of all he could find. Instead of Charles moving to join Rupert, he was obliged to summon his nephew to Oxford. The prince arrived on 4 May accompanied by his brother, Maurice. The following day Lord Goring also arrived, after being summoned to join the king with his forces from Somerset. On the 7th, Charles finally rode out of the city, thereby commencing what proved to be the most important campaign of the Civil War.

By this date Fairfax was likewise on the march, having left Windsor on 30 April with the bulk of the New Model: the rest of parliament's new war machine was in the vicinity of Oxford under Cromwell. On 23 April the New Model had been reported as being 15,000 strong in total, but its strength was now estimated at between 20–21,000 officers and men.

Fairfax moved west, with orders to relieve Taunton. By 7 May he had arrived at Blandford in Dorset. Here he received new orders from the Committee of Both Kingdoms, which had been alarmed by Rupert's arrival at Oxford. He was now to send four regiments of foot, two of horse, and a train of artillery, to relieve Taunton – which was achieved on 11 May – and was to march with the rest of his men towards Oxford and rendezvous with Cromwell with the aim of investing the city.

Hence, after linking up with Cromwell en route, Fairfax proceeded to besiege Oxford later in the month as the Committee of Both Kingdoms had ordered. 'We have designed,' stated the committee, 'this as the main action, to be prosecuted with all such forces as are not already employed elsewhere, unless any special exigency should require these forces to be otherwise employed'.

Though the king was no longer in Oxford the decision to besiege the city was a good one. Charles' opponents were perturbed over which way he would strike and generally believed that a full-scale siege of his principal base would compel him to abandon whatever designs he had in order to defend the city and the Royalist womenfolk who had been left there.

As for the king, following his departure from Oxford he journeyed to Woodstock where he spent the night. The next day he moved to Stow-on-the-Wold. Here he held a council of war. The combined Royalist forces totalled 6,300 horse and 5,300 foot and opinion was divided over strategy. Rupert wished to head north, partly with the aim of tackling a Scottish army in Yorkshire under the Earl of Leven which had crossed into England in January 1644 and had recently lost some regiments which had been recalled to serve against Montrose. If such a course were adopted the Royalists had a chance of saving besieged garrisons, avenging Marston Moor, and recovering the north where recruits and money would no doubt be forthcoming. Charles seems to have favoured Rupert's counsel. Others, however, most notably the king's Secretary of State Lord Digby, and Goring, wished to move against Fairfax and the New Model, known to be moving to the relief of Taunton. A compromise resulted. Goring was sent to harass Fairfax with 3,000 horse, while Charles and the bulk of his men headed north. Lord Clarendon attributed this decision to jealousy on the part of Rupert. The prince and Goring were not on the best of terms and Clarendon states that the former feared that the eloquent Goring, 'a man of ready wit', would undermine his authority and get the better of him in future debates on how best to prosecute the war.

Charles left Stow-on-the-Wold on the 9th. Two days later he arrived at Droitwich. Since leaving Oxford he had moved north-west and the Committee of Both Kingdoms was therefore of the opinion that he was heading 'towards Cheshire and those parts' where a number of Royalists garrisons were besieged.

Charles did indeed move north from Droitwich – where he lingered until the 14th – intent on relieving the town of Chester. At Market Drayton, however, he was joined by Lord Byron who informed him that the siege had been abandoned. This news, and intelligence that Leven was moving from Yorkshire into Westmorland, made Charles change direction for he decided to make for Scotland (where Montrose had recently gained another victory) via the eastern side of the country.

He arrived at Burton on Trent on the 25th. Here he heard that Oxford had just been invested. Was it necessary for the king to move against the New Model in order to save the Royalist capital? Rupert thought not. He believed that if Charles moved against a place of importance to parliament Fairfax would probably be drawn away from Oxford in order to respond to the challenge. The council of war agreed. It was thus decided to march against the prosperous town of Leicester.

On 30 May Rupert summoned the town to surrender. The Royalist army may now have numbered nearly 11,000 men, having recently been augmented, most notably on the 28th by Sir Richard Willis, the governor of Newark, at the head of 1,200 horse. In contrast, Leicester, whose fortifications had been neglected, was defended by 2,070 men, 900 of whom were simply 'inhabitants capable of bearing arms'. Nonetheless, the summons was refused. Hence at about 3.00pm the Royalists commenced a cannonade. Then, at around midnight, they charged the town's battered defences and, after some ferocious fighting, Leicester was in Royalist hands. Clarendon tells us that 'the conquerors pursued their advantage with the utmost license, and miserably sacked the whole town without distinction of people or places to the exceeding regret of the King'. Two or three hundred Royalists lost their lives storming Leicester, but the number of defenders and townsfolk in general who perished must have been greater.

Charles left Leicester on 4 June at the head of an army which had been depleted somewhat by the losses sustained, the desertion of troops laden with loot, Willis' departure for Newark at the head of 400 of his horse, and by his own decision to garrison the town. (The bulk of Leicester's new garrison was made up of local men, but in addition to the raw country recruits the force, over 1,000 strong, included experienced units of Charles' army).

On the 5th Charles arrived at Market Harborough, for he had decided to move south to the relief of Oxford, a decision which according to his secretary, Sir Edward Walker, was 'much against the will of prince Rupert'. The latter believed that the New Model would move north in view of the storming of Leicester.

He was right. The Committee of Both Kingdoms feared that Charles would now move towards East Anglia, a prosperous region of great importance to parliament. Consequently, on 5 June Fairfax abandoned the siege of Oxford and commenced moving north-east to intercept the king. He was pleased to do so. Only the previous day, just prior to receiving new orders, he had lamented in a letter to his father: 'I am very sorry we shall spend our time unprofitably before a town whilst the king hath time to strengthen himself and by terror to force obedience of all places where he comes....It is the earnest desire of the army to follow the king..'.

On the 7th Fairfax arrived at Sherrington, a mile north-east of Newport Pagnell. Two days later he moved to Stony Stratford, a short distance to the south-west, where he halted until the 11th when he advanced north to Wootton near Northampton. By now he had received welcome news from his superiors that the future conduct of the campaign would be left 'wholly' to him and his council of war, a decision made by the Committee of Both Kingdoms on the 9th. Moreover, Fairfax had just received permission from the Commons to recall Cromwell from East Anglia, where he had been strengthening its defences since the beginning of June, to serve as his lieutenant-general of horse.

By this time Fairfax knew that Charles was not moving towards East Anglia, for he had moved south-west from Market Harborough and had arrived at Daventry on, or by, the 7th. Here the king heard that the siege of Oxford had been raised. This, and the expected imminent arrival of reinforcements under Sir Charles Gerard and Goring who had been summoned to his side from Wales and the West Country respectively, put Charles in a very optimistic mood. On the 8th he stated in a letter to his wife: 'I may without being too much sanguine affirm that since this rebellion [began] my affairs were never in so hopeful a way'.

That the king was in a relaxed frame of mind is indicated by his decision to send a large number of impounded cattle and sheep, with an escort of 1,200 cavalry, to provision Oxford. Consequently, for some days he remained at Daventry with his weakened army, awaiting the escort, and passing his time by hunting.

The delay played into the hands of his enemies. Fairfax was closing in at the head of the New Model. On the 12th he left Wootton and moved west to Kislingbury, only nine miles from Daventry. That afternoon cavalry patrols skirmished with Royalist outposts – Charles' days of hunting in the neighbourhood were over.

News of the proximity of the New Model was an unwelcome surprise to the king who had just been rejoined, on the night of the 11/12th, by the escort. As quickly as possible the Royalist army, which had been relaxing, was assembled on Borough Hill just to the east of Daventry, where it stood to arms till day-break. The Royalists then commenced moving off towards Market Harborough for at this juncture Charles and Rupert did not wish to engage the New Model and had decided to make for Newark, where they could receive reinforcements from that and neighbouring garrisons. They reached Market Harborough after a day's march of some twenty miles.

Fairfax was in pursuit. He had the upper hand and was determined to retain it. He also knew that Goring was not moving to join the king. At about 5.00am on the 13th (while still at Kislingbury) Scoutmaster-General Lionel Watson had brought him an intercepted letter from Goring to Rupert which stated that the Royalist commander was not marching to join the king, for among other things, he claimed that ill-health had prevented him from leaving the West Country. Moreover, shortly after receiving this welcome information, and just prior to setting off in pursuit of the king, Fairfax had been joined by Cromwell at the head of 600 cavalry and Joshua Sprigge, the chief Parliamentarian source for Naseby, relates that Cromwell had been received 'with the greatest joy' by Fairfax 'and the whole army'.

The New Model quartered for the night at Guilsborough, some thirteen miles from Market Harborough after marching via Northampton. However a strong body of horse under Henry Ireton pressed on, and surprised a Royalist rearguard at Naseby while the men were playing quoits or having supper.

At about 11.00pm Charles, who was at Lubenham two miles west of Market Harborough, heard of this incident and made his way to Market Harborough to join Rupert. The prince, who was resting in a chair, was roused and a council of war called for midnight.

To fight, or not to fight. That was the question. It was answered in the affirmative by, among others, two influential courtiers, Digby and Sir John Ashburnham: if Charles tried to avoid battle New Model horse could fall upon the retreating Royalists and badly maul them. Rupert, though, was against fighting. He favoured making for Leicester, sixteen miles away. He was not alone, but was nonetheless overruled. As Sprigge records in his well-informed account, 'the Kings Counsel prevailed against the minde of the most of his great Officers, who were of opinion, that it was best to avoid fighting'. Some comfort, though, could be derived from the fact that the Royalist army was only threatened by the New Model and not by Leven's army as well which – primarily owing to Montrose's continued success in Scotland – had not obeyed summonses from the Committee of Both Kingdoms to move urgently south against Charles.

At 2.00am on the 14th the Royalists began mustering at Market Harborough. This took some time for many of the soldiers had to be brought in from neighbouring villages. After several hours had elapsed they moved south a short distance to 'rising Ground of very great Advantage' as Walker recalled, between East Farndon and Great Oxendon, and were 'put in order and disposed to give or receive the Charge'.

Meanwhile, Fairfax had likewise been on the move. Sprigge relates: 'The General...advanced by three of the clock in the morning from Gilling [Guilsborough] towards Naseby [six miles to the north] with an intention to follow close upon the Enemy....By five in the morning, the Army was at a Rendezvouz near Naseby, where his Excellency received intelligence...that the Enemy was at Harborough'. At this point, we are told, Fairfax was uncertain about the Royalists' intentions. 'But immediately' Sprigge continues, 'the doubt was resolved: great Bodies of the Enemies Horse were discerned on the top of the hill on this side of Harborough, which increasing more and more in our view, begat a confidence in the General, and the residue of the Officers that he meant not to draw away, as some imagined, but that he was putting his Army in order, either there to receive us, or to come to us..'.

Apparently, Fairfax subsequently rode forward from his commanding position, just to the north-east of Naseby, at the head of an escort to reconnoitre the undulating ground between his army and that of the king some four miles or so to the north. Evidently, as he approached Clipston he came across a position with boggy ground beyond it, which he seems to have deemed suitable for the deployment of his army. According to a certain W. G., Cromwell persuaded him against adopting such a course, believing that the waterlogged nature of the ground in front of the position would lead Rupert to decline battle or turn the flank. He thus exclaimed: 'Let us, I beseech you, draw back to yonder hill, which will encourage the enemy to charge us, which they cannot do in that place without absolute ruin'. Fairfax agreed, and began riding back to the Naseby ridge where the bulk of the New Model was assembled. It will be remembered that Sprigge states that the New Model had rendezvoused near Naseby by 5.00am. There can be no doubt, however, that the march from Guilsborough took longer than he believed and stragglers were probably still arriving as Fairfax returned from his reconnaissance.

Fairfax was not the only one who undertook a reconnaissance mission. According to Walker, the Royalist scoutmaster, Francis Ruce, rode forward at about 8.00am, and he evidently did so before Fairfax. Visibility seems to have worsened and the Royalists were uncertain about the New Model's movements. Walker relates that Ruce returned 'with a Lye in his Mouth', stating 'that he had been two or three miles forward, and could neither discover or hear of the Rebels'. At this, states Clarendon, 'a report was raised in the army that the enemy was retired. Rupert now rode forward at the head of a strong body of horse to determine the state of affairs himself.

In so doing, apparently in the neighbourhood of Clipston, he caught sight of Fairfax and his escort riding back towards the high ground about Naseby. Rupert may, as one or two of his contemporaries state, have concluded that Fairfax was intent on withdrawing, or perhaps he believed that he had a chance of falling upon the Roundheads before they were ready to receive him. What is certain is that he sent for the rest of the Royalist army to advance as fast as possible. As the ground before him was largely waterlogged, Rupert turned to his right to find more suitable terrain.

The Royalists' movements were seen by their adversaries. Sprigge continues: 'The Enemies Army...we saw plainly advancing in order towards us: and the winde blowing somewhat Westwardly, by the Enemies advance so much on their right hand, it was evident, that he designed to get the winde of us: which occasioned the General to draw down into a large fallow field on the Northwest side of Naseby, flanked on the left hand with a hedge, which was a convenient place for us to fight the Enemy in'.

Thus if Rupert believed that Fairfax was intent on withdrawal, he was soon disabused of the notion. As the Roundheads took up a position on the north slope of high ground a short distance from Naseby, the Royalists therefore prepared for battle on the south slope of Dust Hill. Between the armies was a shallow valley comprising a large open tract of land known as Broad Moor.

The Parliamentarians, however, soon drew back somewhat so that most of them were concealed from the enemy by the brow of the ridge. Just why Fairfax ordered this retrograde movement is uncertain. Perhaps, as Sprigge comments, he did so in order to prevent the Royalists seeing 'in what form' the New Model was deployed 'nor see any confusion therein'. It has, moreover, been suggested that Fairfax wished to ease the pre-battle tension of his new recruits.

Before discussing events further, it will be profitable to say something about the principal protagonists and the opposing armies.

CHARLES AND THE ROYALIST ARMY

Charles was born in Scotland in 1600 and succeeded his father James VI of Scotland and I of England in 1625. When the Civil War commenced in 1642 he had no taste of battle and at Edgehill appointed an experienced Scottish soldier, Lord Forth, commander-in-chief of his army. As has been noted earlier, Forth held this post until the autumn of 1644 (by which date he had been created Earl of Brentford), when he was replaced by the younger and healthier Prince Rupert. (For a discussion of Rupert, see page 132.) It would, however, be a mistake to conclude that in military matters Charles was merely a figurehead. He attended the vast majority of councils of war and played an important, indeed, decisive part in determining strategy. For instance, it will be recalled that more than once during the Naseby campaign he overruled Rupert over what course to take.

His intervention was not always beneficial. Clarendon, who knew him well, observed of him in connection with military affairs that he was 'very fearless...and...had an excellent understanding, but was not confident enough of it which made him oftentimes change his own opinion for a worse and follow the advice of men that did not judge as well as himself....If he had been of a rougher and more imperious nature he would have found more respect and duty; and his not applying some severe cures to approaching evils proceeded from the lenity of his nature and the tenderness of his conscience, which in all cases of blood made him choose the softer way, and not hearken to severe counsels, how reasonably soever urged'.

On the whole, Charles was undoubtedly compassionate and could be magnanimous. At Lostwithiel, for example, he displayed both when dealing with trapped enemy infantry. Upon their surrender, the wounded were shipped to Plymouth rather than taken prisoner, whilst their able-bodied colleagues were likewise allowed their freedom and marched off towards Portsmouth with officers above the rank of corporal still in possession of their weapons. Furthermore, as noted, during the Naseby campaign Charles was distressed by the sack of Leicester.

In some respects, then, the refined king (he was a great lover of art), was an admirable character, a decent man, with moreover a high sense of duty towards his family, subjects and God. Nonetheless he had some pronounced faults. He was frequently devious, and though capable of concerted action, was often irresolute, a trait touched upon by Clarendon. Furthermore, on the whole he was prone to bad judgement. More often than not he misread a situation: more often than not he was sanguine in circumstances which would have alarmed others. In the short-term this was good for his health: in the long-term it cost him his head.

The size of the Royalist army at Naseby is disputed. On 4 June, shortly after taking Leicester, Charles declared in a letter to Sir Edward Nicholas, 'my army is so weak being not 4,000 foot and 3,500 horse'. The same figures appear on Sir Bernard de Gomme's sketch-map of the Royalist and Parliamentarian dispositions at Naseby. It is thus not surprising that some historians are of the opinion that the king's army on 14 June was approximately 7,500 strong.

Interestingly, however, Lord Belasyse (a veteran of the battle and a member of the council of war), recalled that the Royalist army did not exceed 12,000 horse and foot. Moreover, Sprigge, (who was Fairfax's chaplain, though he may not have been at Naseby), relates that the battle 'was fought much upon equall advantage, whether you respect the numbers on each side, there being in that not 500. odds, or the ground'. Sprigge may have been mistaken, as of course could Belasyse, or he may have inflated the size of the Royalist army to magnify the achievement of the New Model.

It is nonetheless possible, indeed probable, that the Royalists did exceed 7,500 men. True, Charles had not been joined by Gerard and Goring, but it is noteworthy that in a letter of 4 June Charles stated that he intended to 'gather up stragglers'. Some historians have estimated that the Royalist army at Naseby may have been as strong as 11,000 men. The basis for estimates of the army's strength is the known strength of regiments at the siege of Leicester, and from these and estimates of the strength of units at Naseby whose establishment in late May is unknown, Brigadier Peter Young finally concluded in his work on Naseby that Charles had approximately 5,000 horse and 4,600 foot, and these figures seem the most plausible.

Some of the men belonged to regiments which had done little more than garrison duty. The majority, however, belonged to tried and tested units. One such was Rupert's regiment of horse – which was 400 strong at Leicester – a very experienced unit which had fought at Marston Moor and a host of other actions where Rupert was present. At Naseby it was commanded by Sir Thomas Dallison. Among other battle-hardened regiments were those of the Northern Horse – in all amounting to 1,500 troopers at Leicester – under Sir Marmaduke Langdale, a dour and formidable Catholic gentleman from Yorkshire. The Northern Horse had a distinguished record and, not surprisingly, was primarily interested in northern affairs. In fact following the capture of Leicester the Northern Horse had arbitrarily moved north, angered by the king's decision to relieve Oxford, but had soon turned back with the result that the disgruntled troopers were again with Charles when he marched into Market Harborough on 5 June.

Many of the regiments of foot at Naseby were likewise no strangers to battle. The most notable was Prince Rupert's regiment – the Bluecoats – which may have been nearly 500 strong on 14 June.

FAIRFAX AND THE NEW MODEL ARMY

Sir Thomas Fairfax was born in 1612, the son of Ferdinando, second Baron Fairfax of Cameron. 'Black Tom,' as he was nicknamed on account of his complexion, was clever and matriculated from Cambridge in 1626. Three years later he went to the Low Countries to learn the art of war. He served under Sir Horace Vere (who later became his father-in-law), and was present at the siege of Bois-le-Duc in 1629. In 1640, by which date he had returned to England, he received a knighthood.

During the early years of the Civil War Fairfax spent much of his time fighting in Yorkshire under his father. He gained a reputation as a very daring soldier who loved to be in the thick of action, and was moreover an inspirational leader. The Royalist Secretary, Nicholas, writing after Fairfax had been defeated by Goring at Seacroft Moor on 4 April 1643, said that he was 'the man most beloved and relied upon by the rebels in the north'. Another contemporary, the Parliamentarian lawyer, Bulstrode Whitelocke, was to write in 1646 that Fairfax 'was a person of as meek and humble carriage as ever I saw in great employment, and of but few words in discourse or council....But I have observed him at councils of war, that he...hath ordered things expressly contrary to the judgement of all his council; and in action in the field I have seen him so highly transported, that...he would seem more like a man distracted and furious, than of his ordinary mildness, and so far different temper'.

An essentially moderate man, Fairfax did not approve of the subsequent trial and execution of King Charles, and played a part in bringing about the Restoration.

Estimates of the strength of the Parliamentarian army at Naseby vary from approximately 13,000 to about 17,000 men. According to Belasyse, the Royalists believed that Fairfax had about 15,000 men, and it is interesting to note that Sir Samuel Luke, the governor of Newport Pagnell, was of the opinion on the eve of Naseby that the army was not 'less than 8,000 horse and 7,000 foot'.

There were ten regiments of New Model cavalry at Naseby and these were all at or near full strength, 600 men. In addition, there were Colonel John Fiennes' regiment and a contingent known as the Associated Horse. In all, 6,700 thus seems a reasonable estimate for the strength of the cavalry.

The army contained one regiment of dragoons. This was commanded by Colonel John Okey and it is generally assumed to have been at, or near, its full establishment of 1,000.

There were eight regiments of foot present, all of which belonged to the New Model. If they were all at full strength – 1,200 – this would mean that there were 9,600 infantry at Fairfax's disposal. Undoubtedly, however, this was not the case. Desertion, particularly of foot, had always been a problem during the Civil War and it would be unreasonable to suppose that the New Model was immune, especially when it is borne in mind that parliament had had to resort to impressment to fill the ranks of the infantry. The French ambassador, for instance, had seen men set upon in broad daylight in London and carried off to serve in parliament's new war machine. In light of such action, and the general war weariness which prevailed at this date, it is logical to assume that a significant number of soldiers stole away when able to do so. As Ian Gentles has commented: 'Conscripting infantry in 1645–6 was like ladling water into a leaky bucket. During the weeks leading up to Naseby, for example, conscripts...did "daily run away".' Moreover, it has to be borne in mind that armies on campaign were weakened by losses owing to illness brought on by a poor diet and bad living conditions. In view of the above, 7,200 seems a reasonable estimate for the strength of the New Model foot at Naseby. In all, then, Fairfax was probably in command of approximately 15,000 officers and men.

Though parliament had conscripted infantry, this had not been the case with the cavalry. The requisite number of troopers for the New Model establishment of eleven regiments was found from the armies of the Eastern Association, the Earl of Essex, and Sir William Waller. Hence the horse contained many battle-hardened veterans. The troopers of Fairfax and Edward Whalley's regiments are a case in point. They had belonged to Cromwell's celebrated double regiment – the 'Ironsides'. A New Model cavalry regiment consisted of six troops each 100-strong, and the rate of pay for a trooper was a handsome 2s a day.

Evidently Okey's regiment of dragoons, which at least in theory had an establishment of ten 100-strong troops, was primarily made up of recent conscripts: it had been little over 400-strong at the beginning of May. The daily rate of pay for the men was 1s 6d.

There were ten companies in a regiment of foot. The colonel's was theoretically 200-strong, the lieutenant-colonel's 160, and the major's 140, while those of captains were each 100 strong. The companies were manned by musketeers and pikemen and the former outnumbered the latter by two to one, or more. The daily rate of pay for infantrymen was a mere 8d, no more than could be earned by labourers.

The proposed strength of the New Model foot was 14,400. The army of the Eastern Association had provided 3,578 men, Essex's 3,048 and Waller's army, 600. As has been noted, parliament had had to resort to conscription to make up the numbers. London and the county committees of the east and south-east were given quotas to raise, but these had not all been achieved. To illustrate the point, a week before Naseby the Eastern Association had provided less than three-fifths of the men required from it. Hence when Fairfax left Windsor on 30 April his infantry was not quite at full strength, and though he was evidently augmented during the Naseby campaign, the reinforcements will have done little more than offset losses through sickness or desertion, if that.

In the chapter on Marston Moor, (which contains a brief account of the tactics, weaponry, etc of the period), it was noted that regiments on both sides wore coats of various colours and consequently that the armies did not have a uniform appearance. The infantry regiments of the New Model, though, all wore coats which were Venice red and were distinguished from each other by the colour of their facings.

It is fairly common to view the soldiers of the New Model as psalm singing Christians who staunchly upheld biblical standards of behaviour. God fearing men of this sort were certainly present, but not all their comrades were as devout. In fact, only four days before Naseby Sir Samuel Luke stated in a letter to his father that drunkenness was prevalent. 'I think these New Modellers knead all their dough with ale' he wrote 'for I never saw so many drunk in my life in so short a time'. Perhaps Luke was exaggerating, but it is evident that the New Model was not as disciplined and formidable a war machine as it was to become in the course of time. Fairfax had, however, already demonstrated a desire to make it such. On 5 May, for instance, shortly after taking the field, he had hanged two wayward soldiers near Andover and had marched the army past the tree on which they were hung.

The quality of officers was generally high. At the beginning of the Civil War most officers had come from the upper echelons of society and though often brave, were not necessarily competent. But as the war progressed the view gained ground that men should hold positions of responsibility through merit, and many officers serving in the New Model had worked their way up through the ranks, with the result that Luke commented it was hard to distinguish the officers from ordinary soldiers. It must be emphasised though, that at the senior level the majority of officers were of good birth. This is of course true of Fairfax. It is also true of Cromwell, who is often erroneously referred to as a yeoman. He was a country gentleman – admittedly of small estate – whose father had been a younger son of Sir Henry Cromwell, one of the wealthiest men in Huntingdonshire.

DESCRIPTION

Naseby lies in the heart of England and is situated on a plateau which contains a number of low hills and valleys. The battle which made this Northamptonshire village notable, was fought on Saturday 14 June 1645 a short distance to the north-west of Naseby, for as noted earlier the Royalist and Parliamentarian armies had respectively taken up positions to the north and south of a shallow valley – Broad Moor.

The Royalists were drawn up on Dust Hill, about half a mile from the Roundhead position, and over one and a half miles from Naseby itself. As usual, the foot was in the centre with horse on the wings.

The right wing was drawn up in two lines with six squadrons in the first line and five in the second, and each line was supported by bodies of musketeers. The wing was commanded by Prince Rupert and probably comprised over 1,600 cavalry and 200 musketeers. The left wing was led by Sir Marmaduke Langdale and was also drawn up in two lines with musketeers in support. Its composition and strength is uncertain. Some are of the opinion that its troopers all belonged to the Northern Horse, which may have been nearly 1,500 strong at Naseby. Others are of the opinion that the wing also contained troopers belonging to the Newark Horse, a view followed here. Furthermore, according to Sir Bernard de Gomme, Sir Horatio Cary's regiment – which had been 200 strong at the siege of Leicester – was with this wing. In all, then, there were probably nearly 2,000 troopers supported by 200 musketeers.

The redoubtable Lord Astley, who had been Sergeant-Major-General of the foot since the commencement of the Civil War, led the centre. Here were per-

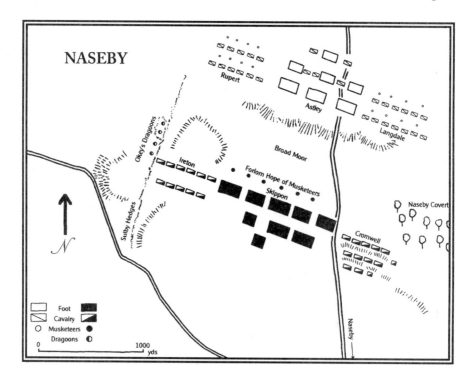

164

haps nearly 3,500 infantry deployed in two lines. The first, and strongest, contained from left to right, the brigades of Sir George Lisle, Sir Henry Bard, and Sir Barnard Astley, Lord Astley's son. The foot of the second line was interspersed by about 880 horse of Colonel Thomas Howard's brigade who were in three 'divisions'.

To the rear was King Charles and the reserve. Its composition and strength are disputed. In part, it is known to have consisted of the king's Lifeguard of Foot and Prince Rupert's regiment, the Bluecoats. According to Walker, these units totalled 800 men. However this seems rather high. 700 men is perhaps nearer the mark. And what of the cavalry? Some are of the opinion that the only unit of horse in the reserve was the king's Lifeguard commanded by Bernard Stuart, the Earl of Lichfield. At Leicester this had been 130-strong, but Walker states that at Naseby it was about 500-strong, a figure which is hard to credit, even allowing for the addition of numerous courtiers and gentlemen volunteers. Other historians are of the opinion that the reserve also contained the 800 or so Newark Horse known to have been at the battle. This may have been the case, but there is reason to believe that at least some of these troopers were with Langdale's Northern Horse for Walker comments that the Royalist left wing consisted of both the Northern and Newark Horse. To conclude, if the foregoing discussion of the king's reserve is correct, Charles probably had about 500 Newark Horse and a Lifeguard perhaps 300-strong in addition to the foot referred to.

It is said that in their march from the East Farndon ridge the Royalists had 'made so much haste, that they left many of their Ordnance behinde them' (Sprigge). What few guns they did have on Dust Hill were undoubtedly sakers.

The Parliamentarian left wing facing Prince Rupert was commanded by Henry Ireton, 'a grave and solid person' according to a contemporary, Lucy Hutchinson. He was to become Cromwell's son-in-law. Fairfax had made Ireton second-in-command of the horse earlier in the morning at Cromwell's bidding. The newly appointed 34-year-old had approximately 3,200 horse deployed in two lines, with six squadrons in the first and five in the second. The wing consisted of five regiments of New Model cavalry and a squadron of the Associated Horse. Ireton opted to ride with his first line.

The right wing was led by Cromwell. It was drawn up in three lines and the ground before it was rough, included a rabbit warren, and fell away more steeply than elsewhere. In the front line were five squadrons under his kinsman Edward Whalley. Like the majority of troopers under his command, Whalley had served in the 'Ironsides'. To the rear of the squadron on the right of the line, and somewhat to the right, was half of Colonel Edward Rossiter's regiment – the regiment had just arrived on the scene in time to participate in the battle. Then came the second line under Cromwell. This consisted of four squadrons covering the intervals between those of the first line. Behind, three squadrons made up the third line. This consisted of the remainder of Rossiter's regiment, half of

Colonel Fiennes' regiment (the rest of which was in the second line), and a squadron of the Associated Horse. It will be remembered that Fiennes' regiment and the Associated Horse were non-New Model units. In all, Cromwell probably had about 3,500 men.

Sprigge relates that a forlorn hope 'consisting of about 300' musketeers was deployed in front of the infantry in the centre, 'down the steep of the hill towards the enemy, somewhere more than Carbine shot from the Main battail, who were ordered to retreat to the battail, whensoever they should be hard pressed upon by the enemy'. Behind, the infantry under Skippon was marshalled in two lines, with five regiments in the first line and two in the second, together with half of Edward Harley's regiment: the rest of his regiment formed the reserve. As for the artillery, the majority of guns were placed in pairs in the intervals along the front line.

And what of Okey's dragoons? Okey tells us that he was giving his men ammunition in a meadow half a mile behind the rest of the army, when Cromwell rode up and ordered him to flank the New Model's left wing. As a result the dragoons took up a position along Sulby Hedges, which ran north from near Ireton's wing towards Dust Hill. The hedges were long and winding, no doubt thicker in some places than elsewhere, and contained at least one close.

It seems that the battle began just after Okey's men took up their position, or indeed before they had fully deployed. It was probably approaching 11.00am when it did so, and it was the Royalists who took the offensive. Their battle cry was 'Queen Mary', (the Parliamentarians' was 'God our Strength'), and presumably the signal for the advance was a salvo from the biggest guns. Events on the west side of the field will be discussed first.

If Okey's account of the battle is accepted at face value, some of Rupert's horse fanned out to the west and advanced on the far side of Sulby Hedges while the remainder moved directly towards Ireton. However, Okey's account is rather garbled and it is generally accepted that Rupert's wing in its entirety advanced to the east of the hedges.

It is sometimes said that Rupert allowed Astley's foot in the centre to progress well across Broad Moor before he moved forward, and that his horse would have been abreast of the infantry within a few minutes. But de Gomme's sketch-map mentioned earlier shows that Rupert's horse were supported by musketeers and it is thus reasonable to suppose that the prince advanced at the same time as Astley, or at most very shortly thereafter.

As cavalry can walk faster than men, especially men encumbered by weaponry etc, Rupert no doubt drew ahead of the infantry and his supporting musketeers. At some point he therefore halted. Sprigge relates that: 'Upon the approach of the Enemies Right wing of Horse, our left wing [drew] down the brow of the hill to meet them,' and that it was this slight advance on the part of Ireton which caused the Royalists to halt 'as if they had not expected us in so ready a posture'.

It seems, rather, that Rupert drew rein in order to let his musketeers catch up, dress the lines of his horse, and allow Astley to draw abreast, or even ahead somewhat. For his part, Ireton likewise halted. Sprigge relates that upon seeing Rupert halt the Parliamentarian commander 'made a little stand also, partly by reason of some disadvantage of the ground, untill the rest of the Divisions [squadrons] of horse might recover their stations'.

Presently, 'the Enemy advanced again', and Ireton responded in kind. Of this phase of the battle, Young has commented: 'The Prince, satisfied that his musketeers had caught up, and that Astley's orderly tertias [brigades] were progressing relentlessly across the valley, gave the signal to continue the advance. Almost at once the opposing regiments were in motion, and in an incredibly short space of time were within range. The panting musketeers doubled into the gaps between the squadrons and loosed off their volleys at the Roundhead horse. This was the moment for the charge..'.

According to Okey's account, as the Royalists drew near, his men 'with shooting and rejoycing received them'. Moreover another New Model officer, Colonel Edward Wogan, states that the dragoons 'did mightily annoy the King's right wing of horse, as they advanced towards us', while a Royalist veteran of the battle, Sir Henry Slingsby, tells us that the Parliamentarians 'possess'd an Hedge upon our right wing wch they had lin'd wth Musqueteers to Gall our horse, (as indeed they did) before we could come up to charge theirs'.

In view of this, it seems likely, contrary to Young's opinion, that the Royalist musketeers did not have an opportunity to fire at the Roundhead horse for their own cavalry, galled somewhat by the fire of Okey's dragoons, must have very soon accelerated to the charge leaving them behind and most, if not all, of them likely fell back to join Rupert's second line.

According to Sprigge, it was the left-hand squadrons of the Royalist front line which clashed first with the enemy. They did so against squadrons on the right of Ireton's first line, i.e., Ireton's own squadron and the right squadron of Vermuyden's regiment, (the regiment was led at Naseby by Major Robert Huntingdon). They did not do well. Prince Maurice's regiment was routed by Ireton, while the left squadron of Prince Rupert's regiment was routed by the other Roundhead unit. Between the Royalist bodies referred to was the Queen's regiment and Sprigge comments that although this did not come to blows with Ireton's second squadron – which failed to charge home – it was nonetheless 'carried away in the disorder' caused by the failure of Prince Maurice's regiment and the left squadron of Prince Rupert's.

Perhaps this was so. But it also seems possible that Ireton's second squadron failed to close with the Queen's regiment because the Roundhead units flanking it advanced with more alacrity than it, and for one reason or another, encroached on the ground over which it would have ridden. If this were so, it would be reasonable to conclude that the Queen's regiment saw some action and that its discomfiture was at least partly due to an assault by troopers belonging to Ireton's own squadron and the right squadron of Vermuyden's regiment, which together outnumbered the combined strength of the three Royalist units referred to.

According to Sprigge, after the failure of the left-hand squadrons of Rupert's front line, Ireton saw 'one of the enemies Brigades of Foot on his right hand, pressing sore upon our Foot,' and thus charged against it at the head of his squadron. When it is borne in mind that the infantry battle was raging further back than where Ireton clashed with Rupert's horse, it becomes clear that such a move would have necessitated a retrograde movement on his part. Perhaps this was the case. It seems more likely, though, that Ireton rode against the right flank of Astley's second line. Whichever view is correct, Ireton's assault must have come as an unpleasant shock to the men he rode against and no doubt caused some disruption. Nevertheless in the encounter the Royalist foot (who were perhaps supported by some of Howard's troopers), evidently came out on top. Ireton himself, had his horse shot from under him, was struck in the thigh by a pike, and hit in the face by an halberd. He was compelled to surrender, but managed to regain his freedom later in the battle.

On the other hand, the right squadron of Vermuyden's regiment had charged on towards Rupert's second line, only to be routed by the opposing Cavaliers. This also seems to have been true of Ireton's left-hand squadron.

And how did events unfold elsewhere on this wing? Did the Roundheads also at least initially prevail against the opposing squadrons, or was it a different story? It was a different story. The left-hand squadron of Vermuyden's regiment clashed with the remainder of Rupert's regiment, while the two squadrons of Colonel John Butler's regiment (which was on the left of Ireton's front line), came to blows with the Lifeguards of the prince and his brother, Maurice: for some reason, perhaps more difficult going, Butler's men had not advanced as far as the squadrons to their right. How long the opposing units were engaged is uncertain. But sooner or later, as Walker notes, and despite the losses sustained by fire from Okey's dragoons, the Cavaliers 'did so well, and were so well seconded [by troopers of the second line which consisted of the regiments of the Earl of Northampton, Sir William Vaughan, and perhaps Sir George Boncle], that they bore all down before them'.

Hence Butler's regiment and the left-hand squadron of Vermuyden's were overcome. So too, for that matter, were the squadrons of Ireton's second line which consisted, from left to right, of the regiments of Colonel Nathaniel Rich and Colonel Charles Fleetwood, and a squadron of the Associated Horse. As Lord Belasyse recalled of events here, the cavalry under Rupert 'beat the enemy off their ground, and pursued them'. The pursuit will be discussed later, but before turning attention to the infantry battle, we should note that by this stage in the proceedings Rupert's supporting musketeers were evidently engaged in a fire-fight with Okey's dragoons, who it seems at some point also received the attention of Royalist horse. Of this more will be said later.

In the centre, a fierce battle was raging. As Astley's foot had drawn near, the Roundhead forlorn hope fired before falling back towards Skippon's front line, and Sprigge relates that: 'Upon the Enemies approach, the Parliaments army marcht up to the brow of the hill....The Enemy this while marched up in good order, a swift march, with a great deal of gallantry and resolution'.

Of the resultant clash, Walker recalled: 'Our Forces advanced up the Hill, the Rebels only discharging five Pieces at them, but over shot them, and so did their Musquetiers. The Foot on either side hardly saw each other until they were within Carbine Shot, and so only made one Volley; ours falling in with Sword and butt end of the Musquet did notable execution; so much as I saw their Colours fall, and their Foot in great Disorder'.

On the right of the New Model front line Fairfax's regiment of foot fared well, for as Sprigge notes it was not 'much pressed upon'. This was because the Parliamentarian front line was longer than that of the numerically inferior Royalists. The rest of the line consisted, from left to right, of the regiments of Skippon, Sir Hardress Waller, John Pickering, and Edward Montagu, and here, as noted, on the whole the Roundheads were in trouble.

It is not just Walker who states that this was so. Sprigge, for instance, wrote: 'Almost all the rest of the main Battail being overpressed, gave ground and went off in some disorder, falling behinde the Reserves; But the Colonels and Officers, doing the duty of very gallant men, in endeavouring to keep their men from disorder, and finding their attempt fruitless therein, fell into the Reserves with their Colours, choosing rather there to fight and die, then to quit the ground they stood on'.

Even if allowance is made for exaggeration, it is clear that the situation was serious for the Parliamentarians. Skippon was one of the New Model officers who did his best to prevent the line from disintegrating. After the battle, Fairfax wrote of him, that though he 'was shot thro' his side...he continued in the ffielde with great resolution', and when told by Fairfax to retire, retorted that 'he would not goe so long as a man would stand'.

It was Fairfax who restored the situation. He ordered forward the remainder of the foot. The regiments in question were those of Edward Harley (commanded by Lieutenant-Colonel Thomas Pride), Robert Hammond, and Thomas Rainsborough. According to Sprigge, the arrival of these units did more than restore the situation. It turned the tide, repelling the enemy and 'forcing them into a disorderly retreat'. That the Royalist foot were sooner or later pushed back in disorder, despite intervention by their second line, is undoubted. But as will be seen, there is reason to attribute this, at least in part, to the action of others.

Why did the Royalist front line initially do so well? It is often said that its success was due to the fact that it was mainly comprised of veterans, in contrast to the Roundhead line it came against. That the bulk of Astley's foot consisted of experienced soldiers is a reasonable view, but it is incorrect to view the New

Model foot as primarily composed of recent conscripts. The majority of Skippon's men had belonged to the three armies merged to form parliament's new war machine and many were thus not strangers to battle.

It is surely more reasonable to attribute the Royalists' success primarily to the speed and ferocity of their assault. Instead of halting when near the enemy and engaging in a fire-fight, they closed in for the kill after firing only one volley. As Barry Denton has commented, 'the volley and quick charge had its success this day'.

Furthermore, Skippon's wounding must have played a part in unsettling the Roundheads, a factor mentioned by Wogan, 'our foot gave ground and were in a manner running away' owing in part, to 'Skippon's being desperately wounded'.

It is time to discuss the clash between Cromwell and Langdale. As has been noted, the ground before Cromwell's position fell away more steeply than elsewhere on the field and was more treacherous. Consequently, it seems likely that Cromwell came to blows with Langdale after Ireton and Rupert had engaged on the other wing.

Sprigge relates that Cromwell, 'not thinking it fit to stand and receive the Enemies charge' advanced against the oncoming Royalists. Edward Whalley's two squadrons on the left of Cromwell's front line were the first to clash with the enemy after they, and their adversaries, had fired their pistols at each other at almost point-blank range. The troopers then set to work with their swords. Whalley's men apparently quickly triumphed, and their opponents fell back towards Rupert's Bluecoats where 'they fled for shelter, and rallied'.

And what of the remainder of Cromwell's command? How did it fare? According to Sprigge, after advancing 'with great difficulty' owing to the presence of gorse bushes and the rabbit warren, the other squadrons of the front line engaged the rest of Langdale's first line before the collapse of the Royalists assailed by Whalley. Weight of numbers soon told. The Cavaliers were pushed back and, to add to their difficulties, were attacked on their left flank by Rossiter. Furthermore, following the success of Whalley, Colonel Sheffield's regiment on the left of the Parliamentarian second line, advanced and evidently attacked the right flank of the hard-pressed Royalists. Thus, not surprisingly, sooner or later the remainder of Langdale's men – who seem to have received support from some of the Newark Horse of the king's reserve – gave up and, like their comrades routed earlier, fell back in disorder. Presumably many of the troopers quit the field altogether.

When describing events on this wing Belasyse comments that the Royalists were 'routed without any handsome dispute'. That the encounter was not very prolonged seems certain. Nonetheless, it is reported by others that the Cavaliers fought with vigour and resolution. Walker, for example, opined: 'I must needs say ours did as well as the Place and their Number would admit, but being flanked and pressed back, they at last gave ground and fled'. Slingsby felt likewise: 'Our Northern Horse who stood upon yt wing, & ye Newark horse who was appoint'd their receive [relief] being out front'd & overpoured...after they were close joyn'd...stood a pritty while, & neither seem'd to yield, till more came up to their flanks and put ym to rout'.

Hence it is reasonable to believe that the failure of the Royalists on this wing was due to the fact that they attacked uphill against a numerically superior force, and that in the heat of battle the hitherto disaffected Northern Horse generally fought with customary valour. Clarendon, however, after acknowledging that the Cavaliers fought as well as circumstances here allowed, commented that once broken 'they fled further and faster than became them'. This was perhaps especially true of the troopers from Newark who were generally not as experienced as the Northern Horse.

Unlike Rupert, Cromwell did not engage in a headlong pursuit of the defeated. Instead, after detailing four squadrons to keep an eye on the broken Royalists, he turned against the left flank of Astley's infantry, thereby helping to turn the tide of battle in the centre.

It was during this phase of the engagement that King Charles decided to play a part in the proceedings. Sir Edward Walker relates what happened: 'the King's Horse-guards and the King at the Head of them were ready to charge those [i.e. the four Roundhead squadrons referred to above] who followed ours, [the broken left wing], when a Person of Quality, 'tis said the Earl of Carnwath, took the King's Horse by the Bridle, turned him about, swearing at Him and saying, Will you go upon your Death?' We shall continue the story by quoting Lord Clarendon: 'Upon this a word ran through the troops that they should march to the right hand; which was away both from charging the enemy, or assisting their own men. Upon this they all turned their horses and rode upon the spur, as if they were every man to shift for himself. It is very true that, upon hearing the more soldierly word Stand, which was sent to run after them, many of them returned to the king; though the former unlucky word carried more from him'.

By now, as noted, Cromwell had turned on the exposed left flank of Astley's doughty infantry. It was not just this flank which came under attack. Okey relates how, after seeing that Cromwell had routed the Royalist left wing, he himself, 'after one houre's battail', ordered his men to mount and proceeded to charge against Astley's right flank.

At some stage prior to this, Okey states that he and his dragoons had given themselves up 'for lost men' and had 'resolved every man to stand to the last'. Perhaps they did so upon the collapse of Ireton's wing. Or they may have thought themselves in dire straits when Royalist cavalry, probably Newark Horse from the king's reserve, subsequently came against them. However, Okey states that in the entire battle he 'lost not one man, and had but three wounded', and if one accepts this it is evident that whatever they may have feared, Okey and his men engaged in little fighting at close quarters either when ensconced in Sulby Hedges or after charging the right flank of the failing Royalist infantry, 500 of whom Okey declares were taken prisoner by his dragoons.

Before discussing the final stages of the infantry battle, mention must be made of Prince Rupert's pursuit. It will be remembered that he quit the field by chasing routed enemy cavalry (a Parliamentarian source, Wogan, relates that many of Ireton's troopers 'went clear away to Northampton and could never be stopt'), and Rupert pursued them for about two miles before rallying his men. He then began returning to the battlefield and en route came across the considerable New Model baggage train, located west of Naseby. He summoned it to surrender but was met by fire from its guards, 'who fired with admirable courage', states Sprigge, 'refusing to hearken to his offer'. Hence Rupert pressed on – Sprigge relates that as the prince did so he was closely followed by some of Ireton's troopers who had rallied – and joined Charles some time after the king's abortive offensive action recounted above, while the pursuing troopers joined Cromwell and proceeded to assist in destroying the Royalist foot.

According to Walker, some of the troopers of the king's reserve who had rejoined Charles following the debacle attributed to the intervention of Carnwath, 'made a Charge, wherein some of them fell'. Not surprisingly, they failed to turn the tide of the battle. And what of Rupert and his men? Walker continues: 'By this time Prince Rupert was come with a good Body of Horse from the right wing; but they having done their part, and not being in Order, could never be brought to charge again'.

Thus the Royalist infantry was left to its fate. Many, perhaps most, of Astley's men had indeed evidently already surrendered. Sooner or later only one tertia continued offering resistance. This probably consisted of Prince Rupert's Bluecoats and the king's Lifeguard of Foot, who had advanced from the reserve to support the rest of the Royalist infantry. Of this action, Sprigge comments that the Royalists fought 'with incredible courage and resolution, although we attempted them in the Flanks, Front and Rear'. They only broke after Fairfax and Cromwell intervened: the former with his regiment of foot (and it seems his Lifeguard); the latter at the head of his victorious troopers and perhaps some of Ireton's.

Bulstrode Whitelocke apparently also refers to this action. He relates how Fairfax, who was 'riding in the field bareheaded' after losing his helmet in action, rode 'from one part of his army to another, to see how they stood', and in so doing came 'up to his own lifeguard commanded by [Captain] Charles D'Oyley'. Fairfax, 'seeing a body of the King's foot stand, and not all broken', asked D'Oyley whether he had charged against it'. Hearing that he had done so twice, Fairfax ordered him to do so again, stating that 'he would take a commanded party, and charge them in the rear at the same time'. The combined onslaught at last prevailed.

Following the total collapse of Astley's infantry, Fairfax reformed his army. Sprigge notes, the cavalry 'were again put in to two wings, within Carbine shot of the enemy, leaving a wide space for the battail of foot to fall in'. Okey's dragoons were evidently placed to the front and his men proceeded to fire at the Royalist horse with Charles which, Sprigge comments, had been 'put again into as good order as the shortnesse of their time, and our near pressing upon them would permit'. Slingsby recalled that the Royalists were 'mightily discourag'd', and so turned about and quit the field. They fled towards Leicester.

They were pursued by the New Model cavalry. Accounts of the pursuit vary. Sprigge wrote: 'Our horse had the Chase of them' to 'within two miles of Leicester...took many prisoners, and had the execution of them all that way'. In contrast, Wogan states that the troopers resented having to chase the Royalists and thus did so in a 'disorderly and discontented' manner: 'We leisurely continued the pursuit till we came within 2 miles of Leicester, where we found part of the King's horse drawn up; but they never offered to charge us, nor we them, but stood and looked on each other till night came on. They marched into Leicester, and we were called back again'. According to Wogan the troopers' resentment was due to the fact that they had had to 'leave all the plunder of the field' to the infantry. Finally, it is interesting to note that according to the Royalist, Richard Symonds, the commander of the king's Lifeguard, the Earl of Lichfield, charged pursuing Roundheads 'with half a score' of men at Great Glen 'and beate them back'.

Of Royalist losses at Naseby, Belasyse recalled: 'Not 200 lost their lives in this battle, so ill it was disputed'. On the other hand, according to Colonel Thomas Herbert and Colonel Harcourt Leighton, two 'commissioners of parliament' with the New Model, some 600 Royalists were slain while Parliamentarian losses were 'not above 200'. However their report was written immediately after the battle (which lasted between two and three hours), and it is certain that even if these figures are correct – and that for Roundhead losses seems rather low – other individuals will have been killed during the pursuit or would have died in the days and weeks to come from wounds they had sustained.

The number of prisoners taken was substantial. Leighton and Herbert report that the figure was nearly 4,000. Sprigge relates that some 5,000 Royalists were taken, of whom 4,500 were common soldiers. The majority of the captives were marched to London to be triumphantly paraded through the streets.

The Roundheads also captured all the king's ordnance, 8,000 arms, a rich haul of colours, and the entire baggage train – which afforded them a much needed supply of cheese and biscuit – as well as some of the treasure taken at Leicester. Furthermore, Charles' private papers were seized and this provided his enemies with proof that he was, among other things, planning to bring Catholics from Ireland to fight on his behalf and attempting to gain military and financial backing from continental rulers. Parliament soon published this vital correspondence, claiming that the king was a traitor.

Mention must be made of the fate which befell womenfolk with the Royalist baggage train. Over a hundred were slaughtered by Parliamentarian soldiers, while others had their noses slit and their faces slashed: savage action later defended on the grounds that the victims were whores or Irish papists. It has, however, been plausibly suggested that the women assumed to be Irish were most probably Welsh or Cornish.

Upon arriving at Leicester, following his flight from Naseby, Charles paused briefly before pressing on that evening north-west to Ashby-de-la-Zouch with the bulk of his cavalry. There he was joined the following day by Sir Henry Slingsby and Belasyse, who had met at Leicester after flying from the battlefield. Slingsby tells us that Ashby-de-la-Zouch's garrison was 'well stor'd wth good victuals & a good Cellar'. Nonetheless Charles and what was left of his army, did not dally there. On the 15th they moved to Lichfield, and then headed south-west to Bewdley where they arrived on the 18th. Charles was intent on joining Gerard and raising a new army in Wales. Hence he proceeded to Hereford and then made for Raglan Castle in South Wales. Moreover, on the 23rd, whilst at Hereford, he wrote to the Earl of Glamorgan, whom he had sent earlier in the year to enlist forces in Ireland, stating that he hoped to receive 'succor' from that quarter.

Instead of moving to Wales (where he spent most of July), it would have been wiser for Charles, as Clarendon later wrote, to have 'immediately repaired' to the West Country 'where he had an army already formed'.

And what of Fairfax? After Naseby he moved to Market Harborough, where he spent the night. The next day he made for Leicester which he proceeded to invest. It surrendered on 18 June. He then marched south to deal with Goring's army in the West Country and destroyed it at Langport on 10 July.

Only some days before this engagement, on the 6th to be precise, Charles wrote at Raglan that he hoped 'to be at the head of the greatest army within two months that I have seen this year'. It was not to be and almost a year later, after several other reverses, the Royalists decided that enough was enough and surrendered Oxford on 24 June 1646, thereby bringing an end to the war.

Naseby was undoubtedly the decisive engagement of the Civil War. It tore much of the heart out of the Royalist cause and was a massive psychological boost to the king's opponents, whose new war machine had most emphatically won its spurs. That the battle was of unusual significance was immediately apparent to Leighton and Herbert. 'God Almighty' they wrote, 'give us thankful hearts for this great victory, the most absolute as yet obtayned'.

As William Seymour has commented, 'Naseby was a battle which need never have been fought'. The Royalists found themselves committed to an engagement against a numerically superior army owing to mistakes on their part. At the beginning of the campaign the decision to send Goring and 3,000 horse to the West Country from Stow-on-the-Wold was a blunder, as was the garrisoning of Leicester and the decision to let Sir Richard Willis return to Newark on 4 June at the head of 400 cavalry. Sending provisions to Oxford was another mistake. It resulted in Charles' dalliance at Daventry, something which enabled Fairfax to close in with the New Model and endanger any subsequent Royalist moves. Not for nothing did Symonds lament 'the unhappy stay at Daventry so long'.

These errors must be attributed to Charles. Even if the decision to send Goring to the West Country was instigated by Rupert as Clarendon states, Charles could have overruled him, as he reportedly did for instance at the council of war at Market Harborough on the eve of Naseby when, swayed by the advice of courtiers who had a dismissive view of the New Model, he unwisely rejected the view of Rupert and other senior officers that battle be avoided.

Prince Rupert likewise made mistakes. The most notable was surely the decision to quit the good defensive position between East Farndon and Great Oxendon, either in the belief that Fairfax was retreating or because he thought that he had a chance of falling upon the New Model before it was ready to receive him. It seems that, after his initial reluctance for battle, the young man became rather overexcited and that this impaired his judgement somewhat.

Moreover, Rupert should not have led the right wing. There were other men present – Prince Maurice for instance – who were perfectly capable of doing so. It would have been wiser for Rupert to have been with the reserve, where he would have gained an overall view of the battle, and where he would no doubt have been more effective than was Charles. Perhaps Rupert was ordered to lead the right wing by the king, but if the decision to do so was his own, it was another error on his part.

Rupert has also been censured for pursuing Ireton's shattered wing instead of assisting the Royalist infantry. This seems just. If the pursuit were simply due to ill-discipline on the part of Rupert's cavalry, and occurred against his wishes, then surely he would have returned to the field post haste after rallying his men. Instead, as has been noted, he attempted to secure the surrender of the New Model baggage train. He did not dally long when faced with opposition, but the very fact that he behaved in such a manner indicates that he was not possessed by a great sense of urgency. As Peter Young has observed: 'It seems extraordinary that a man of his intelligence...should have wasted time in this fashion. If he had won the battle the train would be his for the taking'. Rupert had made the same mistake at Edgehill. That he made it again is amazing. In short, the performance of the commander of the king's forces at Naseby is not particularly edifying.

As for Lord Astley and Sir Marmaduke Langdale, they evidently performed creditably. This cannot be said of Goring. True, he was not at the battle. But he should have been. If this brave but increasingly dissolute Cavalier had marched to join the king as ordered following the decision to recall him from the West Country, the outcome of Naseby might very well have been different.

And what of the New Model commanders? Ireton fought bravely, though his decision to turn against the Royalist foot before ensuring that Rupert's wing had been routed was a mistake. Skippon's performance, on the other hand, is faultless, for although seriously wounded he did not quit the field, even when exhorted to do so by Fairfax, anxious not to undermine morale.

Cromwell likewise deserves praise. That he routed Langdale's numerically inferior wing is not surprising. Nonetheless, as at Marston Moor, he showed a cool head and a sound tactical brain: he was an inspirational leader and a highly capable one.

So too was Fairfax, who deserves great commendation. From the outset of the campaign he showed that he intended the New Model Army to be a disciplined force, for it will be remembered that on 5 May he hanged two wayward soldiers near Andover and marched the army past the tree on which they were hung. Throughout the rest of the campaign Fairfax showed himself conscientious and capable. For example, he spent much of the night of 12/13 June, when his army was at Kislingbury, riding from outpost to outpost to ensure that all was well and that any attempted surprise attack by the Royalists would be thwarted.

At Naseby itself, Fairfax showed that he was prepared to act upon the advice of subordinates, and during the engagement rode from one part of his army to another to encourage his men and ascertain how events were unfolding. Moreover, as he had shown on previous occasions, he was prepared to enter the thick of the fray. Joshua Sprigge records of him: 'when he hath come upon action, or been near an engagement, it hath been observed, another spirit hath come upon him, another soul hath lookt out at his eyes; I mean he hath been so raised, elevated, and transported, as that he hath been not unlike himself at other times, but more like an Angell, then a man. And this was observed of him at this time'.

When his performance and Cromwell's is compared with that of Rupert and Charles, one has to agree with Maurice Ashley's comment that: 'What most emphatically differentiated the two armies was the quality of the generalship'.

As has been noted, Naseby was the decisive engagement of the English Civil War. Never again was Charles able to raise an army comparable to that so soundly defeated on 14 June 1645. Nonetheless, he remained frequently optimistic in the months and years which followed, hoping that he would emerge triumphant either through a change in his military fortunes or by exploiting the differences of his opponents, differences which became increasingly pronounced. In the end his hopes came to nothing, and he was tried and condemned to death by his most extreme opponents who had tired of his intrigues and held him accountable for all the blood which had been shed.

Charles had behaved courageously at Naseby when he wished to ride against the troopers following Langdale's men, and in his reluctance to forsake the field. He had shown courage in the past, and he was to show it again, most notably on the day of his execution, 30 January 1649. 'I fear not death' he said. 'Death is nothing terrible to me'. Shortly after saying this he calmly knelt down, placed his head upon the block, prayed, signalled with his arms, and awaited the axe.

24

DUNBAR

3 SEPTEMBER 1650

The execution of Charles I in January 1649 profoundly shocked a considerable number of people in England and elsewhere. The Scots, for instance, were appalled even though most had opposed the king's religious policies, and they proceeded to recognise his exiled eldest son as Charles II on condition that he accepted the National Covenant.

Charles landed in Scotland in June 1650 and was proclaimed king the following month. Events north of the border caused alarm in ruling circles in England and produced a speedy response – Cromwell was sent to deal with the situation. He entered Scotland on 22 July with 5,000 horse and 10,000 foot of the New Model Army (of which he had just become commander-in-chief), and began marching towards Edinburgh.

The Scottish commander, David Leslie, who had fought alongside Cromwell at Marston Moor, led a stronger army but his men were mainly raw recruits and the quality of the officers was not high: religious zeal rather than military ability had secured many of them their positions.

Leslie avoided giving battle, and so in late August Cromwell withdrew from the vicinity of Edinburgh to Dunbar, for he was short of supplies. By 1 September he only had 11,000 'sound men' left owing to Scottish harassment, desertion and sickness. He began fortifying Dunbar and placed some of the sick on ships of a supporting fleet which was too small to transport the army home.

On the 1st, Leslie took up a position on Doon Hill a short distance south of Dunbar. The following morning, at the urging of the Committee of the Kirk, he moved to less bleak ground between the hill and the ravine of a burn a short distance to the north. He had at least 22,000 men: cavalry on the wings, foot in the centre.

Cromwell noted that because of the lie of the ground the Scottish left flank would not be able to quickly support the right, and so decided to attack the latter. At about 4.00am on the 3rd the English began crossing the burn near where it joins the sea. The vanguard under Colonel Lambert then clashed with a detachment guarding a position on the Berwick road to the right of the Scottish army. After routing it, Lambert's brigade was attacked by the Scottish right wing and recoiled somewhat. Then, supported by other units, Lambert's horse and foot rallied and the Scots were overcome, as were infantry units on the right of Leslie's centre. The rest of the foot fled rather than make a stand, and many were cut down by English cavalry who rode among them. The victorious troopers then overwhelmed the demoralised Scottish left. By 7.00am the battle was over. 3,000 Scots were slain and 10,000 taken prisoner. English losses are said not to have exceeded twenty men. As Ian Gentles states, at Dunbar 'Cromwell again demonstrated his ability as a field commander by massing overwhelming force against a single point'.

Leslie retreated to the strategic town of Stirling, while Cromwell proceeded to secure Edinburgh and Glasgow. Then, in February 1651 he fell ill and was unable to continue campaigning for several months, during which his adversaries consolidated their position in and around Stirling and in other ways prepared for renewed conflict: the Worcester campaign was soon to begin.

25

WORCESTER
3 SEPTEMBER 1651

After Cromwell's stunning victory at Dunbar, the power of the Covenanting party declined, and before and after his coronation at Scone on 1 January 1651, Charles II raised a new 'uncovenanted' army which would not have to act upon the dictates of Presbyterian zealots and in which non-Presbyterians could serve.

In the summer of 1651 Cromwell retook the field, by which time the English army in Scotland was over 21,000 strong, larger than Charles' force. Cromwell wished to lure the Scots from their strong defensive position in and around Stirling and thus crossed the Firth of Forth at Queensferry, with the bulk of his army, and moved towards Perth whose surrender he received on 2 August. The Royalists reacted the way he hoped. They began marching south in the belief that once across the border they would receive support from Englishmen faithful to Charles. Cromwell set off in pursuit in early August, intending to link up with forces under able subordinates, and eager to destroy the enemy before they got close to London.

On 22 August Charles entered Worcester unopposed at the head of a tired army of 12,000 men demoralised by the unenthusiastic welcome they had received in England, and the desertion of many colleagues en route. However, Charles hoped for support from Wales and the south-west.

While the Royalists rested, Cromwell closed in. He arrived outside the city on 28 August at the head of a powerful force soon to number 31,000 men.

The River Severn flows through Worcester and is joined a short distance to the south by the Teme flowing from the west. Cromwell deployed the bulk of his army on high ground to the east of the city, whose fortifications had been hurriedly strengthened 'beyond imagination' by Charles, and sent 11,000 men to cross the Severn via a bridge captured by Lambert nine miles to the south at Upton.

Cromwell delayed taking the offensive until 3 September, the anniversary of Dunbar. Early that morning the men on the west bank of the Severn (under General Fleetwood), began moving north from Upton. Their advance was slow. They had to haul against the current twenty 'great boats' needed to make bridges across the Teme and the Severn. They arrived at the confluence of the rivers at about 1.00pm and the bridges were constructed: one to enable Fleetwood to cross to the north side of the Teme, the other to enable reinforcements to reach him from across the Severn.

Fleetwood sent some of his men about a mile west to force their way across the Teme at Powicke Bridge, but the attempt failed. Meanwhile, Cromwell had joined Fleetwood and was engaged with him in a fierce fight on the north side of the river. After about two hours enemy resistance collapsed and the Scots fled back into Worcester. Charles then moved against men Cromwell had left east of the Severn, and began driving them back. However, the New Model commander returned and drove his gallant adversary back into Worcester, where fierce street fighting subsequently ensued after sundown. The battle was over by 8.00pm

Between 2,000 and 3,000 Royalists were killed and many more were taken captive. Parliamentarian losses were put at less than 200 but this is surely too low for Cromwell himself said that the engagement was 'as stiff a contest for four or five hours as ever I have seen'. As for Charles, he avoided capture and fled abroad.

26

SEDGEMOOR
6 JULY 1685

On 6 February 1685 Charles II died and was succeeded by his brother, James II. The accession of this staunch Catholic was followed by plotting by people who wished to overthrow him. One such was the Earl of Argyll, a strong Protestant who had fled into exile some years before when James, then Charles' lieutenant in Scotland, had had him sentenced to death for treason following a dubious trial. Argyll and other opponents of James now encouraged the late king's exiled illegitimate son, the Duke of Monmouth, to return to England and lead a rising which would synchronise with one the earl was planning to head in Scotland. Against his better judgement, Monmouth agreed.

On 11 June the duke landed at Lyme Regis with a small following, after sailing from Holland a few weeks after Argyll had left for Scotland. Monmouth soon received enthusiastic support from the ordinary people of the West Country. On the 19th he entered Taunton and was proclaimed king. He then tried to secure Bristol but failed, and harassed by government forces, made his way to Norton St Philip near Bath. Here, on the 27th, his rustic army came off best in a clash with a force under Lord Feversham, and then moved south to Frome. While here Monmouth received bad news. Argyll had been captured and executed in Scotland. This, and the fact that few persons of consequence had joined him, made Monmouth despondent. He thus retired to Bridgewater.

Feversham followed, and on 3 July, reached Somerton. He then proceeded north-west to Westonzoyland where he made his headquarters on the 5th. He had about 2,700 regular soldiers. A report that Feversham was only four miles away soon reached Monmouth. The duke and his lieutenants therefore decided to carry out a night attack. At about 11.00pm the rebel army of over 3,500 men left Bridgewater. At first it moved north-east, but then turned south, skirting Chedzoy – where a government detachment was stationed – moving silently over Sedgemoor toward Westonzoyland. Suddenly, as the rebels approached their target, the silence was shattered by a pistol shot, probably fired by a government sentinel, and Feversham hurriedly prepared for battle. It was about 1.45am.

Unfortunately for the rebels, between them and Westonzoyland was a formidable ditch, the Bussex Rhine, which greatly impeded their advance. About 300 of Monmouth's cavalry tried to force their way over the uppermost of the ditch's two crossing places but were repulsed by the enemy. Many of them therefore quit the field, as did the bulk of the rest of Monmouth's raw cavalry when fired on. This hampered the infantry coming up in support. Nonetheless they proceeded to line up and fire across the ditch, but did little damage. As the infantry exchanged fire, Feversham's horse made their way over the crossings and moved against the flanks of the rebels. Assailed from the sides, and from the front by the government infantry which proceeded to cross the ditch, the rebels began falling back and then commenced fleeing. Many were cut down as they did so, while many others were captured and executed by Feversham or subsequently received little or no mercy at the hands of Judge Jeffreys.

Monmouth fled the field before the collapse of his army. However, he was soon captured and on 15 July the kind and malleable 36-year-old died bravely on Tower Hill at the hands of a man wielding an axe with singular incompetence.

27

SHERIFFMUIR
13 NOVEMBER 1715

'Argyle, the State's whole thunder born to wield,
And shake alike the Senate and the Field.'
— Alexander Pope

In June 1688 the wife of James II gave birth to a son. This was not welcome news
to the majority of the king's subjects. They were Protestants, whereas James was
an ardent Catholic intent on restoring Catholicism to a position of supremacy in
Britain. Hitherto, most of his subjects had hoped that his rule would be a temporary aberration and that upon his death the throne would pass to Mary (a
Protestant daughter by a previous marriage), who had married William of
Orange. But now it seemed certain that the newly born prince would be schooled
by his father to perpetuate his policy of Romanisation and that the hopes of
Protestants would come to nought. Consequently, on 30 June seven 'persons of
quality' signed an invitation to William of Orange, the champion of Protestantism, asking him to cross from Holland and help overthrow James. He was
willing to do so, and landed in Devon in early November at the head of an army.

James found himself deserted by many of those closest to him, including his
most able soldier, John Churchill, (the future Duke of Marlborough), and soon
fled to France where he was sure of support from Louis XIV, an ardent Catholic
and a bitter enemy of William of Orange. James died in France in 1701 and following his death his adherents – the Jacobites – immediately recognised his thir-
teen-year-old son as James III of England and VIII of Scotland.

Meanwhile, William and Mary had been reigning jointly in Britain. Mary
had died in 1694 and William was to follow her to the grave in 1702, whereupon he was succeeded by his Protestant sister-in-law, Anne, who like his former wife was the offspring of James II's first marriage.

Who would be Anne's successor? This was the all important question during,
and indeed, before her reign. In 1683 she had married George of Denmark, but
although the marriage had been fruitful death had carried off the youngsters
with unfortunate regularity. Hence, according to the Act of Settlement of 1701,
in the event of Anne dying without surviving issue the throne was to pass to the
Protestant Electress of Hanover, Sophia, (a granddaughter of James I of England) and her descendants.

However, the Jacobites had other ideas. They were determined to place James
Stuart on the throne his father had lost. Schemes to bring about such an event

thus occurred. Moreover, at a later date, an important member of the government, Viscount Bolingbroke, attempted to build up a Jacobite clique at the centre of affairs but was overtaken by the course of events. The queen died on 1 August 1714 before he had been able to set the stage for a Jacobite restoration and so George of Hanover (the late Sophia's son), succeeded to the throne as George I.

He was a middle-aged man of little charm who could speak no English, and following his arrival in England on 18 September he made it clear that he had serious doubts about the loyalty of the Tory party (to which Bolingbroke belonged), for he believed it to be pro-Jacobite. Thus he snubbed a number of leading Tories and soon dismissed them from office.

One of the men who fell foul of the king was the Earl of Mar. On 24 September he was dismissed from his position as Secretary of State for Scotland. He subsequently tried to ingratiate himself with the king but did not succeed, and by the summer of 1715 evidently believed it in his best interests to foment a Jacobite rising in Scotland which, in conjunction with risings expected elsewhere, most notably in the south-west of England, would oust the dour and unpopular George.

On 1 August Mar slipped away from the court and boarded a collier bound for Newcastle at Gravesend. From Tyneside he continued travelling north by sea until he reached Fife.

Following his arrival in Scotland Mar invited a number of prominent Jacobites to a hunt at Braemar. On 26 August he is said to have made a stirring speech to the assembled notables in which, according to Peter Rae, he denounced the Hanoverian succession and stated his intention of restoring 'the Chevalier de St George' (James Stuart), for he had the only 'undoubted right to the Crown'. Then, on 6 September, Mar raised the Pretender's standard at Braemar.

Soon afterwards a party of Jacobites tried to take Edinburgh Castle, which contained a large quantity of arms and ammunition, but failed despite support from a few pro-Jacobite members of the garrison. Nevertheless, the rebels did make progress elsewhere, for on 14 September John Hay secured Perth with a party of horsemen. Mar arrived there on the 28th at the head of a growing army, and received word that James would soon arrive from France and that powerful support could be expected from that quarter.

The man appointed to command the government forces in Scotland was the Duke of Argyll. He arrived in Edinburgh on 14 September after travelling from London and found its loyal inhabitants desperately concerned by events. They were not the only ones in a pessimistic mood. Argyll was likewise far from sanguine for he only had about 1,800 regular soldiers with which to oppose Mar. He thus wrote to London, begging for urgent reinforcement. On 24 September, for instance, he wrote to a senior member of the government, Lord Townshend, and concluded: 'I must end with insisting on considerable reinforcements, for without it, or a miracle, not only this country will be utterly destroyed but the rest of his Majesty's dominions put in the extremest danger'.

While awaiting the arrival of more troops at his headquarters at Stirling, Argyll did what he could. For example, he encouraged people in positions of responsibility loyal to the government, such as Glasgow's magistrates, to enlist men and sent his brother the Earl of Islay west to protect Campbell territory in Argyll and to ensure that members of the Campbell clan, (of which the duke was chief), did not join Mar.

Mar likewise had problems. Arms, ammunition, gunpowder and money, were scarce. Moreover, there was little love lost between sections of his army – which was over 6,000 strong by the end of the first week of October – for it contained men from many clans, some of which were traditional enemies, as well as Lowlanders, many of whom viewed Highlanders with disdain and were in turn looked down on by many clansmen. To solve his financial difficulties, Mar resorted to various measures such as sending out parties of men to raise money in the surrounding counties.

Despite his problems, Mar was in a better position than his opponent. Nonetheless he dallied in Perth awaiting the expected French reinforcements and the Pretender. It would have been wiser to have moved against Argyll: a strategy which if pursued vigorously would almost certainly have resulted in the destruction of the government army.

By the second week of October Mar was aware that a Jacobite rising had just commenced in Northumberland – it did so on the 6th – and that Argyll thus faced the possibility of being attacked from the rear. He therefore decided to send part of his army south under Brigadier Macintosh of Borlum with the intention, it seems, of reinforcing the English rebels.

On the 9th, Borlum left Perth and made his way through Fife. He then crossed the Firth of Forth by boat, and by the morning of the 14th the bulk of his command of about 2,000 men had gathered at Haddington after coming ashore at various places to the east of Edinburgh: the remainder had either been captured by a man-o'-war during the crossing or been driven back.

Borlum's crossing of the Firth of Forth caused consternation among the loyal citizens of Edinburgh, and in the belief that the city was in danger, they urgently requested help from Argyll. He reacted swiftly. He sent part of his army post haste to the capital and soon followed himself. Borlum did indeed move on Edinburgh, but when he saw that preparations were being made to oppose him, he made for Leith instead and occupied a disused fortress. On the 15th he was called upon by Argyll to surrender. He refused, and the duke returned to the capital. Later that day Borlum moved east, and then subsequently began moving south after being ordered to do so urgently by Mar.

By this date another rising, this time in the south-west of Scotland, had commenced and on 22 October Borlum joined the rebels (and the Northumbrian

Jacobites with whom they had become associated), at Kelso. Though it would undoubtedly have been wise to move against Argyll, something which Mar hoped would happen, the combined force crossed into England in the erroneous belief that it would find much support in the north-west, with the result that the small insurgent army surrendered to government forces at Preston on 14 November following a battle in the streets of the town.

Meanwhile, Argyll had dashed back to Stirling from Edinburgh on 17 October (he left Major-General Wightman with some men to hold the capital), after hearing that Mar had advanced from Perth. The earl did so on 16 October and arrived at Dunblane, five miles north of Stirling, late on the 17th. The following day, however, he began retracing his steps rather than confront Argyll.

Hence Mar dallied once again at Perth. Here, in early November, he received expected reinforcements. The Earl of Seaforth, for instance, the chief of the MacKenzies, arrived with a force from the north on the 4th or 5th.

By the second week of the month, with winter approaching, Mar at last decided that it was time for decisive action. On 10 November he marched out of Perth (leaving three battalions to hold the city), with the intention of joining the Jacobite force which was to surrender at Preston. On the 11th he reviewed his army at Auchterarder, where he had just been joined by a body of Highlanders under General Alexander Gordon who had been sent from Perth to rally the western clans. On the other hand, Mar had been weakened by the desertion of the Frasers and a battalion of Gordons during the night of the 10/11th. Nevertheless his army was still formidable. He was reluctant however, to fight a pitched battle: it had been decided before leaving Perth that three diversionary attacks would be made in the vicinity of Stirling to occupy Argyll while Mar and the bulk of his army crossed the Forth further upstream.

Unfortunately for the Jacobites, Argyll had a number of spies in their camp and thus soon received information about their advance and plans. His response was bold. He ordered Wightman to join him from Edinburgh with his men and then, after leaving militia to hold Stirling, took the offensive at the head of an army which though reinforced was still weaker than that of his opponent. Argyll left Stirling on 12 November and later that day encamped just to the east of Dunblane, beneath wild and windswept Sheriffmuir.

On the same day Mar moved south from Auchterarder, with General Gordon commanding an advance guard. Argyll's unexpected march from Stirling thwarted an attempt by Gordon to secure Dunblane and so he halted at about 4.00pm at Kinbuck two miles to the north and awaited Mar who appeared on the scene at around 9.00pm.

Before dawn the following morning, the Jacobites drew up just to the east of Kinbuck. Then, as the sun rose at about 8.00am they saw, as the Master of Sinclair recalled, 'a command of horse on the high ground to the south'. As Robert Patton states, the horse were 'on the Height of the West End of the Sheriff Muir'.

What the Jacobites were looking at was a reconnaissance party led by Argyll. For some time both sides looked at each other. Mar then sent cavalry and foot to drive away the enemy and so the reconnaissance party moved off. A council of war was then held in the Jacobite camp and it was decided to give battle. Consequently, after 11.00am, the Jacobites commenced moving and soon began ascending Sheriffmuir.

Argyll responded by leading his men up onto the moor to confront the Jacobites. In the past Highlanders had routed government soldiers by charging furiously down on them and he did not wish to let that happen again.

Before discussing events further, something needs to be said about the character and background of the respective commanders and the composition, weaponry and tactics of the armies they led.

ARGYLL AND HIS ARMY

The Duke of Argyll was born in 1678. His military career began as a teenager when he was appointed to command the regiment founded by his father, the Argylls. He soon showed signs of great promise, and in later years enhanced his reputation at Ramillies (1706), Oudenarde (1708) and Malplaquet (1709), where he held high rank under Marlborough.

Argyll was brave and daring. At Malplaquet, for example, he led an audacious charge which drove the French from the woods of Sart and though he escaped injury, his coat, hat and periwig were hit by shot. In the Highlands exploits such as this made him a respected figure, and he was known as 'Red John of the Battles'.

Argyll did not only cut a fine figure on the battlefield. He made his mark in the political field – he played a prominent part in bringing about the Act of Union of 1707 which united Scotland and England – and was noted for his fine oratory. Indeed, Lord Chesterfield said of him that he was the most 'persuasive and applauded speaker I ever saw'. His abilities in both fields were commemorated by Pope in the couplet quoted at the beginning of this chapter. Nevertheless, despite his ability, he was prone to bouts of depression and self-doubt.

On the whole, it is probably fair to say that Argyll has not had a good press. He was certainly proud and ambitious. However, he was an essentially decent man, less cold and manipulative than some of his line: his actions were often motivated by passion, and though intelligent, he was significantly described by a contemporary as a weak reasoner.

In later life he said of himself: 'I have, ever since I set out in the world...served my prince with my tongue. I have served him with any little interest I had; and I have served him in my trade, and were I tomorrow to be stripped of all the employments I have endeavoured honestly to deserve, I would serve him again to the utmost of my power, and to the last drop of my blood'.

Argyll's army was composed of regular soldiers save for some gentlemen volunteers. Some of the regiments were raw, having been newly raised; the remainder, though well below full strength, contained many veterans who had fought under Marlborough.

Officers of this period were usually of gentle birth and though some did not take their duties very seriously, many were competent and dedicated soldiers who displayed a high degree of professionalism. The rank and file were mostly of dubious background. Few respectable members of society found the idea of enlisting attractive owing to bad pay and poor living conditions.

At Sheriffmuir Argyll had some 900 or so cavalry, 60 gentlemen volunteers, and about 2,200 infantry.

The cavalry consisted of five regiments of dragoons. These rode inferior mounts to those of the higher ranking cavalry of the line – the Horse – who were not among the duke's small army. In the past dragoons had usually dismounted to fight but by this date it had become common for them to serve as cavalry. The dragoon was principally armed with a carbine and a straight sword. In appearance he looked like an infantryman, except for his riding boots.

The bulk of Argyll's army consisted of eight regiments of foot. These were single battalion regiments, as were most of the regiments of foot in the British Army, comprising thirteen companies. Of these one was a grenadier company, the remainder contained musketeers.

Grenadiers were the tallest and strongest infantry and were often used as shock troops. They were usually armed with three hand grenades, a musket, bayonet and sword, and also possessed a hatchet.

Musketeers were armed with flintlock muskets (which had an effective range of about 60 yards), swords, and socket bayonets which fitted over the muzzle and thus allowed the musket to be fired with the bayonet in place, unlike earlier bayonets which had plugged into the muzzle thereby rendering the weapon inoperative as a firearm. The principal task of the infantry was to rout the enemy foot. A regiment advanced to the attack in line, drawn up three ranks deep, then, when within effective range, halted and began firing systematically with the front rank kneeling.

Mar and his Army

The Earl of Mar was born in 1675 into an illustrious but impoverished aristocratic Scottish family. He was a politician, not a soldier, and held high office as Secretary of State for Scotland during the reign of Anne and participated in the events which brought about the Act of Union.

A contemporary, George Lockhart of Carnwath, wrote that Mar's 'greatest talent lay in the cunning management of his designs and projects...and thus he showed himself to be a man of good sense but bad morals'. He was undoubtedly ambitious and proved himself ready to change his allegiance when he believed it in his best interests to do so. It is said that his nickname, 'Bobbing John', derived from his jerky gait and willingness to change his coat when he saw which way the tide was turning. It is only right however to note that Mar was not the only one prone to tergiversation, for treachery and double dealing in political circles were about as commonplace as severed heads in Revolutionary France. Moreover, although capable of decisive action, Mar was essentially weak and had difficulty converting stirring oratory into real achievements.

At Sheriffmuir he had approximately 800 horse, most of whom were Lowlanders, and about 6,290 foot, the majority of whom were clansmen from the Grampian Highlands.

Though not regular soldiers, many clansmen had seen action in inter-clan conflicts. They were brought to battle by their chief, or one of his representatives, and it would thus be a mistake to conclude that all Highlanders who fought for the Stuarts did so out of devotion to the Jacobite cause for many would have been compelled to serve.

The principal weapon of well-equipped Highlanders was the broadsword, a single-handed basket-hilted weapon of continental origin which, incidentally, was also used by many cavalry of the British Army. Clansmen also possessed dirks. These were usually 18in long, and for many Highlanders served as a substitute for a sword. Those who could afford to do so also had a musket and/or, a pair of pistols. Hay forks, scythes, and sometimes even sticks, were used by the humblest members of Highland society. For protection many clansmen carried a round shield known as a targe. When lined up for combat the best equipped individuals were naturally placed to the fore.

The normal tactic was to charge towards the enemy on foot, screaming clan war-cries. On the eve of Falkirk in 1746 General Henry Hawley, a veteran of Sheriffmuir, recalled that when within 'three score yards' of their opponents charging clansmen in the front rank would fire and then discard their muskets. They, and their colleagues, would then continue on 'in a cluster with their swords and targes making a noise and endeavouring to pierce...the battalions before them'.

Though generally courageous, it was uncommon for clansmen to indulge in senseless heroics. If things went wrong they usually withdrew. 'Better is a good retreat than a bad stand' was one of their proverbs.

The virtues of the Highland warrior were courage and toughness. The failings were a strong tendency to desert with loot and a general lack of discipline.

As far as dress is concerned, the majority of clansmen would have been wearing, as their chief item of clothing, the belted plaid. This was a large tartan garment belted at the waist so that the lower portion hung to the knees as a roughly pleated skirt, while the remainder was either wrapped around the upper part of the body or fastened to the left shoulder by a brooch or pin. No doubt trews were worn instead by some of those present.

As has been noted, Lowlanders also served in Mar's army. Most were infantry, but there were mounted country gentlemen and their retinues from Aberdeenshire, Fife, Stirlingshire and elsewhere.

DESCRIPTION

It was approaching midday when the armies began deploying for battle on Sheriffmuir. Mar's army – which had advanced in several columns from near Kinbuck – was evidently the first to arrive at the battlesite. The exact deployment of the Jacobites is uncertain. Apparently, though, the host became rather disorganised for Mar recalled that 'they fell in some confusion in forming up for battle'.

According to the Master of Sinclair, as horse were making their way to deploy on the left flank, aides de camp rode up as they were nearing their position and ordered that all the horse were to go 'to the right of the whole army'. Hence at least some of the horse in question moved to the right. Furthermore, a squadron under the Earl Marischal ended up somewhere in the centre. Marischal's brother, James Keith, a veteran of the battle, recalled that 'one column of foot' inclined to the right 'and another to the left of the Earl Marischal's squadron of horse' with the result that the squadron, 'which should have been on the right,

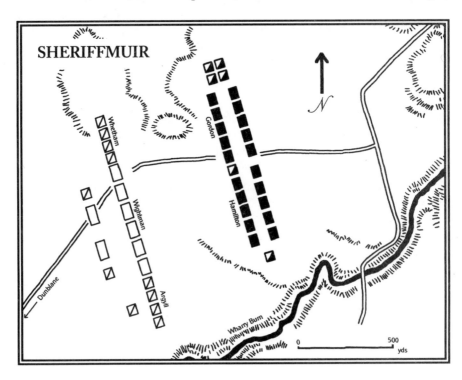

found itself in the centre'. Similarly, Mar recorded that 'some of the horse for-m'd near the centre'.

The army was drawn up in two lines. General Gordon was in command on the right, and General Hamilton on the left. Mar, who was in overall command, took up a position somewhere on the right.

And what of Argyll's army? The right wing was under the personal command of the duke. It seems to have consisted of two squadrons of Evan's dragoons and two squadrons of the Royal Scots Greys with, to the rear, the gentlemen volunteers. General Wightman commanded the centre. This consisted of six regiments of foot in the front line – these were, probably, from left to right, Clayton's, Montagu's, Morrison's, Shannon's, Wightman's and Forfar's Buffs – with Orrery's and Egerton's regiments of foot to the rear. On either flank of the second line was a squadron of Stair's dragoons. The left wing, under General Whetham, consisted of Carpenter's and Kerr's dragoons.

Interestingly, the right wings of the armies overlapped the enemy left wing. This was due to the lie of the ground, which led to neither commander being entirely sure of his opponent's dispositions, and the speedy nature of the preparations for battle.

We are told that the Jacobites were eager to fight, confident of victory: at last the weeks of frustration were over. As for Argyll's men, some probably drew comfort from the fact that their commander was one of the most admired soldiers in the British Army, while others perhaps dwelt on the fearsome reputation of the Highlanders and drew little comfort from doing so.

And what of the terrain? Today much of the battlesite is well-wooded but in 1715 Sheriffmuir was wild and desolate. Moreover, towards the south, where the land falls to a stream known as the Wharry Burn, some of the ground was waterlogged, though at least some of this appears to have been rendered passable by a heavy frost.

Reportedly, the Jacobite right wing could have fallen upon the opposing government soldiers before the latter were prepared to receive them. Sinclair tells us that Gordon was told by 'Captain Livingstone of Dumbarton's Regiment, with great oaths, To attack the enemie before they were formed'. Gordon, however, was unwilling to do so without consulting Mar and the resultant delay enabled the vulnerable government soldiers to deploy, or at least be in a better state of readiness than had been the case.

When the Jacobite right wing did charge it momentarily faltered when Allan MacDonald, the popular and courageous Captain of Clanranald, was cut down by enemy fire. At this point however, Alexander MacDonnell of Glengarry rushed forward, shouting: 'Revenge! Revenge! Today for revenge, and tomorrow for mourning!' and in so doing urged the Highlanders on.

Soon they clashed with the ranks of their outnumbered opponents and set to work with their dirks and broadswords. Fear rapidly spread among their adversaries. It was not long before resistance collapsed and the soldiers began fleeing towards Dunblane. Whetham, on the extreme left with Carpenter's dragoons, reportedly fought courageously but his efforts to inspire his men came to nothing and he too was soon falling back. Not surprisingly, the fleeing horse and foot were pursued. Mar himself, was among those who gave chase, in the belief that the battle was won. But was it? How had the Jacobites fared elsewhere?

Here things were going well for Argyll. Hamilton's men charged at about the same time as their colleagues on the right, but met stiffer resistance. After inconclusive fighting between the infantry, Argyll sent his dragoons under Colonel Cathcart against the Jacobite left flank and this threw the latter onto the defensive. They began to be pushed back and then broke. The gallant young Earl of Strathmore perished at this juncture. Deserted by many of his men, he fought on doggedly until, having been struck by a musket shot, he was cut down by a dragoon. Of him Sinclair wrote: 'He was the young man of all I ever saw who approached the nearest to perfection'.

Though the government soldiers in this sector had gained the upper hand their opponents did not take to headlong flight. They rallied on several occasions, thirteen in all it is said. However, Argyll ensured that they received little respite and slowly drove them back in a two-mile semicircle to Allan Water. Here, in the vicinity of Kinbuck, three hours or so after the battle's commencement, some of the tired and dispirited Jacobites managed to escape by crossing the river. Others drowned while attempting to do so, or chose to surrender instead. It seems that Argyll tried to minimise casualties as much as possible, for at some stage after his men had gained the upper hand he reportedly cried out 'Oh! Spare the poor Bluebonnets'.

One of the Jacobites who did manage to cross Allan Water was John Cameron, the commander of the Cameron regiment. He subsequently stated in a letter to his formidable father, Lochiel, that shortly after doing so he 'percieved Rob Roy MacGregor' and his men marching toward him, 'coming from the town of Doune'. Cameron continues: 'I marched towards him with the few I had got together, perceiving Argyll opposite to us, I entreated...that we would join and cross the River to attack Argyll; which he absolutely refused'. But whether Cameron can be trusted on this point is uncertain (it has been suggested that he was trying to assure his father that his performance at Sheriffmuir was a creditable one), for accounts of Rob Roy's actions on the 13th differ, though all agree that he did not take part in the fighting.

As for Argyll, from Allan Water he commenced retracing his steps to confront Mar, who had returned to the field with the victorious Jacobite right wing. Upon returning, Mar had found the Master of Sinclair and the bulk of the Jacobite horse – which had not come to blows – on a small hill known as the Stoney Hill of Kippendavie, to the west of their position at the time of the battle's commencement. Of the horse in question Peter Rae commented: 'They stood without attempting any Thing, with their swords drawn, for near four hours space'.

From the Stoney Hill of Kippendavie Mar watched Argyll approach. The duke may have had nearly 1,500 soldiers – the figure is often put at 1,000 – and either way he was substantially outnumbered. He reformed with the Scots Greys on the right, the infantry in the centre, and Evan's and some of Stair's dragoons on the left. According to his biographer, Robert Campbell, his position was among 'some Enclosures and mud Walls, which would serve for a Breast-work in Case they were attack'd'. It was about 4.00pm.

A stalemate ensued. Sinclair recalled that the opposing forces 'stood looking at one another about four hundred yards distance, for half an hour'. At least some in the Jacobite camp wished to take the offensive. According to Sinclair, one such was John Gordon of Glenbucket who, frustrated by Mar's inaction, exclaimed: 'Oh! For one hour of Dundee'. A reference to the courageous leader of the Jacobite revolt of 1689 who, it is safe to assume, would not have dithered if he had been in Mar's shoes.

Sinclair states that 'with night comeing on, the Duke of Argyle seem'd first to make a feint as if he was moveing towards us, and inclined after to Dunblain, and it being almost dark, we soon lost sight of them'. The duke and his men spent the night in and around the town. Then, the following morning, they returned to Sheriffmuir where they collected a large quantity of discarded arms, as well as some cannon which had played no part in the battle. They then returned to Stirling.

As for Mar, after Sheriffmuir he moved to Ardoch where he spent the night. With an army weakened by desertion, he then fell back to Perth.

John Baynes has calculated that Argyll's casualties at Sheriffmuir were roughly as follows: 377 killed, 153 wounded, and 133 taken prisoner (most of whom were soon released owing to lack of means to feed and accommodate them). In contrast, Mar's casualties are said to have been 60 killed, 90 wounded and 82 taken captive. Even if the figures for the number of Jacobites killed or wounded err somewhat on the low side, it is evident that Argyll's losses were greater than those of his opponent. However, Mar did lose more people of note – the Earl of Strathmore, the Captain of Clanranald and Patrick Lyon of Auchterhouse. On the government side the most notable fatality was the Earl of Forfar who died of his wounds following the battle.

The end of the rising is soon told. On 22 December James Stuart landed at Peterhead near Aberdeen, having sailed to Scotland from Dunkirk. On the 27th he was met by Mar and a party of leading Jacobites at Fetteresso Castle, the seat of the Earl Marischal, and was subsequently escorted to Perth.

He entered Perth on 9 January 1716. However, his long awaited arrival failed to raise the spirits of the depressed and depleted Jacobite army for he had come to Scotland without arms or men save for a few companions. Moreover, although brave – he had conducted himself with great gallantry at the Battle of Malplaquet – James was not an inspirational character. Nonetheless, it was something of a miracle that he arrived in Scotland at all for the government of France's new king, Louis XV, had tried to obstruct him while the British ambassador in Paris, Lord Stair, had arranged an assassination attempt. Furthermore, bad weather had added to James' difficulties.

By this date Argyll had been joined by General Cadogan (with whom he was on bad terms), and substantial reinforcements. Hence in late January he marched out of Stirling once again, and moved north against the Pretender. Faced with his advance, the Jacobites left Perth – having burned to the ground villages between Dunblane and Perth in order to hamper Argyll – and fell back to Dundee. From there they retreated to Montrose. Here, on 4 February, James, Mar and some other leading Jacobites, boarded a ship, the *Marie-Therese*, and sailed for France in the early hours of the 5th.

Before departing, James appointed General Gordon commander-in-chief of the Jacobite army, and Gordon proceeded to lead the dispirited force north to Aberdeen. He was closely pursued by Argyll, despite inclement weather. Shortly after this, in mid February, what remained of the army fell apart after entering the Highlands when the clansmen melted away into the hills and glens, heading for home. As for Argyll, he set out for London leaving his successor, Cadogan, a more ruthless character, to pacify the Highlands.

Sheriffmuir is sometimes described as an inconclusive engagement. This view is wrong. It was a victory for Argyll, albeit a costly one. The battle was a major reverse for the Jacobite cause. When the Pretender arrived at Perth he found an army filled with despondency and plagued by desertion. This was primarily due to the outcome of Sheriffmuir. The battle highlighted more clearly than ever before Mar's incapacity for generalship and led to widespread disaffection, something which James with his uninspiring personality and lack of resources could not allay. Not for nothing did Peter Rae observe of Sheriffmuir, 'by this battle the heart of the Rebellion was broke'. It was a view shared by others. James Keith, for example, declared in his memoirs that the engagement 'was the entire ruin of our party'. Moreover, Sheriffmuir had a long-term effect. In future years fewer Scots were to rally to the Jacobite cause, and this is undoubtedly partly attributable to the outcome of the events that occured on and about Sheriffmuir on 13 November 1715.

Mar's performance during the campaign and battle has been highly criticised and rightly so. His lengthy stay at Perth before advancing south was a major blunder. True, during this period his army was augmented by reinforcements, but then so too was Argyll's. As a result of the delay, much of Mar's army became increasingly disillusioned by the quality of his leadership and this led to desertion even before the crowning failure of Sheriffmuir.

At Sheriffmuir itself Mar again demonstrated his incapacity for generalship when, after routing part of Argyll's army, he failed to move against what remained. As Christopher Sinclair-Stevenson has commented, he 'could have swept down to deliver the coup de grace at any moment of his choosing'. Instead, he did nothing, and his failure to act clearly demonstrates his weakness and incompetence.

In short, there can be little doubt that in 1715 Mar squandered the best chance the Jacobites ever had of bringing about the restoration of the House of Stuart. To be fair, it is only right to mention that he showed courage and determination by initiating the rising in the first place. Furthermore, he was not the only Jacobite who failed to distinguish himself. The Master of Sinclair, for example, who subsequently poured scorn on Mar, simply watched proceedings at Sheriffmuir instead of coming to blows with the enemy. Not for nothing did Rae comment that the quality of the Jacobite leadership was such that it 'counteracted the warlike spirits of the clans', leaving the rank and file amazed.

And what of Argyll? He has justly been criticised by John Baynes for not positioning 'himself where he could control the whole of his forces' at Sheriffmuir. However, his overall performance during the rising is worthy of commendation, not disparagement, and it is clear that some historians (though not Baynes) have underestimated the difficulties he faced. For a start, his own clan, the Campbells, was divided. It is true that the majority followed his lead and supported the House of Hanover, but hundreds joined the ranks of Mar's army and in so doing must have caused Argyll some distress.

Furthermore, throughout much of the campaign he received little material support from the government which, fearing Jacobite insurrections in England, was unwilling to send him large numbers of reinforcements. Thus Argyll found himself facing the threat posed by an opponent commanding a stronger army than he, in a country which was largely pro-Jacobite. Nonetheless, on the whole he met the threat with skill and resolution. For instance, he reacted promptly to the news that Borlum was threatening Edinburgh, and later, boldly advanced to confront Mar, thereby forcing his opponent off balance.

As noted, this was a courageous move. True, Mar's force was made up of irregular soldiers, but it is also true that in 1689 clansmen under Dundee had routed a numerically superior government force at Killiekrankie, something of which Argyll was no doubt well aware. Furthermore, when it is borne in mind that in later years Highlanders were to rout regular soldiers again (including of course part of Argyll's army at Sheriffmuir) it becomes clear that the duke deserves commendation for driving much of Mar's army back to Allan Water for it was no foregone conclusion.

Following his arrival in London, Argyll received appropriate thanks for his services. However, as Robert Campbell relates, 'this sunshine did not last long' for he was soon 'turned out of all his places' by the government. His downfall was due to the spite of persons such as Cadogan who accused him of being too magnanimous to the king's enemies. Nevertheless, Argyll was later restored to favour and created Duke of Greenwich. Upon his death in 1743 he was buried in Westminster Abbey and his splendid monument bears the following inscription honouring a brave, able, and compassionate soldier who, admittedly assisted by his opponent's ineptitude, saved Scotland for the House of Hanover. It reads:

'In memory of an Honest Man, a Constant Friend,
John the Great Duke of Argyle and Greenwich.
A general and orator exceeded by none in the
Age in which he lived'.

28

CULLODEN
16 APRIL 1746

'I am come home, sir'
— Bonnie Prince Charlie

Despite the failure of the '15 rebellion, hopes of the restoration of the House of Stuart continued in the hearts of many Jacobites and resulted in subsequent risings. The greatest of these was the '45, which culminated in the Battle of Culloden, one of the most famous engagements in British history and one surrounded by an aura of romance.

The rising was led by Charles Edward Stuart – Bonnie Prince Charlie – whose father, James, had belatedly participated in the '15 rebellion and was known as the Old Pretender. Charles was born in Rome in 1720 and grew up to be intensely proud of his Stuart blood and determined to oust the Hanoverian dynasty from the domains which his grandfather James II and VII had lost.

Determined he certainly was, for he overcame setbacks which would have daunted other men. For instance, initially it seemed as though he would receive great French assistance. France was a major participant in a war known as the War of the Austrian Succession (1740–48), and in 1743 a French army was defeated by a British and Hanoverian force under George II at Dettingen. Following this reverse, the French planned to weaken Britain's war effort by stirring up a Jacobite rebellion in Scotland (which was to be led by a veteran Scottish Jacobite, Lord Marischal, who was living as an exile in France), and by threatening to invade England from Dunkirk with an army under Marshal Maurice de Saxe. Word of this was leaked to the Old Pretender who thus sent Charles from Rome to Paris to play a part in the proceedings.

By March 1744 Charles was at Gravelines waiting to embark. As for Marischal, he believed that the French were simply playing a selfish game and so refused to play along with their schemes. Moreover, he wrote to Charles while the latter was at Gravelines urging him to 'guard against being made a tool of France'. Marischal was right. The French had no intention of supporting a Jacobite rising in Scotland, and their planned invasion of England was merely a feint to force the British government to recall troops from Flanders and lift a blockade of the main French fleet at Toulon. Hence, upon hearing that the blockade had ended and that soldiers had been recalled from Flanders, Saxe left Dunkirk (on about 16 March) with the bulk of his men and marched into Flemish territory.

Charles remained at Gravelines for some weeks after receiving the disappointing news of Saxe's departure, and then returned to Paris. As time passed it became increasingly apparent that waiting for French assistance was a waste of time. Charles thus faced a stark choice: he could either give up and accept that nothing was going to happen, or he could lead a rising himself in Scotland in the hope that success there would propel the French into rendering assistance and helping to administer the coup de grace to the Hanoverian dynasty in Britain. Boldly, he chose the latter.

Consequently, on 5 July 1745, he set sail for Scotland from Belle-Ile (near St Nazaire) on board an 18-gun frigate, *Du Teillay,* one of two vessels provided by Jacobite owners: the other ship was a 68-gun man-o'-war, the *Elizabeth.* With Charles was a small group of companions, one of whom was a notorious Irish soldier of fortune, Colonel John O'Sullivan. The vessels also carried arms and ammunition Charles had acquired himself. It was a tremendously daring enterprise upon which they were set, but the prince and his associates must have been encouraged by the knowledge that on 11 May Saxe had defeated a British army and its allies at Fontenoy. Not all was going well for the British abroad: it was Charles' intention that British forces would now suffer reverses at home.

After five days at sea *Du Teillay* and the *Elizabeth* were intercepted off Lizard Point, Cornwall, by a 64-gun man-o'-war, HMS *Lion.* A vicious struggle ensued between the *Lion* and the *Elizabeth* in which the captains of both perished. When night fell, the *Lion* sailed off, after which the *Elizabeth* commenced returning to France taking with her the bulk of the arms Charles had acquired for she was too damaged to press on.

Despite this, the prince continued sailing towards Scotland, and experienced stormy weather as he did so. On 23 July he landed on the impoverished island of Eriskay off the west coast of Scotland. The following day he was met by Alexander MacDonald of Boisdale who told him that two important chiefs upon whom the prince was relying for support, Sir Alexander MacDonald of Sleat and Norman MacCleod, were not prepared to 'come out' in rebellion on the grounds that Charles had arrived without French troops. This was a major blow to the prince, who was bluntly told by Boisdale to go home, to which he retorted, 'I am come home, sir'.

The likelihood that Charles could lead a successful rising certainly did not seem high. True, the English government was unpopular in Scotland, even among non-Jacobites, and there were other factors in favour of a successful rebellion, but on the whole the chances of a rising succeeding were not as good as they had once been. For a start, in the 1720s and 1730s a chain of strategically placed forts, linked by military roads, had been created in the Highlands by General Wade, thereby making the region more accessible and easier to police for government forces. Furthermore, the failure of previous Jacobite risings, especially the '15, must have added to any feelings of apprehension felt by potential rebels.

On the 25th Charles came ashore on the mainland at Lochailort in Arisaig. Again, the prince and his companions met with disappointment. Other senior MacDonalds refused their support, influenced by the stance of MacDonald of Sleat. But despite entreaties from the clan luminaries and his companions to throw in the towel, Charles remained adamant and managed to win over a number of the unenthusiastic MacDonalds, such as young Ranald of Clanranald.

Shortly after this, Charles was visited by Donald Cameron of Lochiel, chief of the Camerons. Exactly what was said at their meeting is unknown. What matters is that Lochiel finally yielded to the prince's entreaties and gave his conditional support, one of the conditions being that the Young Pretender promised him security for his estates if the rising failed: the prince pledged jewels which had belonged to his late mother. Lochiel's decision was a major boost to Charles for he was one of the most influential figures in the Highlands and his continued adherence to the Jacobite cause inspired other chiefs to rally likewise to the prince's side.

On 19 August the Stuart standard was raised at Glenfinnan, at the head of Loch Shiel, and Charles' father, James, was proclaimed king. Looking on were about 1,300 Highlanders, many of them Clanranald and Keppoch MacDonalds. The remainder – approximately 700 men – were Camerons, for Lochiel had promised the prince that 'every man over whom nature or fortune' had given him any power would be committed to the rising and had been as good as his word, having had to resort to threatening many of his reluctant clansmen with burning their bothies over their heads. It was a momentous day for Charles and his feelings of excitement were no doubt enhanced by knowledge that other chiefs and their men were marching to join him.

By this date news of the prince's landing had arrived in London. George II was in Hanover and thousands of British troops were likewise on the continent. The government reacted by recalling regiments and by offering a reward of £30,000 for the apprehension of the Young Pretender. Then, in late August, George returned to England 'in good humour', confident that the rising would come to nothing.

Regular forces in Scotland only numbered 3,750 men in scattered garrisons. Their commander was General Sir John Cope, an experienced soldier who had fought at Dettingen. He marched north from Edinburgh towards Fort Augustus in the Highlands, intending to bring the Jacobites to battle before they grew stronger. Charles, however, whose force had been augmented since the standard had been raised at Glenfinnan, decided to move north-east to the Corrieyairack Pass to block Cope's route. Fearful that his men would be ambushed as they made their way through the pass, Cope thus changed his mind and headed north to Inverness in the hope of rallying loyal clans. Hence the Jacobites made their way down the pass and proceeded to Perth – which they entered on 4 September – having obtained recruits en route. At Perth itself the Jacobite army was again augmented. One of those who joined Charles was Lord George Murray, a 51-year-old veteran of the '15 and '19 risings, and a man who enjoyed a significant degree of prestige in Scotland.

On 11 September the Jacobites marched southward to Dunblane, en route to Edinburgh. Tuesday, 17 September, was one of the most momentous days of the Young Pretender's life for he entered the Scottish capital in style and was welcomed by enthusiastic crowds. He made a notable impression and it was on this occasion that the sobriquet 'Bonnie Prince Charlie' was first used. At Edinburgh Charles was joined by some volunteers from the city, as well as by men from elsewhere such as Lachlan MacLachlan of MacLachlan who arrived with 150 of his clansmen.

Meanwhile Cope had marched from Inverness to Aberdeen, from where he shipped his army south with the aim of defending Edinburgh. However, by the time his men disembarked at Dunbar the capital, (though not the castle, which was held by government soldiers), was in enemy hands. Cope now hurried towards Edinburgh determined to engage the Young Pretender.

Aware of his approach, Charles left Edinburgh on 19 September and moved to Duddingston at the head of an army about 2,400 strong, intent on battle. On the 20th he came across Cope at Prestonpans. Although Cope was in a strong defensive position, his army of 2,000 foot and 500 dragoons, was overwhelmed in less than fifteen minutes early on the 21st by Highlanders fighting 'like enraged furies'.

Following the battle, in which he fought bravely, Cope fled south to Berwick. On the other hand Charles returned to Edinburgh. Although his instinct was for a swift advance on England, he was prevailed upon to wait in Edinburgh for some weeks, primarily in the hope that large-scale French assistance would be forthcoming. A messenger was despatched to Versailles with the task of securing just that.

As far as Scotland was concerned, Charles' victory at Prestonpans made a number of hitherto reluctant Jacobites decide to throw in their lot with him, though this was offset somewhat by the desertion of victorious clansmen who headed home with loot they had stripped from the bodies of fallen government soldiers.

While at Edinburgh the prince established a permanent cabinet or Grand Council, which included men who had accompanied him to Scotland from France such as O'Sullivan, as well as the leaders of clan regiments such as Lochiel, and men of substance such as Lord George Murray. The council met daily and, in addition to discussing strategy, dealt with matters such as raising further troops and equipping the army. It is interesting to note that in mid October their task was eased somewhat by the arrival of artillery and stores sent from France. Moreover, one of the vessels also brought the Marquis d'Eguilles who had been sent to Scotland – prior to Prestonpans – on a fact-finding mission.

Meanwhile, the government had been strengthening its position. More troops were recalled from Flanders, and some of these were sent north to Newcastle where they augmented an army under Wade, who was now a field marshal.

On the 30th and 31st of October, Charles and his council decided to invade England and bypass Wade by advancing into the north-west of the country. The decision was only arrived at after an acrimonious debate. The prince was eager to move south. For one thing, it was evident that the Jacobite army was growing restless and such a move would counter any boredom. Moreover, Louis XV was an indecisive character and as Frank McLynn has commented, it was thus 'vital not to give [him] a plausible excuse for doing nothing'. On the other hand, Charles was opposed by a faction led by Murray which argued that it would be a mistake to invade England with their small army, especially without any guarantee of large-scale French military support, and that it would be wiser to retreat into the Highlands where forts still in government hands could be dealt with, and where pressure could be put on clan chiefs who had not committed themselves to the Jacobite cause to do so, thereby making any subsequent descent on England more likely to succeed. The prince's faction, however, just managed to win the vote. But a compromise ensued. Charles wished to move against Wade in the belief that a second victory, particularly one on English soil, was needed soon to maintain momentum, but acceded to Murray's wish that Wade be bypassed.

At the beginning of November the Jacobites began moving south. They did so in two columns, one led by Charles, the other by Murray. The prince headed south-east, giving the impression that he was making for Newcastle, and then made his way westward and down Liddesdale to join up with Murray near Carlisle. On 8 November the prince forded the Esk, thereby entering England, and linked up with Lord George the following day. The combined force numbered approximately 500 horse and 5,000 foot. It would have been stronger, but significant desertion had occurred during the march through the Lowlands.

On 18 November, after a brief siege, Charles secured the surrender of Carlisle: Wade had attempted to save it but had found the roads across the Pennines unpassable due to snow. From Carlisle the Jacobites advanced south in two columns, one under Murray and the other, a day behind, under the prince. The army was without tents – they had been 'lost' at Moffat – and this division of the force was intended to ease billeting problems in the towns through which the army passed. It was planned to join at Preston, the first sizeable town, and on the 26th Charles met up with Murray there. The Jacobites had hoped for significant support in Lancashire but so far this had not been forthcoming. Nonetheless, the decision to press on was made. On the afternoon of 29 November the prince rode into Manchester. Here he received his first significant English support, 300 or so men, mainly down and outs, who were formed into the Manchester Regiment. Charles had hoped for a greater response but remained undaunted, determined to continue making for London. His determination was not shared by Murray.

Things came to a head after the Jacobites reached Derby on 4 December – en route Lord George had cleverly outmanoeuvred the Duke of Cumberland, who was in command of a government army in Staffordshire, by giving the impression that the Jacobites were making for Wales. At Derby acrimonious meetings of the Jacobite council were held on the 5th. The prince entreated his followers to hold their nerve and press on towards panic-stricken London, 120 miles away. They were, after all, closer to the capital than either Cumberland or Wade: the latter was many miles behind making his way through Yorkshire. But Lord George was adamant that they should commence retreating. Significant English Jacobite support had not been forthcoming; there was no sign of a French invasion, (one was in fact being planned); a government army was assembling to confront them at Finchley near the capital; and to cap it all, according to an English spy, Dudley Bradstreet, another army – which did not exist – was barring the route south at Northampton. In the past Charles had been able to persuade reluctant members of his council to support him, but on this occasion he was about as effective as a chocolate fireguard. Indeed, he later commented that 'he could not prevail upon one single person to support him'. Consequently on 6 December, 'Black Friday', the Jacobites began retracing their steps with the prince in despondent mood. Discipline in the ranks of his army also began faltering as morale declined.

The retreating Jacobites were pursued by Cumberland, and on the 18th at Clifton, near Penrith, English dragoons clashed with the rearguard under Murray. The dragoons were driven off, and following this skirmish Cumberland halted and awaited reinforcements.

On 19 December the Jacobites reached Carlisle. Here, contrary to the wishes of his lieutenants, Charles left a garrison of 400 men to hold the castle, most of whom belonged to the Manchester Regiment. The following day he entered Scotland by fording the swollen River Esk. On the 26th, Charles arrived at Glasgow, a strongly pro-Hanoverian city, and remained there for a week, raising money from its unwilling citizens. He also conducted a review of his army on Glasgow Green which showed that no more than two dozen men had been lost during the days in England.

The Jacobites then moved east, and secured Stirling on the 8th, by which date the Young Pretender had fallen ill with influenza and lay ill nearby at Bannockburn House. During this period around 4,000 reinforcements under the command of Lord John Drummond arrived. Most were Highlanders, including MacKintoshes, Farquharsons and MacKenzies, but about 1,100 were troops of the Irish brigade who had sailed to Montrose with Drummond from France, before linking up with the Highlanders in question at Perth.

Though Charles' men had occupied the town of Stirling, the castle was held for King George. Thus the prince now ordered that the fortress be besieged using artillery brought by Drummond.

As for Cumberland, he had secured the surrender of the garrison at Carlisle on 30 December, and had then returned to London leaving an elderly general, Henry Hawley, to pursue the Young Pretender. On 15 January Hawley marched west from Edinburgh to relieve Stirling Castle at the head of about 8,000 men. Charles moved against him with a force of comparable strength. Hawley had been wounded at Sheriffmuir in 1715 and should have treated the Jacobite army with greater respect than he did. His general ineptitude resulted in the defeat of his force in a short battle at Falkirk on the 17th in which his men attacked uphill, with rain blowing into their faces. Though defeated, Hawley managed to retreat to Linlithgow with the bulk of his force, and then fell back to Edinburgh.

Meanwhile, bitter arguments had occurred among the victors over the fact that Hawley's army had not been dealt with as decisively as could have been the case. Moreover the feelings of tension and gloom in the Jacobite camp were heightened by an unfortunate incident which occurred shortly after the battle. Angus MacDonell of Glengarry, the son of a chief, was accidentally shot at Falkirk by a Keppoch MacDonald who was therefore executed despite entreaties on his behalf by the dying Glengarry, something which alienated many of the Keppoch MacDonalds. It was thus a rather dispirited Jacobite army which made its way back to Stirling – some had wished to move on Edinburgh – where the siege of the castle was resumed.

For his part, Charles returned to Bannockburn House. Once again he was ill, for he had suffered a relapse after Falkirk. On 30 January he was presented with a document signed by Murray and six clan chiefs which strongly urged that the ineffectual siege of Stirling Castle be abandoned and that the army, which had experienced fairly substantial desertion since Falkirk, should withdraw into the Highlands for the remainder of the winter. There the clansmen could spend time with their families, deserters could be rounded up and returned to the fold, and where future successes against forces loyal to George II would likely induce hitherto reluctant people to throw in their lot with the prince. The Young Pretender disagreed. For one thing, he sensibly argued that withdrawal would further undermine morale and lead to more desertion. Nonetheless he complied with the desire to withdraw, stating that he had an army which he could not 'command any further than the chief officers please' and that he washed his hands of the 'fatal consequences' which would ensue.

On 1 February the Jacobites began moving north in a state of disarray, largely owing to a decline in morale. Some dispirited clansmen, for instance, set off without waiting to hear further instructions. The army crossed the Forth at the Fords of Frew. A very heated council of war followed at Crieff. Murray wished to retreat through the Highlands to pro-Jacobite Inverness which was held for the government by the Earl of Loudoun. Charles, though, wished to head for Inverness via the north-east of Scotland, partly in expectation of the arrival there of French support. A compromise thus occurred. The prince reluctantly agreed to make for Inverness through the Highlands while Murray would make his way there via the ports of Montrose and Aberdeen.

The advances of both were undertaken in bitter weather. The prince arrived at Inverness first – Loudoun abandoned the town on the 17th as Charles drew near – and was joined by Lord George on the 21st.

Meanwhile, following Falkirk, Cumberland had been sent north again to take command of operations. He arrived in Edinburgh in late January and shortly thereafter made his way to Perth following the Jacobites' withdrawal from Stirling. On 20 February, after building up his commissariat to ensure that his army was adequately supplied with food, he began advancing towards Aberdeen which he entered on the 27th. He was to remain there until early April awaiting improved weather conditions.

During the weeks which followed Charles' arrival at Inverness, contingents of his army undertook several military ventures. On 3 March Fort Augustus was invested, and surrendered two days later. Then, on the 7th, Fort William was likewise besieged, though the operation was to prove unsuccessful. Furthermore, Lord Loudoun and his men were pursued in Sutherland. Initially the Earl of Cromarty had the task of doing so, but he was soon replaced by the Duke of Perth who surprised Loudoun on 20 March, with the result that the Highland companies comprising the earl's force were scattered. Loudoun and some of his associates managed to escape by sea to the Isle of Skye. March also witnessed a generally successful operation by Lord George Murray in Atholl country, though he failed to take Blair Castle.

On the other hand, March also witnessed a significant reverse for Charles – who was afflicted with scarlet fever for much of the month. On the 25th a Jacobite vessel, *Prince Charles*, was sighted by four Royal Navy cruisers in the Pentland Firth. She had sailed from France carrying men, supplies, and money – £13,600 in English gold and 1,500 guineas – destined for the Young Pretender. Upon being sighted, she was pursued and ran aground in the Kyle of Tongue while trying to escape. The money was brought ashore, only for it to fall into the hands of the pro-government MacKays who, under their chief Lord Reay, ambushed the Jacobite party the following day.

Charles responded by sending a force under Cromarty to regain the money, but the expedition proved a failure. The financial loss could not simply be dismissed as a misfortune. It was a bitter blow. The prince was desperately short of funds and this was undermining morale: desertion owing to lack of pay was becoming increasingly serious. Morale dropped even further when the siege of Fort William was abandoned on 3 April. Then, to make things worse, the Jacobite commissariat began to fail.

As for Cumberland, on 8 April he resumed his advance. By the 11th he had reached Cullen. He then crossed the Spey, and arrived at Nairn on the 14th, about twelve miles east of Inverness. The crossing of the Spey had been uncontested. A Jacobite force under Lord John Drummond and John Roy Stewart, numbering 2,000 men and lacking cannon, withdrew rather than attempt a delaying action. It is sometimes maintained that if the crossing had been contested in strength and with artillery, the Jacobites could have inflicted very significant losses on Cumberland. Although the inexperience of the Jacobite gun crews gives pause for thought, the argument nonetheless carries weight.

Cumberland's approach produced a rapid response on the part of the Jacobite leadership. Outlying forces were recalled – though some failed to return in time for Culloden – and on the 15th Charles took up a position on Drummossie Moor a short distance east of Inverness, and one mile south-east of Culloden House where the prince had spent part of his time since arriving in the region in February. Here the Jacobites awaited Cumberland. But the duke did not come. The 15th was his birthday and he had decided to celebrate the event with his men at Nairn.

While Cumberland and his soldiers celebrated, the Jacobite leaders discussed strategy. Though the Young Pretender and O'Sullivan favoured confronting the duke on Drummossie Moor this was not to the liking of Lord George Murray, an abler and more experienced man than either of them. He rightly believed it to be too exposed a position for lightly armed clansmen to engage a larger and better equipped force and, with the support of the clan chiefs, proposed moving to rougher ground near Dalcross Castle 'such as the Highlanders would have liked very well'. He was, however, overruled by the prince.

Later in the day, though, following the arrival of reinforcements and in the knowledge that Cumberland was still at Nairn, the Jacobite leadership discussed strategy again. It was suggested that they should march that night against Cumberland and launch a surprise attack on his camp before dawn. The idea appealed to both Prince Charles and Murray. As the latter recalled: 'I thought we had a better chanse by doing it then by fighting in so plain a feeld'. The attack was on.

At about 8.00pm, or perhaps slightly later, the Jacobites commenced marching, guided by MacKintoshes who knew the country. The army was in two columns, the first led by Murray, the second by the prince. However the daring advance did not go according to plan, partly because the men were famished. As they trudged through the darkness and mist many of them collapsed through exhaustion due to 'want of food'. Hence, much to the prince's annoyance, Murray and other senior figures, Lochiel for one, decided to forgo the attack and so the weary and dispirited Jacobites turned around and began retracing their steps. At about 6.00am the bulk of the army arrived back on Drummossie Moor. Many were soon fast asleep: others probably found rest elusive, fearing that Cumberland would presently move against them.

A debate now ensued in the Jacobite camp about what to do. Lord George argued strongly in favour of avoiding battle, but held that if Charles were set on fighting it would be best to fall back across to the south side of the River Nairn and take up a position favourable to the Highlanders' mode of fighting reconnoitred the previous day by two officers, Brigadier Walter Stapleton and Colonel Ker of Graden. But the prince adamantly rejected such counsel, even after exhorted not to fight on Drummossie Moor by the French envoy, the Marquis d'Eguilles.

In the meantime Cumberland had received word of the Jacobites' disastrous night march, and had ordered his men to advance. Consequently, at about 10.00am, the Jacobites were roused when they received news that Cumberland was only four miles away and steps were urgently taken by officers to prepare their men. It can be imagined how despondent many must have felt in the prince's army when, at about 11.00am, they saw Cumberland's impressive force of Redcoats drawing near with pipers of the Campbell Militia to the fore.

CHARLES AND HIS ARMY

John Murray of Broughton wrote of Charles: 'the eldest son of the Chevalier de St George [the Old Pretender], is tall, above the common stature, his limbs cast in the most exact mould, his complexion has in it somewhat of an uncommon delicacy; all his features are perfectly regular and well turned, and his eyes the finest I ever saw'.

His appearance was certainly prepossessing. But there was more to the prince than good looks. He was for example endowed with great stamina, and as has been seen, could behave with resolution. Moreover he was very compassionate. At Prestonpans, for instance, he called out to the clansmen to spare Cope's routed men. Furthermore he could be extremely charming and courageous, qualities which he displayed at an early age for in 1734 when only thirteen, while present at the siege of Gaeta, Italy, he stood in the front line trenches with the Duke of Liria who recorded: 'Neither the noise of the cannon, nor the hiss of bullets could produce any sign of fear' in the 'bewitching' youngster.

But like all mortals Charles had foibles. Frank McLynn has commented: 'Always in the prince's personality there was the lack of a middle path or a golden mean. He was too trusting and lacked normal shrewdness and suspicion when dealing with flatterers. When his suspicions were aroused, they quickly toppled into paranoia'. Although more intelligent than is often maintained, Charles' judgement of men and situations was at times strikingly poor and no doubt his susceptibility to flattery was partly responsible. Owing to his mercurial temperament, he could swing quickly from supreme optimism and confidence to despair and then an obstinate, self-destructive streak would manifest itself.

How strong the Jacobite army was is uncertain. Some historians have stated that it numbered as much as 7,000 men – Charles' opponents held that it was over 6,500 strong – but others feel 5,000 is more probable. In contrast, Susan Maclean Kybett is of the opinion that: 'The 4,500 figure usually given for his force at this time is outrageously charitable. A more reasonable estimate is that the Prince had but two thousand bone-weary men left for the Battle of Culloden'. The army had undoubtedly been weakened by desertion and absenteeism but, all things considered, it seems reasonable to conclude that the prince's force was at least 4,000 strong and perhaps approached 5,000 men.

Highlanders formed the bulk of the army. Tactically, they still favoured the old approach of charging ferociously toward the enemy, discharging and then discarding firearms as they did so, before employing swords, dirks and targes in close combat.

On other the hand, as far as the clansmen's appearance is concerned, it is interesting to note that since the '15 rebellion the belted plaid (see page 189) had begun to be superseded by the little kilt.

The remainder of the army consisted of Lowlanders, such as the members of Ogilvy's Regiment raised in Angus, and Franco-Irish troops such as FitzJames' Horse, an experienced fighting unit which had recently seen extensive service in Italy and on the Rhine with the French Army. Unfortunately for the Young Pretender only about 70 members of FitzJames' Horse were present at Culloden, partly owing to the fact that many of the regiment bound for Scotland had been captured by the Royal Navy. Carbines or muskets, pistols and straight brass-hilted swords, were employed by FitzJames' Horse, and Scottish cavalry regiments in the prince's army such as Elcho's Life Guards would have been similarly armed. In addition to FitzJames' Horse, the Franco-Irish contingent included infantry such as the Irish pickets, drawn from Irish regiments in the service of France and veterans of Fontenoy.

The Jacobite artillery train consisted of thirteen guns of varying calibre, the largest was a four-pounder, and some of the cannon had been captured at Prestonpans. The differing calibre of the guns must have created an ammunition supply problem.

CUMBERLAND AND HIS ARMY

The Duke of Cumberland was born in 1721 and was the third son of George II. Like his cousin, the Young Pretender, William Augustus was keen on military matters from boyhood, but unlike Charles, was allowed to pursue a career as a professional soldier. At Dettingen in 1743 he fought on the left of the first line of infantry against the French and as James Wolfe (who was later to gain fame on the heights of Abraham) wrote, 'behaved as bravely as a man could do....He gave his orders with a great deal of calmness and seemed quite unconcerned'. Two years later Cumberland was in sole command of the British contingent of an allied force at Fontenoy, and although the battle was lost, received credit for the way in which he enabled his men to withdraw in order.

A methodical and conscientious commander, Cumberland familiarised himself with the Highlanders' manner of fighting and did not underestimate them: he was determined that he was not going to be humiliated as Cope and Hawley had been.

Physically Cumberland was the antithesis of the Young Pretender. He was fat and ungainly, and in some respects his personality was as unattractive as his appearance. He was, for instance, a harsh, unforgiving character. On the other hand, though not noted for magnanimity to his enemies, he did concern himself with the welfare of his men and was popular with them. Certainly Wolfe's comment regarding Hawley that: 'The troops dread his severity, hate the man and hold his military knowledge in contempt' could not be said to apply to Cumberland as well.

At Culloden Cumberland commanded three regiments of cavalry, fifteen regiments of foot, a company of the Royal Regiment of Artillery, and several companies of Campbells. It was a well equipped, well-fed, and generally highly trained force of around 9,000 men with a formidable artillery train.

On the whole the record of the British Army during the 18th century testifies to its having been a professional and redoubtable force, and despite the humiliating reverses at Prestonpans (where many of the soldiers were raw) and Falkirk, this was true of the army during this period.

There were two types of cavalry: horse and dragoons. The former were big men on large mounts and carried out charges at a fast trot, with the sword being their principal weapon. The latter were expected to fight on foot as well as when mounted and were proficient in musketry, though they also carried a sword.

Infantry comprised the bulk of Cumberland's force. Theoretically, infantry regiments were to total 850 officers and men in ten companies, but in reality they were often well below this. At Culloden, for example, many of the regiments were little over 400 men strong.

The principal weapon was the flintlock musket, especially the recently introduced 'Brown Bess', and the introduction of the iron ramrod in about 1725 meant that at least three effective volleys could probably be fired a minute, a faster rate of fire than had been possible hitherto. In addition to a musket, bayonet and sword, grenadiers – the elite infantry – also carried three hand grenades.

In appearance British soldiers of this period differed little from those who had served in 1715. With the exception of members of the Royal Regiment of Artillery, the soldiers still wore red coats, but regimental facing colours, lace patterns and distinctive badges, had been regularised since the accession of George II in 1727.

The Royal Regiment of Artillery was founded in 1716 and consisted of eight companies, and as noted, one such was present at Culloden. Members of the regiment wore blue coats and their principal weapon was the three-pounder, a gun with a range of about 500 yards.

Cumberland was well aware how devastating a Highland charge could be, and so in the weeks prior to Culloden he trained his infantry to meet such an assault. Each soldier was drilled so that when it came to hand-to-hand fighting he would thrust his bayonet towards the clansman to his right, a move which meant that the bayonet would have a greater chance of striking home than if the soldier thrust at the man in front of him, for the Highlander's right side was more exposed than the left which was protected to some extent by the targe. Moreover, such a move would take the enemy by surprise.

Finally, as has been noted, Cumberland's army included Campbells. They were members of the Argyll Militia, a regiment raised by the 3rd Duke of Argyll at the commencement of the rising. The regiment was approximately 630 officers and men strong at Culloden. The men wore Highland dress, but were identified as being on the government side by having a black cockade and a large red cross on their bonnets.

Prince Charles had unrealistically hoped that the Campbells, the most powerful clan in the Highlands, would support his rising. The fact that they opposed him has helped fuel the antagonism some people have towards the clan. It is only right, however, to bear in mind that some other clans (the MacKays, Munros and Gunns, for example), served on behalf of the government during the rising and that the loyalties of others were divided. After all, the fighting potential of the Highlands was estimated at 32,000 men, and the Young Pretender never enjoyed the support of even a third of that figure.

DESCRIPTION

On Wednesday, 16 April 1746, the battlesite comprised moorland and was bounded to the north and south by walled enclosures. In recent years, under the auspices of the National Trust for Scotland, the site has been largely returned to its appearance on the day of the battle, something which necessitated the removal of many trees planted by the Forestry Commission, thereby rendering an overall view of the site possible again.

For a variety of reasons, including hunger and disenchantment with Charles' leadership, Jacobite morale was not high. The MacDonalds in particular were discontented. Traditionally they fought on the right of the line but this position had been given to Murray's Atholl brigade by the prince who refused to change his mind though entreated to do so by three senior MacDonalds, Clanranald, Lochgarry and Keppoch.

Hence the Atholl brigade formed the right wing of the front line. To its left, and also under Murray's command, were Camerons and Stewarts of Appin. The centre of the line was commanded by Lord John Drummond. Here were Frasers, and members of Clan Chattan, (a confederation of clans which included the MacKintoshes, MacBeans and MacGillivrays), then, beyond a battery of cannon, were more members of Clan Chattan, as well as a regiment of MacLeans and MacLachlans. Next in line was a non-clan unit, John Roy Stewart's regiment consisting of Edinburgh volunteers. Then came the Chisholms. The left wing, which consisted of three MacDonald regiments, was under the Duke of Perth and included some Grants. Cannon were placed on the flanks of the line.

The second line was not as substantial. From right to left it evidently comprised Lord Ogilvy's regiment, that of Lord Lewis Gordon, Gordon of Glenbucket's, the Duke of Perth's regiment, the Royal Scots, (a regiment in the service of France), and the Irish pickets.

Charles' cavalry units appear to have all been deployed in a third line, though by this date many of the 'cavalry' fought on foot owing to lack of mounts. The prince, who had assumed command for the first time, evidently took up a position behind the second line, accompanied by a small mounted escort.

300 yards or more away from the Jacobite front line was that of Cumberland's army. (Owing to the alignment of the armies the distance between the Jacobite left and the duke's right was greater than elsewhere).

As finally deployed – Cumberland made minor alterations to his dispositions during a cannonade which opened the battle – the duke had seven infantry regiments in his front line, from left to right, Barrell's, Munro's, Campbell's, Price's, Cholmondley's, St Clair's and Pulteney's. Another regiment, Wolfe's, was

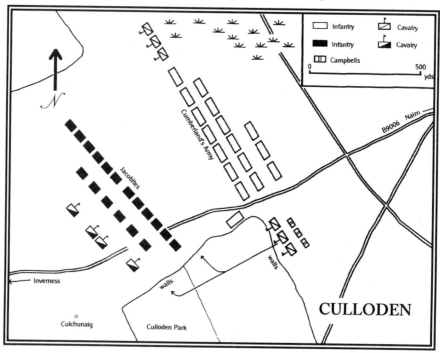

placed a little to the fore at the left end of the line, and at right angles to it, so that flanking fire could be poured into the ranks of attacking Highlanders. The second line had six more infantry regiments, and another such formed a reserve towards the left of the centre.

On the right flank of the front line were Kingston's Horse and sixty of Cobham's Dragoons under General Bland, while on the left flank of the front line, though further from the infantry, were the remainder of Cobham's Dragoons and Lord Mark Kerr's Dragoons, under General Hawley, together with companies of Argyll Militia.

Colonel William Belford, a veteran of Dettingen and Fontenoy, was in command of the artillery which principally comprised ten three-pounders. These were placed at intervals between the regiments of the front line. Moreover, six coehorn mortars were placed in batteries of three to the rear of the right and left of the front line.

Cumberland took up a position to the rear of the front line. He was mounted on a grey horse, confident that his 'brave boys' would bring him victory.

It was just after 1.00pm on this cold, rainy day, that the battle commenced. It did so when the Jacobite guns opened fire. Cumberland's gunners, who were more proficient, responded with sustained fire. As Surgeon Grainger recalled: 'The thunder of our cannons was perpetual'. It was not long before the Jacobite guns had been almost entirely put out of action. Furthermore, fire from Belford's guns cut swathes in the massed ranks of the men waiting for the order to charge. Not for nothing did Grainger record: 'Most of our shots took effect'.

The trajectory of at least two of the guns was deliberately such that shot flew over the first and second lines with the intention of hitting the Young Pretender. Soon his horse was wounded and his groom decapitated. Following this the prince withdrew to a safer position and one of his escort, John Daniel, tells us that as he did so he repeatedly looked around 'to see how his men behaved'. Just where Charles stationed himself is uncertain, but it was probably near the Culchunaig farm steadings just to the south-west of the battlefield.

Meanwhile his army continued receiving punishment from Belford's gunners (who switched from ball to grape-shot during the course of the cannonade), and as Lord George Murray later wrote: 'The regiments in the front rank were turned so impatient that they were like to break their ranks'. His men, on the right, likely suffered most severely, for they were closer to the enemy than their colleagues further down the line.

While the cannonade was occurring, the Campbells and dragoons on the left of Cumberland's army entered an enclosure in front of their position, (the Campbells pulled down sections of dry stone walling to make way for the dragoons), and some of the Argyll Militia then made their way northward up the sloping ground until they came to the north wall of the enclosure where they halted, ready to pour flanking fire into the Jacobite right flank if it charged. On the other hand, after entering the enclosure, some of the Campbells headed west, accompanied by the dragoons, and made their way through another wall, thereby entering an enclosure close to the right flank of the Jacobite army. Seeing this, Lord George Murray ordered Ogilvy's regiment on the right of the second line to face them and a fire-fight evidently ensued with the Campbells. The dragoons continued westward, accompanied by other members of the Argyll Militia, evidently with the aim of exiting the enclosure and threatening the right flank or rear of the Jacobite army.

By about this stage the men facing the bulk of Cumberland's army had had more than enough of a pounding – they had endured the cannonade for at least ten minutes – and in desperation Murray sent Kerr of Graden to find Charles, requesting that the order to charge be given. The prince evidently responded positively by sending one of his aides-de-camp, young Lachlan MacLachlan, forward with the order to charge but before he could deliver the order he was decapitated by a cannonball. Sir John MacDonald and Brigadier Stapleton were then sent by the prince to give the order.

Evidently, though, Clan Chattan in the centre of the front line under the chief of the MacGillivrays, Alexander MacGillivray of Dunmaglas, commenced charging without having received the order to do so. Soon Murray and the right of the line were charging too. However, on the left, the MacDonalds initially refused to charge after receiving the order to do so and, when they finally moved forward, did so with little vigour.

Hail and rain caused the charging clansmen some discomfort, as did smoke which blew into their eyes, but this was nothing compared to the grape-shot which continued bringing death and destruction into their ranks. Nonetheless they kept charging, 'like troops of hungry wolves', states a government soldier, Private Alexander Taylor.

As the men of Clan Chattan charged they suddenly veered to their right onto firmer ground, and in so doing hampered somewhat the advance of Murray's regiments. Indeed, Maxwell of Kirkconnel relates that the resulting congestion was such that many of the clansmen 'could make no use of their firearms' and so discarded them. On and on the densely packed Highlanders charged. Those on the extreme right, the Athollmen, not only had to brave the grape-shot but also fire from Campbells in the enclosure to their right, and then the fire of Wolfe's regiment. Thus, not surprisingly, few of them managed to close with Cumberland's front line. When twenty yards from the waiting Redcoats the oncoming clansmen in general suffered yet more losses when the government soldiers fired a well-timed volley. Many fell, but others pressed on relentlessly and came to blows with the regiments on the left of the line, Barrell's (which had distinguished itself at Falkirk) and Munro's.

The Highlanders' hearts were filled with anger. Their own ranks had been decimated and they now dealt out death and destruction themselves, wielding their dirks and broadswords with terrible ferocity. Lord Robert Kerr was one of the government soldiers who did not survive. After reportedly bayoneting a Cameron, he was struck down by a Highlander who cleaved his head open to the collarbone. Kerr belonged to Barrell's regiment, whose commander, Colonel Robert Rich, had his left hand cut off and shortly thereafter his right arm was severed at the elbow.

Though hard pressed, Barrell's regiment fought courageously, as did Munro's, but despite this some of the Highlanders managed to hack their way through the front line only to be killed by the men of Sempill's and Bligh's regiments of the second line. One of those who fell was MacGillivray of Dunmaglas. Other clansmen, who outflanked Barrell's regiment, were likewise dealt with by the same regiments.

The regiments in the centre of Cumberland's front line were not subjected to such a ferocious onslaught. Few of the clansmen (and members of John Roy Stewart's regiment) who charged towards the government soldiers in question managed to reach their adversaries owing to the grape-shot and musket fire which tore into their ranks. For instance, none of the MacLeans and MacLachlans closed with the enemy. Old Lachlan MacLachlan of MacLachlan, the father of Charles' late ADC, was among those who perished.

And what of the regiments on the left of the Jacobite front line? They likewise failed to come to blows. Cumberland relates what happened: 'I had placed myself [on the right] imagining the greatest push would be there, they came down there several times within a hundred yards of our men, firing their pistols and brandishing their swords, but the Royals [i.e., St Clair's] and Pulteney's hardly took their fire-locks from their shoulders, so that after those feint attempts they made off: and the little squadrons on our right were sent to pursue them'.

Although some of the ground between them and the enemy was waterlogged, the performance of the MacDonalds was nonetheless a bitter blow to Keppoch, whom the Chevalier de Johnstone – who was present – describes as 'a gentleman of uncommon merit'. Hence Keppoch despairingly cried: 'My God, have the clansmen of my name deserted me?' He then courageously charged with other determined individuals, most of whom soon fell under a hail of bullets, Keppoch among them. The rest, including Clanranald, who was wounded, joined their fellows in flight.

The MacDonalds, and those with them such as the Chevalier de Johnstone, were not the only members of the Jacobite army falling back for it was obvious that the day was lost. Even on the right, where as noted fairly significant losses had been inflicted on the government troops, the men were retreating under enemy fire, including grape-shot from Belford's guns. Reinforcements from the second line brought forward by Murray, who had returned from the charge to bring them forward, failed to turn the tide. As Kirkconnel recalled, 'nothing could stop the Highlanders after they had begun to run', while Johnstone later wrote: 'What a spectacle of horror! The same Highlanders, who had advanced to the charge like lions, with bold, determined countenances, were in an instant seen flying like trembling cowards in the greatest disorder'.

Nevertheless, pursuing government troops did encounter some resistance. The cavalry on the right, for example, after chasing after the collapsed left of the Jacobite front line, found themselves opposed by the Irish pickets and the Royal Scots of the second who stood firm, and were checked as a result until their doughty opponents also commenced retreating.

The Argyll Militia also sustained casualties during this stage of the proceedings for upon seeing the Jacobites falling back in confusion, many of the Campbells who had entered the enclosures referred to above, climbed over the wall between them and the enemy – Ogilvy's regiment had been unwisely withdrawn to form a reserve – and moved in for the kill with the result that several of their own number were cut down.

Meanwhile, the dragoons in the westernmost of the enclosures had made their way out onto the moor through gaps made for them in the west wall. Seeing this, FitzJames' Horse and Elcho's Lifeguard were ordered by Murray to counter the threat. The dragoons were about 500 strong: their opponents no more than 160 men, if that. For a while a standoff occurred in the vicinity of Culchunaig, partly owing to the nature of the ground for a sunken road lay between them. Then, emboldened by the sight of the Jacobite army in flight, the dragoons moved forward. Saddles were emptied on both sides as shots were exchanged, and though the dragoons drove back their opponents, the delay which had occurred enabled many of the fleeing Jacobite right to escape the field.

The Young Pretender seems to have been dazed by the rout of his army. Early in the campaign he had promised his followers that he would conquer or die, but in the event he allowed himself to be led from the field. According to Johnstone, following the battle the prince 'was in total prostration, lost to all hope of being able to retrieve his affairs...and giving up every design but that of saving himself in France as soon as he possibly could'.

On the other hand Cumberland was elated. He rode around the field congratulating his men and was in turn applauded by them. Though cheerful, he was not in a magnanimous mood. Wounded Highlanders were thus systematically butchered. Most were bayoneted or shot but some who had sheltered in barns and huts were burnt alive when the buildings were set alight. In his dispatch, Cumberland reported that he had 'made a great slaughter and gave quarter to none but about fifty French officers and soldiers'.

Government casualties were said to be 50 killed, 259 wounded and one missing. According to Cumberland, rebel fatalities amounted to about 2,000 killed on the field or during the pursuit. That they were very high is undoubted. For instance, only three of Clan Chattan's 21 officers survived the battle, while half of the Atholl brigade perished.

Lord George Murray, who fought with typical courage at Culloden and perforce largely conducted the battle, blamed Charles for the disaster and gave vent to his feelings in a letter to the prince written the day after Culloden. For a start, he declared, it was 'highly wrong' of the prince 'to have set up the royal standard [at Glenfinnan] without having positive assurance' that France would fully back a rising. Moreover, among other things he lamented the prince's reliance on the incompetent O'Sullivan, who had been entrusted 'with the most essential things' in regard to operations and whose choice of ground, Drummossie Moor, the prince had accepted to do battle with Cumberland.

Drummossie Moor had undoubtedly been a disastrous choice of battlesite. To make matters worse, the prince had compounded the error by making others. Prior to the battle's commencement, he overruled a suggestion by Murray that a close inspection of the terrain be undertaken. Consequently, unbeknown to the Jacobites, some of the ground before their position was boggy and thus hindered the clansmen's subsequent charge. Furthermore, the prince blundered by allowing the enemy to secure the enclosures to the right of his position. Murray had wanted to partly demolish their walls but had been overruled by the prince.

During the battle itself, Charles appears to have displayed chronic indecision. His only chance of victory was launching a ferocious charge, but by the time it commenced his ranks had been seriously weakened by the cannon fire to which they had been subjected for far too long. In fairness to the prince, he later maintained that he had given the order to advance on eight occasions. This seems rather unlikely, but if true, would of course nullify or at least weaken the accusation that he was indecisive, while indicating that the standard of communications in the Jacobite army was abysmal.

Although we have to deplore the savagery Cumberland showed to the defeated Highlanders, (savagery which earned him the sobriquet, 'Butcher'), it must be conceded that his overall performance deserves respect. Though he generally despised Highlanders, he did not underestimate their prowess. Hence, as noted earlier, in the weeks prior to Culloden he drilled and redrilled his men, training them to withstand a Highland charge and ensured through this and other measures that morale was high. Moreover, he behaved with alacrity upon hearing of the Jacobites' abortive night march on Nairn, and led his men competently when they came face to face with their adversaries on Drummossie Moor.

George II received the news of his son's victory on 25 April and was overjoyed. The defeat of the Jacobites was also well received by the majority of his subjects, some of whom now felt compassion for the routed. Shortly after Culloden young Edmund Burke wrote, 'how the minds of people are in a few days changed, the very men who but awhile ago, while they were alarmed by [the prince's] progress so heartily cursed and hated those unfortunate creatures are now all pity and wish it could be terminated without bloodshed'.

Cumberland, however, remained implacable. 'All the good we have done', he wrote to the Duke of Newcastle, 'is a little blood-letting, which has only weakened the madness, not cured it. I tremble for fear that this vile spot may still be the ruin of this island and our family'. He was determined to continue the work of destroying Jacobitism, which he had commenced at Culloden.

One objective was of course the apprehension of the Young Pretender. But much to their chagrin, the government forces failed to arrest the fugitive prince, for on 20 September 1746, after many adventures in the Highlands and the Western Isles, he sailed for France on board *l'Heureux* accompanied by a few companions, one of whom was Cameron of Lochiel. Charles' high hopes of ousting the House of Hanover had come to nothing and Jacobitism was a spent force: he was a sad and disillusioned man.

In their endeavours to capture him, and cow the Highlanders into permanent submission, the government forces inflicted great suffering; killing people for little or no reason, ransacking and destroying property, and slaughtering livestock. As Kybett comments: 'Added to the toll of lives taken at Culloden and the reprisals of that summer were many stillbirths and deaths from starvation in the winter of 1746. It was the beginning of the decimation of the Highland population, from which they never recovered'.

The harshness of the government forces, and measures such as an Act of Parliament of 1747 prohibiting the wearing of tartan or any item of Highland dress other than by soldiers serving in regiments of the British Army, had a profound effect on Highland society. Many of those who had dreamt of the restoration of the House of Stuart found that the dream had become a nightmare: they must have bitterly lamented the day Charles Edward Stuart ever had cause to say: 'I am come home, sir'.

BIBLIOGRAPHY

In addition to primary sources, the following have been used:

Abels, R. P., *Lordship and Military Obligation in Anglo-Saxon England*, 1988

Ashdown, C. H., *Armour and Weapons in the Middle Ages*, 1925.

Ashley, M., *The English Civil War*, 1990.
— *The Battle of Naseby and the Fall of King Charles I*, 1992.

Asquith, S. A., *The Campaign of Naseby: 1645*, 1979.
— *The New Model Army*, 1981.

Aylmer, G. E., *Rebellion or Revolution*, 1986.

Barlow, F., *William I and the Norman Conquest*, 1966.

Barthorp, M., *The Jacobite Rebellions, 1689–1745*, 1982

Bates, C. J., 'Flodden Field', *Archaeologia Aeliana*, Vol 16 New Series, 1894.

Baynes, J., *The Jacobite Rising of 1715*, 1970.

Becke, A. F., 'The Battle of Bannockburn', *Complete Peerage*, XI, Appendix B, 1949.

Bennett, M., *The Battle of Bosworth*, 1985.
— *Traveller's Guide to the Battlefields of the English Civil War*, 1990.

Bernstein, D., 'The Blinding of Harold and the Meaning of the Bayeux Tapestry', *Anglo-Norman Studies*, V, 1983.
— *The Mystery of the Bayeux Tapestry*, 1986.

Black, J., *Culloden and the Forty-Five*, 1990.
— 'Could The Jacobites Have Won?', *History Today*, Vol 45 (7) July 1995.

Boardman, A. W., *The Battle of Towton*, 1994.

Bone, P., 'The Development of

Anglo-Saxon Swords from the Fifth to Eleventh Century', *Weapons and Warfare in Anglo-Saxon England*, ed. S. C. Hawkes, 1989.

Bradbury, J., 'Battles in England and Normandy, 1066–1154', *Anglo-Norman Warfare*, ed. M. Strickland, 1992.

Brown, H., *History of Scotland*, Vol III, 1911.

Brown, R. A., 'The Battle of Hastings', *Anglo-Norman Warfare*, ed. M. Strickland, 1992.

Burne, A. H., *The Battlefields of England*, 1950.

Campbell, J., 'Some Agents and Agencies of the Late Anglo-Saxon State', *Domesday Studies*, ed. J. Holt, 1987.

Carpenter, D. A., *The Minority of Henry III*, 1990.
— 'English Peasants in Politics, 1258–1267', *Past and Present*, No 136, August 1992.

Chibnall, M., 'Military Service in Normandy before 1066', *Anglo-Norman Warfare*, ed. M. Strickland, 1992.

Contamine, P., *Warfare in the Middle Ages*, 1984.

Cornish, P., *Henry VIII's Army*, 1987.

Davies, G., *The Early Stuarts, 1603–1660*, Second Edition, 1959.

Davies, R. C. H., 'Did the Anglo-Saxons have Warhorses?', *Weapons and Warfare in Anglo-Saxon England*, ed. S. C. Hawkes, 1989.

Denton, B., *Naseby Fight*, 1988.

Douglas, D. C., *William the Conqueror*, 1964.

Firth, C., *Cromwell's Army*, 1912.
— *Rupert*, 'Dictionary of National Biography,' Vol XLIX, 1897.
— *Thomas Fairfax*, ibid, Vol XVIII, 1889.

— *William Cavendish, Duke of Newcastle*, ibid, Vol IX, 1887.

Fisher, A., Wallace and Bruce: 'Scotland's Uneasy Heroes', *History Today*, February 1989.

Fletcher, A., *The Outbreak of the English Civil War*, 1981.

Foss, P. J., *The Battle of Bosworth: Towards a Reassessment*, Midland History' XIII, 1988.

— *The Field of Redemore: the Battle of Bosworth, 1485*, 1990.

Fraser, A., *Cromwell, our Chief of Men*, 1973.

Gardiner, S. R., *History of the Great Civil War*, Vols I and II, 1893.

Garrett, R., *Clash of Arms: The World's Great Land Battles*, 1976.

Gentles, I., *The New Model Army in England, Ireland and Scotland, 1645–1653*, 1992.

Gillingham, J., *William the Bastard at War*, 'Anglo-Norman Warfare' ed. M. Strickland, 1992.

Goodman, A., *The Wars of the Roses*, 1981.

Goodman, A., and Tuck, A., *War and Border Societies in the Middle Ages*, 1992.

Gransden, A., '1066 and All That Revised', *History Today*, September 1988.

Grant, N., *The Campbells of Argyll*, 1975.

Gravett, C., *Hastings 1066: the Fall of Saxon England*, 1992.

Griffiths, R. A., and Thomas, R. S., *The Making of the Tudor Dynasty*, 1985

Hammond, P. W., and Sutton, A. F., *Richard III: the Road to Bosworth*, 1985.

Hampton, W. E., 'Sir Robert Brackenbury of Selaby, County Durham', *The Ricardian*, Vol VII No 90, September 1985.

Harris, O. D., 'The Bosworth Commemoration at Dadlington', *The Ricardian*, Vol VII No 90, September 1985.

— '"Even Here in Bosworth Field", a Disputed Site of Battle', *The Ricardian*, Vol VII No 92, March, 1986.

Henderson, T. F., 'John Campbell, Second Duke of Argyll and Duke of Greenwich', *Dictionary of National Biography*, Vol VIII, 1886.

— 'John Erskine, Earl of Mar', *Dictionary of National Biography*, Vol XVII, 1889.

Hirst, D., *Authority and Conflict: England 1603–1658*, 1986.

Hodgkin, T., 'The Battle of Flodden', *Archaeologia Aeliana*, Vol 16, New Series, 1894.

Holden, M., *The British Soldier*, 1974.

Hollister, C. W., *Anglo-Saxon Military Institutions*, 1962.

Hooper, N., 'The Housecarls in England in the Eleventh Century', *Anglo-Norman Studies*, VII, 1985.

— 'The Anglo-Saxons at War', *Weapons and Warfare in Anglo-Saxon England*, ed. S. C. Hawkes, 1989.

Horrox, R., *Richard III: a Study in Service*, 1989.

Hutton, R., *The Royalist War Effort, 1642–46*, 1982.

Jacob, E. F., *The Fifteenth Century 1399–1485*, 1961.

James, A. J., 'A Personal View of the Road to Bosworth Field', *The Ricardian*, Vol VIII No 105, June 1989.

— 'An Amended Itinerary to Bosworth Field', *The Ricardian*, Vol IX No 113, June 1991.

John, E., *Orbis Britanniae*, 1966.

— 'The End of Anglo-Saxon England', *The Anglo-Saxons*, ed. J. Campbell, 1982.

Kenyon, J., *The Civil Wars of England*, 1988.

Kinross, J., *The Battlefields of Britain*, 1979.

Kishlansky, M., *The Rise of the New Model Army*, 1979.

Kitson, F., *Prince Rupert – Portrait of a Soldier*, 1994.

Koch, H. W., *Medieval Warfare*, 1978.

Kybett, S. M., *Bonnie Prince Charlie: a Biography*, 1988.

Lander, J. R., *Conflict and Stability in Fifteenth-Century England*, Third Edition, 1977.

Lander, J. R., *Government and Community: England 1450–1509*, 1980.

— *The Wars of the Roses*, Second Edition, 1990.

Lang, A., *History of Scotland*, Vol IV, 1907.

Lemmon, C. H., *The Field of Hastings*, 1957.

Lenman, B., *The Jacobite Risings in Great Britain 1689–1746*, 1980.

Lovatt, R., 'A Collector of Apocryphal Anecdotes: John Blacman Revisited', *Property and Politics: Essays in Later Medieval English History*, ed. A. J. Pollard, 1984.

Loyn, H. R., *The Norman Conquest*, Third Edition, 1982.

Lucy, B., *Twenty Centuries in Sedlescombe*, 1978.

MacDougall, N., *James IV*, 1989.

MacFarlane, K. B., *England in the Fifteenth Century*, 1981.

MacKenzie, W. M., *The Battle of Bannockburn*, 1913.

— *The Secret of Flodden*, 1931.

MacKie, J. D., *The Earlier Tudors, 1485–1558*, 1952.

MacKie, R. L., *King James IV of Scotland*, 1958.

MacLean, F., *Bonnie Prince Charlie*, 1988.

McKisack, M., *The Fourteenth Century 1307–1399*, 1959.

McLynn, F., *The Jacobites*, 1985.

— *Bonnie Prince Charlie: Charles Edward Stuart*, 1988.

Magnusson, M., *Vikings!*, 1980.

Moreton, C. E., 'A Local Dispute and the Politics of 1483: Roger Townshend, Earl Rivers and the Duke of Gloucester', *The Ricardian*, Vol VIII No 107, December 1989.

Morgan, E. O., ed., *The Oxford History of Britain*, 1984.

Morrill, J., *The Revolt of the Provinces*, 1980.

— ed., *Reactions to the English Civil War, 1642–49*, 1982.

Myres, A. R., *England in the Late Middle Ages*, Eighth Edition, 1971.

Newman, P., *Marston Moor, 1644*, 1981.

Nicolle, D., *The Normans*, 1987.

Norman, A. V. B., and Pottinger, D., *English Weapons and Warfare 449–1660*, 1979.

Ollard, R., *This War Without An Enemy*, 1976.

Oman, C., *A History of the Art of War in the Middle Ages*, Second Edition, 1924.

Pollard, A. J., 'Memoirs of a Yorkist Civil Servant', *The Ricardian*, Vol VII No 96, 1987.

— *Richard III and the Princes in the Tower*, 1991.

Poole, A. L., *From Domesday Book to Magna Carta, 1087–1216*, Second Edition, 1955.

Potter, J., *Good King Richard*, 1983.

Powicke, F. M., *The Thirteenth Century, 1216–1307*, Second Edition, 1961.

Prebble, J., *The Battle of Culloden*, 1964.

Prestwich, M., *The Three Edwards*, 1980.

— *Edward I*, 1988.

Richmond, C., 'The Battle of Bosworth', *History Today*, August 1985.

— 'Note on Bosworth', *The Ricardian*, Vol VII No 92, March 1986.

Roberts, K., *Soldiers of the English Civil War (1) Infantry*, 1989.

Rogers, H. C. B., *Battles and Generals of the Civil Wars, 1642–1651*, 1968.

— *The British Army of the Eighteenth Century*, 1977.

Ross, C., *Edward IV*, 1974.

— *The Wars of the Roses*, 1976.

— *Richard III*, 1981.

Russell, C., *The Causes of the English Civil War*, 1990.

Scott, R. M., *Robert the Bruce: King of Scots*, 1982.

Seward, D., *Richard III: England's Black Legend*, 1983.

Sinclair-Stevenson, C., *Inglorious Rebellion: the Jacobite Risings of 1708, 1715 & 1719*, 1971.

Smurthwaite, D., *The Ordnance Survey Guide to Battlefields of Britain*, 1984.

Stenton, F. M., *Anglo-Saxon England*, Third Edition, 1971.

Tetlow, E., *The Enigma of Hastings*, 1974.

Tincey, J., *Soldiers of the English Civil War (2), Cavalry*, 1990.

Verkaik, J. W., 'Note on Bosworth', *The Ricardian*, Vol IX No 119, December 1992.

Warner, P., *British Battlefields: the North*, 1972.

— *British Battlefields: the South*, 1972.

Wedgewood, C. V., *The King's War*, 1958.

White, G. H., 'The Battle of Hastings and the Death of Harold', *Complete Peerage*, XII, Part I, Appendix L, 1953.

— 'Problems of the Bayeux Tapestry', *Complete Peerage*, XII, Part II, Appendix K, 1953.

White, R., 'The Battle of Flodden', *Archaeologia Aeliana*, New Series, Vol III, 1859.

Williams, B., *The Whig Supremacy, 1714–1760*, Second Edition, 1962.

Williams, D., '"A Place Mete For Twoo Battayles to Encountre": the Siting of the Battle of Bosworth, 1485', *The Ricardian*, Vol VII No 90, September 1985.

Wise, T., *1066: Year of Destiny*, 1979.

— *The Wars of the Roses*, 1983.

Wolffe, B., *Henry VI*, 1981.

Wood, M., *In Search of the Dark Ages*, 1981.

Woods, J., 'Was Bosworth worth a Mass?', *The Ricardian*, Vol IX No 113, December 1991.

Woolrych, A., *Battles of the English Civil War*, 1991.

Young, P., & Holmes, R., *The English Civil War*, 1979.

Young, P., *Marston Moor 1644: the Campaign and the Battle*, 1970.

— *Naseby, 1645: the Campaign and the Battle*, 1985.

INDEX